Linda C. Smith, PhD
Ruth C. Carter, PhD
Editors

Technical Services Management, 1965-1990
A Quarter Century of Change and a Look to the Future

Pre-publication
REVIEWS,
COMMENTARIES,
EVALUATIONS . . .

" **I**t is quite appropriate that the festschrift for Kathryn Henderson should be a survey of technical services over the last twenty-five years, since that coincides with the time during which she taught cataloging and other courses on technical services. What makes such a survey valuable is the revolutionary nature of the changes that the technical services have experienced since 1965. Each paper in this collection is valuable in its own right, but the entire collection is much more than the sum of its parts, giving as it does a panoramic view of technical services during a time when they have been fundamentally transformed. The editors have made an excellent choice of topics, giving appropriate emphasis to such traditional subjects as acquisitions and descriptive cataloging, but also including activities such as preservation and indexing, which have only recently surfaced as major concerns within technical services.

Each reader will of course have her/his own favorites among the many fine papers within this collection. Robert Burger's treatment of authority control is marked by clarity and precision, and presents a thorough, balanced treatment of this crucial subject by one who is this country's leading expert. All of us who lived through the raging controversies that attended the publication and implementation of AACR2 will be fascinated by the description of the very similar controversies that centered on Lubetzky's Code of Cataloging Rules. The detailed description of the political maneuverings that defeated that code will be very familiar to veterans of the AACR2 wars. Arguably the most valuable paper in the collection is Richard Meyer's 'The Effect of a Transition in Intellectual Property Rights Caused by Electronic Media on the Human Capital of Librarians.' He carefully analyzes the probable effect of electronic publishing on every aspect of technical services, from acquisitions through cataloging to preservation. This collection will be essential reading for every thoughtful student of technical services."

Arnold S. Wajenberg, MA
*Former Principal Cataloger
and Professor Emeritus,
University of Illinois Library
at Urbana–Champaign*

"**U**nlike many festschrift, this collection is both readable and useful. Coverage is broad, for the authors examine a variety of areas, including acquisitions, cataloging, serials control, preservation, the public catalog, and technical services education.

The papers are well written, and they share at least a couple of themes. One theme is historical. Many of the papers describe the history of technical services and related areas. Even without looking at the authors' names, the reader knows right away that many of these papers are written by people who themselves experienced some of this history. At the same time, many of the papers have sections that look into the future. And all papers have references to materials of the 1990s or late 1980s.

Another theme is the role of automation. From binding to bibliographic control, to indexing to intellectual properties rights, to users' accessibility to information, we read here that electronic media have raised many questions and provided some answers in this field.

The Haworth Press, Inc.

Technical Services Management, 1965-1990

A Quarter Century of Change and a Look to the Future

Festschrift for Kathryn Luther Henderson

HAWORTH Cataloging & Classification
Ruth C. Carter, Senior Editor

New, Recent, and Forthcoming Titles:

Cataloging and Classification for Library Technicians by Mary Liu Kao

Technical Services Management, 1965-1990: A Quarter Century of Change and a Look to the Future by Linda C. Smith and Ruth C. Carter

Technical Services Management, 1965-1990
A Quarter Century of Change and a Look to the Future

Festschrift for Kathryn Luther Henderson

Linda C. Smith, PhD
Ruth C. Carter, PhD
Editors

The Haworth Press
New York • London

The Haworth Press, Inc., 10 Alice Street, Binghamton, NY 13904-1580

Library of Congress Cataloging-in-Publication Data

Technical services management, 1965-1990 : a quarter century of change, a look to the future : festschrift for Kathryn Luther Henderson / Linda C. Smith, Ruth C. Carter, editors.
    p.   cm.
    Includes bibliographical references (p.   ) and index.
    ISBN 1-56024-960-9 (hard : alk. paper)
    1. Processing (Libraries)–History–20th century. 2. Processing (Libraries)–United States–History–20th century. I. Smith, Linda C. II. Carter, Ruth C.
    Z688.5.T39   1995
    025'.02–dc20   95-20463
                                                                    CIP

CONTENTS

PART IV: CATALOGING

PART V: SUBJECT ACCESS

Chapter 11. Subject Cataloging   211
Tschera Harkness Connell

Chapter 12. The Dewey Decimal Classification: 1965-1990   223
John P. Comaromi

PART VI: INDEXING

Chapter 13. Indexing, in Theory and Practice   241
Marie A. Kascus

ABOUT THE EDITORS

Linda C. Smith, PhD, is Professor in the Graduate School of Library & Information Science at the University of Illinois at Urbana-Champaign where she has been a member of the faculty since 1977. She is active in several professional associations, including the Association for Library and Information Science Education and the American Society for Information Science. She is co-editor of the text *Reference and Information Services: An Introduction,* a member of the editorial board of *Library Quarterly,* bibliographic editor of the *Annual Review of Information Science and Technology,* and author of many articles and book chapters.

Ruth C. Carter, PhD, is Assistant Director for Automated and Technical Services at the University Library System, University of Pittsburgh. She has been at the University of Pittsburgh in varying capacities in automated and technical services since 1972. Her professional activities include being editor of *Cataloging & Classification Quarterly,* a term as President of the Association for Library Collections and Technical Services, and membership on the OCLC Users Council and the National Information Standards Organization Standards Development Committee. She is also active in the Urban History Association and holds membership in several historical societies and associations.

Contributors

Lawrence W. S. Auld is Associate Professor and Chair, Department of Library Studies & Education Technology, East Carolina University, Greenville, NC 27858-4353.

Robert H. Burger is Head, Slavic and East European Library, University of Illinois at Urbana-Champaign, 1408 W. Gregory Drive, Urbana, IL 61801.

John P. Comaromi (now deceased) was Editor, Dewey Decimal Classification, Decimal Classification Division, Library of Congress.

Tschera Harkness Connell is Assistant Professor, School of Library and Information Science, Kent State University, 124 Mount Hall, 1050 Carmack, Columbus, OH 43210.

Mary Ellyn Gibbs, Librarian, Thornwood High School Library, 17101 S. Park Ave., South Holland, IL 60473.

William T Henderson is Preservation Librarian, University of Illinois at Urbana-Champaign, 1408 W. Gregory Drive, Urbana, IL 61801.

Edgar A. Jones is Assistant Professor, Graduate School of Library & Information Science, Rosary College, 7900 W. Division Street, River Forest, IL 60305.

Marie A. Kascus is Librarian and Head of Serials, Central Connecticut State University, Elihu Burritt Library, 1615 Stanley St., New Britain, CT 06050.

Richard W. Meyer is Director, Trinity University Library, 715 Stadium Drive, San Antonio, TX 78212.

Larry Millsap is Head, Bibliographic Records and Automated Systems, University Library, University of California, Santa Cruz, Santa Cruz, CA 95064.

Carolynne Myall is Head, Library Materials Services, University Libraries, Eastern Washington University, MS-84, Cheney, WA 99004-2495.

James Orr is President, Hertzberg-New Method, Inc., 617E Vandalia Road, Jacksonville, IL 62560-3599.

Lori L. Osmus is Head, Serials & Monographs Original Cataloging Department, Iowa State University, 204 Parks Library, Ames, IA 50011.

Mary Piggott, 14 District Road, Wembley, Middlesex, HA0 2LD, England.

Marion Taylor Reid is Director of Library Services, California State University, San Marcos, 820 West Los Vallecitos Blvd., Suite C, San Marcos, CA 92069-1477.

Kathleen L. Shannon is Librarian, Thornwood High School Library, 17101 S. Park Avenue, South Holland, IL 60743.

Debora Shaw is Associate Professor, School of Library & Information Science, Indiana University, Main Library 011, Bloomington, IN 47405.

Mary Ellen Soper is Assistant Professor, Graduate School of Library & Information Science, University of Washington, 133 Suzzallo Library FM-30, Seattle, WA 98195.

Andrea L. Stamm is Acting Head, Catalog Department, Northwestern University Library, Evanston, IL 60208-2300.

Arlene G. Taylor is Associate Professor, School of Library & Information Science, University of Pittsburgh, 135 N. Bellefield Avenue, Pittsburgh, PA 15260.

Eloise M. Vondruska is Head, Catalog Department, Northwestern University, Law School Library, 357 E. Chicago Avenue, Chicago, IL 60611-3069.

Introduction

Linda C. Smith
Ruth C. Carter

This Festschrift, *Technical Services Management, 1965-1990: A Quarter Century of Change and a Look to the Future,* honors Kathryn Luther Henderson, inspirational teacher, colleague, and friend. Through a quarter century plus of teaching at the University of Illinois at Urbana-Champaign, "Kathie" has dedicated herself to educating about the "hidden" user service–technical services. Her students take it for granted that acquisitions, cataloging, and preservation of library materials are public services. In any course Kathryn Henderson teaches, the question "Why are we doing this?" is always asked. And, the answer always is, "For the user."

We are delighted with this opportunity to recognize Mrs. Henderson in this lasting manner. While Kathryn Henderson probably is most identified with teaching cataloging, her talents, interests, and areas of instruction do not stop there. From the mid-1960s she began teaching cataloging, adding technical services in 1981 and preservation in 1988. Together Mrs. Henderson and her husband, William T Henderson (Preservation Librarian with the University of Illinois Library at Urbana-Champaign), devote incredible energy to teaching the need to preserve the holdings of our nation's libraries and methods to accomplish this.

Above all, the more than 25 years in Kathryn Henderson's teaching career coincide with rapid change in libraries, in library catalogs, in library management, and in user expectations. In 1965 MARC records were an embryonic dream, computers were avail-

The Editors would like to note that the articles in this *Festschrift* were submitted during or before 1992 and that any delays in reaching publication are due to the editors rather than either the authors or The Haworth Press.

able but limited to a few bulky mainframes, punched cards were the primary input form, and printed lists or tapes the major outputs. AACR1 much less AACR2 had not appeared. United States research libraries were in the golden age of collection building. Interlibrary loan was reserved for scholars, and users expected to find most items of interest locally.

Kathryn Henderson has taught, steadfastly, through the past turbulent quarter century that we acquire, catalog, and preserve materials so that they can be used. Cataloging rules have changed, serial prices have escalated, online public access catalogs ("OPACS") are now a commonly understood phenomenon, and there is growing recognition of the vulnerability to disintegration of America's great treasure, its collective library holdings. Through all these changes, Mrs. Henderson has led and challenged her students to help the user find what she or he needs.

This Festschrift is a collection of essays by 21 of Kathryn Henderson's students and colleagues, including her most important associate, with the opportunity to recognize someone so dedicated, so giving, so insightful, so caring. Kathie has been a tremendous influence in our lives and careers. With this effort we acknowledge her and all she has given us and the profession.

MANAGEMENT OF TECHNICAL SERVICES

The essays review the past 25-year period of 1965-1990 for library technical services, broadly defined. Most are historical, combined with a firm grasp of the present and a glimpse or more at the future. One critical topic, management of technical services, is, however, missing from the contents as a separate essay. How indeed does one review management of technical services as it has evolved between 1965 and the early 1990s? When Mrs. Henderson began her teaching career, technical services was normally a slightly mysterious kingdom to itself. And, a very people-intensive kingdom at that. Large libraries had separate files of holdings or acquisitions data spread between serial departments, acquisitions departments, and catalog departments. It was not uncommon for one library to have three or four codes used in differing files to represent one library location.

The filing rules were perhaps the most used technical services reference tool. Countless staff spent hours filing catalog cards that could be used only in a catalog's single location. Revising filing seemed a necessity, for if the card was misfiled it negated all the effort of cataloging. Catalogers commonly spent many hours laboring over spaces and indentations trying to achieve the "perfect" catalog card although, it must quickly be noted, Mrs. Henderson stressed content of the catalog record over format. Preservation, in 1965, received little attention in American libraries. Acquisitions, both serials and monographs, was normally slow and labor-intensive. My how things have changed! Kathryn Henderson has always been at the cutting edge in conveying to students the changes and the trends. And always, the relentless questions: why? how? for whom?

Like public services with its CD-ROM networks, online databases, online public access catalogs, and a rapidly multiplying menu of options for access, technical services has undergone an evolutionary revolution during the quarter century plus that Kathryn Henderson has taught. Management skills are the same in part, but different in part. In the early years of Kathie's teaching tenure, a manager probably had to be worried about the accuracy of record keeping; supervising original catalogers who could successfully adapt copy or more likely catalog the same thing a librarian in another research library was also cataloging; reporting by paper to the National Union Catalog; using paper-intensive acquisitions procedures requiring placement of orders; making sure that new serial holdings got reported to *New Serial Titles;* and having glue and Scotch tape on hand to repair books.

Twenty-five years later, technical services managers are concerned with coordinating upgrades to the integrated automated system or components of linked systems of their choice; many are committed to national cooperative programs so that we can share cataloging and librarians perform only "original" cataloging; we have approval plans and use a healthy mix of vendors and direct orders; prices of materials and costs of highly trained staff have both gone up; one worries about cost effectiveness and how to streamline; MARC records have become "godlike" and it becomes difficult to remember to communicate with key components of technical services operations; and preservation needs have been recognized.

Technical services managers in the past 25 years have had to adapt rapidly. At the same time that technical services managers are concerned with the business and production aspects of libraries, they also connect outward toward a national and international community. Not because the user in the home institution is not important. We have learned Mrs. Henderson's lesson well. Everything we do, we do for the user. But, we depend on our colleagues nationally and internationally to do their fair share of original contributions as well as national databases such as OCLC and RLIN; we depend on international as well as national vendors; we depend on our national bibliographic utilities to carry the information about our preservation decisions and those of other libraries; and we care about standards: standards for cataloging, for communication exchange, for holdings representation, for permanent paper, for preservation microfilming, for claim data elements, and for numbering, to name just a few.

Yet all of the above depend on people; people who, in technical services, work closely together in often crowded conditions with poor lighting, no windows, and with an increasing number of machines or electronic linkages of one sort or another. Technical services managers must like and care about people. They should enjoy machines and what they can do; they need a zest for continuous learning; they must care about getting information to the user; and, perhaps above all, they must have a sense of humor. As technical services sometimes seems a blur with other parts of the library, it must be remembered that there will always be needs to create, to organize, to preserve, and to retrieve information. The technical services manager continues to play a crucial role in both organizing and preserving information. Reflecting this, the essays in this Festschrift suggest directions for the future as well as document the past.

FESTSCHRIFT ESSAYS

The 20 essays in this volume are grouped to reflect the various aspects of technical services: trends in technical services, acquisitions and collection development, catalogs, cataloging, subject access, indexing, preservation, education and professional development, and the future. To begin the volume Carolynne Myall reviews the growth and format of technical services literature, particularly in the English language, during the period 1969-1990; the journals in which technical services literature appeared; and patterns in the extent of publication about some important topics. Kathleen L. Shannon and Mary Ellyn Gibbs describe the major changes in technical services in school libraries since 1967: (1) cataloging principles and practices, from earlier codes to AACR2; (2) types of materials acquired, cataloged, and processed, from mainly hardback books to a variety of audiovisual materials including laser disks and videodisks; and (3) automation, which has allowed many school libraries to take advantage of shared cataloging and to provide more standardized bibliographic control of materials.

In her essay on acquisitions and collection development Marion T. Reid describes changes in the past 25 years in selection, funding, acquisitions tools, procurement methods, and staffing. She concludes with a number of predictions, in particular exploring the implications of the increasing focus on access rather than ownership.

Looking at the emergence of OPACs, Larry Millsap traces the history of the online catalog in North America from the early in-house automation efforts of the 1960s to the enhanced catalogs of the 1990s. Debora Shaw contrasts early library automation efforts such as the development of the MARC format and bibliographic utilities with the creation of databases by indexing and abstracting services. She concludes that today's attempts to provide unified bibliographic access to the library's entire collection must find ways to integrate this plethora of independently developed access tools. Robert H. Burger assesses the development of authority control thinking and practice, especially over the past quarter century.

Cataloging depends on cataloging codes and Edgar A. Jones explores the politics of catalog code revision by tracing the history of the treatment of "institutions" as the 1949 ALA code was revised. Mary Ellen Soper discusses the development of descriptive cataloging practice with the implementation of AACR1 and AACR2 and their revisions. Lori L. Osmus contrasts the world of the serials cataloger in 1965 and 1990 marked by the growth of bibliographic utilities and increased standardization. She notes new challenges as serials are being issued in a greater variety of formats than can be easily described by the current cataloging rules and demands are made on library catalogs for more in-depth access to serial contents. Andrea L. Stamm explores the past, present, and future of minimal level (MLC) or less-than-full cataloging, used to speed up processing and save costs. Her discussion of MLC at Northwestern University provides concrete examples of the kinds of decisions libraries must make.

Subject access can be accomplished using entries from subject heading lists and classification schedules. Tschera Harkness Connell discusses established approaches to subject access using subject headings and the demands for improved subject access associated with the widespread availability of online catalogs and the evidence of problems experienced by catalog users in subject searching. John P. Comaromi traces the development of one widely used classification scheme, the Dewey Decimal Classification, over the past quarter century. He explains that the marked philosophic differences between Editions 17 and 20 result from the differing philosophies of their respective editors with regard to the means and extent by which assistance is provided for classifiers.

Marie A. Kascus sketches the events and people that have impacted the field of indexing, considering the indexing literature, indexers as professionals, professional organizations, machine indexing, and indexing evaluation. Mary Piggott focuses more specifically on some post-war developments in indexing in Great Britain.

Over the past 25 years preservation of library materials has been a growing concern in librarianship. William T Henderson describes the techniques in use to preserve books and the challenges posed by new media, especially computer-based materials. James Orr traces changes in binding techniques, including the role of automation and mechanization.

While education for technical services begins in the library school, technical services librarians continue learning through participation in continuing education and involvement in professional associations. Arlene G. Taylor analyzes changes in cataloging education in library schools, noting major additions to the course content and changes in teaching methods. Eloise M. Vondruska illustrates the need for continuing education in technical services and explores some approaches. Lawrence W. S. Auld describes COLA (the Committee on Library Automation) and the LARC (Library Automation, Research, and Consulting) Association, two little-known professional organizations, and investigates their impact on technical services.

Although most essays in this volume include some discussion of the future, the final essay by Richard W. Meyer explores in some detail the new roles for librarians that may emerge in an electronic environment where ownership of intellectual property rights is retained by the institutions in which scholars work. He terms these the communication role, the gatekeeper role, the archival role, and the human capital role. Meyer agrees with other authors in this volume in his observation that librarians will have to acquire additional skills on top of the old ones; those tasks and skills required to handle printed resources will need to be augmented by skills for the special handling of electronic materials.

KATHRYN LUTHER HENDERSON:
BIOGRAPHICAL AND BIBLIOGRAPHICAL NOTES

Kathryn Luther Henderson began teaching cataloging full-time at the University of Illinois at Urbana-Champaign in 1965, but her association with the community and university actually began several years earlier. She grew up on a farm in rural Champaign and earned all her degrees at the University of Illinois: an AB in history and English in 1944, a BS in library science in 1948, and an MS in library science in 1951. A founding member and first national secretary of Beta Phi Mu, the international honor society in library science, she held positions in the University of Illinois Library, first as a clerical assistant from 1944-1946 and then as a serial cataloger from 1950-1953. Following her marriage to William T Henderson in 1953, she moved to Chicago where she held positions as circulation librarian (1953-1956) and head cataloger (1956-1965) at McCormick Theological Seminary.

As a faculty member at Illinois, Kathryn Henderson has been involved in teaching a variety of courses. She is most closely associated with four courses that she has taught for several years: Cataloging and Classification I and II, Technical Services Functions, and Preservation of Library Materials (taught jointly with William T Henderson). She developed the latter two to better equip students to work in these areas in all types of libraries. Other contributions to the curriculum include her development of the syllabus for the core course Introduction to Services Relating to Organization of Library Materials and for the doctoral seminar on The Bibliographic Organization of Information and Library Materials, both of which she also taught for several years. In 1992 she and William T Henderson introduced a course on Issues in Preservation Management.

Kathryn Henderson "redevelops" her courses each time they are offered to reflect current trends and to incorporate the newest readings from the literature. Her lengthy course syllabi integrate descriptions of topics, structured in a logical progression. Students find the syllabi of much value during and after the courses. Instruction in each course employs a variety of teaching methods–lecture, student presentations, discussion, small group work, guest speakers, demonstrations. Mrs. Henderson developed computer-assisted instruction lessons for cataloging using PLATO as early as 1971 and more recently has included assignments that allow students to make use of automated systems widely used in cataloging. Regularly receiving outstanding ratings from students on course evaluations, in 1991 she was recognized at the campus level for her significant contributions as a teacher with the Urbana-Champaign Campus Award for Excellence in Graduate and Professional Teaching. In addition to her teaching she is frequently involved in supervision of research carried out by master's, certificate of advanced study, and doctoral students. In 1993 she received the Distinguished Alumnus Award from the Library School Association, the alumni association of the Graduate School of Library and Information Science at the University of Illinois at Urbana-Champaign, in recognition of her many contributions as an educator. In addition she was recognized at the 1993 American Library Association conference as the winner of the 1993 Beta Phi Mu Award citing her "distinguished record of teaching and service that has defined an uncommon level of excellence and has challenged and inspired a generation of librarians and library educators." In 1995 the Association for Library and Information Science Education recognized her with the ALISE Award for Teaching Excellence in the Field of Library and Information Science Education.

Kathryn Henderson is a longstanding member of the American Library Association, the Illinois Library Association, the American Association of University Professors, the American Theological Library Association, the American Society for Information Science, and the Association of Library and Information Science Education. She has served on and chaired numerous committees related to technical services, cataloging, and classification. Since 1984 she has been a member of the Editorial Board for *Cataloging & Classification Quarterly*. Her tenure as a faculty member includes service on many committees within the School, especially those dealing with admissions and curriculum. At the campus level she was the School's representative to the campus Senate for several years and served on two Senate committees.

Kathryn Henderson's first contribution to the library literature dealt, most appropriately, with the teaching of cataloging and classification at the University of Illinois.[1] Since joining the faculty at the University of Illinois, she has planned a number of conferences and edited the proceedings. Topics dealt with include trends in American publishing,[2] MARC records and their uses,[3] major classification systems,[4] conservation and preservation of library materials,[5] and the special problems in preservation of nonbook formats.[6] She has also been a frequent contributor to other publications of the School, including papers on serial cataloging,[7] the history of descriptive cataloging,[8] competencies for technical services,[9] the history of automation in technical services,[10] and the history of technical services education at Illinois.[11] Other publications include journal articles and conference papers on the topics of authority control,[12] human factors in library automation,[13] issues in cataloging education,[14] and education for serials cataloging,[15] as well as an encyclopedia article on subject headings.[16]

While Kathryn Luther Henderson has made numerous research and service contributions, her most valuable legacy is the hundreds of students whom she has taught and to whom she dedicated her paper "Some Persistent Issues in the Education of Catalogers and

Classifiers."[17] Both past and present students are inspired by her example to be enthusiastic about librarianship as a profession, to recognize the importance of problem solving and professional users of libraries, and to strive for excellence in other work just as she is uncompromising in her quest for excellence in teaching. New students frequently report that Kathryn Henderson's former students have been influential in their choice of Illinois as a graduate school and cataloging as an area of specialization. As a conclusion to this Festschrift introduction, it is fitting to quote her assessment of the challenge facing cataloging educators:

> Cataloging educators should recognize current problems and needs of all types of libraries and be knowledgeable about present and emerging technologies as well as codes, schemes, and lists, but they, as do all other library educators, have to keep in mind their unique responsibilities to lead the profession not only in research and publication but through the preparation of students who leave their schools. In the final analysis, teaching and learning are very personal endeavors that occur between two persons both of whom should always be learners. The other aspects will not get across as well if teachers fail at this level.[18]

As her many students can testify, Kathryn Luther Henderson has enjoyed continued success in sharing these learning experiences.

REFERENCE NOTES

1. Kathryn Luther [Henderson], *The Teaching of Cataloging and Classification at the University of Illinois Library School,* University of Illinois Occasional Papers, no. 5 (Urbana, IL: University of Illinois, Graduate School of Library Science, 1949), 12p.

2. Kathryn Luther Henderson, ed., *Trends in American Publishing,* Allerton Park Institute, no. 14 (Urbana, IL: University of Illinois, Graduate School of Library Science, 1968), 105p.

3. Kathryn Luther Henderson, ed., *Proceedings of the 1970 Clinic on Library Applications of Data Processing: MARC II Records and Their Uses* (Urbana, IL: University of Illinois, Graduate School of Library Science, 1971), 110p.

4. Kathryn Luther Henderson, ed., *Major Classification Systems: The Dewey Centennial, Allerton Park Institute,* no. 21 (Urbana, IL: University of Illinois, Graduate School of Library Science, 1977), 182p.

5. Kathryn Luther Henderson and William T Henderson, eds., *Conserving and Preserving Library Materials,* Allerton Park Institute, no. 27 (Urbana, IL: University of Illinois at Urbana-Champaign, Graduate School of Library and Information Science, 1983), 207p.

6. Kathryn Luther Henderson and William T Henderson, eds., *Conserving and Preserving Materials in Nonbook Formats,* Allerton Park Institute, no. 30 (Urbana, IL: University of Illinois at Urbana-Champaign, Graduate School of Library and Information Science, 1991), 165p.

7. Kathryn Luther Henderson, "Serial Cataloging Revisited: A Long Search for a Little Theory and a Lot of Cooperation," in *Serial Publications in Large Libraries, ed. Walter C. Allen* (Urbana, IL: University of Illinois, Graduate School of Library Science, 1970), 48-68.

8. Kathryn Luther Henderson, "'Treated with a Degree of Uniformity and Common Sense': Descriptive Cataloging in the United States: 1876-1976," *Library Trends* 25 (July 1976): 227-271.

9. Kathryn Luther Henderson, "The New Technology and Competencies for 'the Most Typical of the Activities of Libraries': Technical Services," in *Professional Competencies: Technology and the Librarian* (Clinic on Library Applications of Data Processing, 1983), ed. Linda C. Smith (Urbana, IL: University of Illinois at Urbana-Champaign, Graduate School of Library and Information Science, 1984), 12-41.

10. Kathryn Luther Henderson and William T Henderson, "From Flow Charting to User Friendly: Technical Services Functions in Retrospect," in *Design and Evaluation of Computer/Human Interfaces* (Clinic on Library Applications of Data Processing, 1988), ed. Martin A. Siegel (Urbana, IL: University of Illinois at Urbana-Champaign, Graduate School of Library and Information Science, 1991), 27-52.

11. Kathryn Luther Henderson, "To Become Well Trained and Well Educated: A History of Technical Services at the University of Illinois," in *Ideals and Standards: The History of the University of Illinois Graduate School of Library and Information Science, 1893-1993.* ed. Walter C. Allen and Robert F. Delzell (Urbana, IL: University of Illinois at Urbana-Champaign, Graduate School of Library and Information Science, 1992), 81-114.

12. Kathryn Luther Henderson, "Great Expectations: The Authority Control Connection," *Illinois Libraries* 64 (May 1983): 334-336.

13. Kathryn Luther Henderson, "Human Considerations in Library Automation," in *Summary of Proceedings: Fortieth Annual Conference of the American Theological Library Association,* June 15-20, 1986 (St. Meinrad, Ind.: ATLA, 1986), 185-230.

14. Kathryn Luther Henderson, "Some Persistent Issues in the Education of Catalogers and Classifiers," *Cataloging & Classification Quarterly* 7 (Summer 1987): 5-26.

15. Kathryn Luther Henderson, "Personalities of Their Own: Some Informal Thoughts on Serials and Teaching about How to Catalog Them," *The Serials Librarian* 22 (1992): 3-16.

16. Kathryn Luther Henderson, "Subject Headings," in Encyclopedia of Library History, eds. Wayne A. Wiegand and Donald G. Davis, Jr. (New York: Garland Publishing, 1994), 604-608.

17. Henderson, "Some Persistent Issues in the Education of Catalogers and Classifiers," 23.

18. Ibid., 22.

PART I:
TRENDS IN TECHNICAL SERVICES

Chapter 1

Technical Services Literature, 1969-1990

Carolynne Myall

INTRODUCTION

During the period 1969-1990, the literature of library technical services increased in volume and in degree of specialization. While monographic treatments and library tools comprised an important sector of technical services literature throughout the period, particularly in areas concerned with application of codes, dominance of the journal format became more pronounced. The number of journals publishing technical services articles increased; several new journals established themselves as core publications in their fields. Technical services literature defined itself more precisely in some subject areas (e.g., acquisitions) while its coverage extended into other new areas, notably the application of computer technology to the control and retrieval of bibliographic materials. Some topics experienced a sharp increase in treatment, then leveled off; some topics showed cycles of increased and reduced treatment apparently related to the release of new codes or versions; a few topics (e.g., preservation) seem barely past the heroic stage–no slackening in publication is in sight. Technical services literature included standard tools and handbooks, codes and their revisions, news reports, editorials and opinion pieces, analysis and "think pieces," reports of professional practice in specific institutions, and basic research. Though many authors lamented the relationship (or lack thereof) of research to technical services practice, few explored the exact nature of that relationship in a systematic manner. Few examined libraries and technical services in terms of organizational behavior, external constraints upon decision making, or other perspectives which might illuminate some of the reasons for that relationship's contours and condition.

This chapter reviews the growth and format of technical services literature, particularly in the English language, during the period 1969-1990; the journals in which technical services literature appeared; and patterns in the extent of publication about some important topics. While based in large part on examination of entries in *Library Literature,* much of this study is impressionistic and personal, an expression of the judgment and observations of a practitioner whose library career is virtually coterminous with the period under examination.

METHOD OF STUDY

Studies of library professional literature recognize that review articles in general give evidence of professional consensus.[1] In technical services, "Year's Work" review articles in *Library Resources & Technical Services (LRTS)* have served for many years as the practitioner's traditional means of keeping up with the literature. In addition, *LRTS* was the only library journal primarily devoted to technical services which was published throughout the period under consideration and which was consistently identified as a "core journal" of librarianship in studies of library literature. This study therefore began with an examination of "Year's Work" articles in *Library Resources & Technical Services,* 1970-1991,[2] in areas of library work which professional consensus and most library organization charts tend to place in technical services. These work areas included acquisitions, descriptive cataloging, subject analysis, serials (acquisitions and control), and preservation, but did not include selection/ collection development or reproduction of library materials. I examined "Year's Work" articles partly in order to gain an overview of technical services literature during the period, but especially to identify important topics and to begin to track recurring themes.

Next I undertook a review of some of the principal studies of the literature of librarianship and its technical services specialties. As a group, these studies tended to focus on research literature, though there were exceptions to this pattern (for example, see John J. Boll's article).[3] While these were studies of research literature, little systematic study focused on the relationship between research literature and library practice or indeed between any sort of library literature and library practice. Since it was unclear that research articles were more influential in practice than any others, the entire range of technical services literature seemed worthy of consideration in a study of publication patterns. Similarly, bibliometric methods which focus on "scholarly" materials with citations did not seem the most appropriate choices.

An initial search of *Library Literature* and ERIC on CD-ROM for a few of the major themes identified through review of the "Year's Work" articles suggested that *Library Literature* coverage was generally more complete. *Library Literature* also appeared to have fewer indexing vocabulary problems for these topics. (In the areas of classification and selection/collection development, for example, ERIC's vocabulary remained less clear and less explicit for a longer time period.) *Library Literature* thus seemed the best available source for determining extent of published literature on important technical services topics for the period. Even so, coverage in *Library Literature* did not extend to many publications this practitioner has used extensively: notably, several bibliographic utility and network documents, *Cataloging Service Bulletin,* etc.

After selecting *Library Literature,* I traced ten concepts through printed volumes for 1970-1971 through 1990.[4] I noted number of entries per topic, format of materials cited (journal article, thesis or other degree-related paper, separate publication, section of separate publication or annual, etc.), number of entries per journal title, publishers of separates, number of non-English entries, and changes in and characteristics of the index vocabulary (e.g., number of references to other index terms). I eliminated entries under geographic subheadings but included entries under topical subheadings (in fact, many entries under geographic subheadings were also entered under topical subheadings). Entries under subheadings which were transferred out of the heading during the course of the period under study were eliminated from tabulations.

Another possible approach to reviewing technical services literature might be to study characteristics of works cited in "Year's Work" articles. I opted for the *Library Literature* approach in part because of my interest in changes in amount and format of published literature on specific topics, but also because of the rather idiosyncratic nature of some "Year's Work" pieces. One of the charms and sources of interest of "Year's Work" articles is the tendency of their coverage to reflect the interests of their authors, often prominent librarians or information professionals. "Year's Work" articles also, of course, emphasize specific works the authors considered significant or noteworthy, a distinction I was not willing to make as a starting point. Thus, coverage under specific index terms in *Library Literature* appeared, at least superficially, to be more consistent as well as more complete, than bibliographies of "Year's Work" articles.

Printed volumes of *Library Literature* include some duplicate entries for items indexed in previous volumes. Deriving information from *Library Literature* on WILSONLINE would have been faster, more accurate, and, most important, would have eliminated these duplicate entries. Unfortunately, I could not get sufficient support for access to WILSONLINE in the limited time frame for this project. Since I could not eliminate all possible duplicate entries, I cannot claim total accuracy in tabulation, and therefore present the following observations as suggestive rather than definitive.

LITERATURE ON TEN TECHNICAL SERVICES TOPICS, AS INDEXED IN LIBRARY LITERATURE, 1970-1971 THROUGH 1990 VOLUMES

Note: The first four cumulated volumes of *Library Literature* for this period are biennial, while volumes for 1978 through 1990 are annual; entries for any volume may have publication dates more than a year earlier than the chronological designation of the volume. Thus, without the superseded annual volumes, it was not possible to divide the number of entries in biennial volumes in two in a meaningful way. Therefore some figures in the following discussion are for two years.

Acquisitions

This period saw some increase in acquisitions literature (see Table 1.1). Several journals which included acquisitions in their

TABLE 1.1. Acquisitions

Library Lit. Vols.	Total No. Entries	No. Entries for Per. Articles	No. of Per. Titles
1970-71	38	25	14
1972-73	48	38	22
1974-75	69	54	24
1976-77	55	40	25
1978	31	18	12
1979	20	14	11
1980	39	25	15
1981	26	22	16
1982	24	14	12
1983	25	21	14
1984	23	20	12
1985	33	29	14
1986	34	24	13
1987	41	35	15
1988	34	25	16
1989	41	35	20
1990	42	30	19

scope began publication. Most notably, these include *Library Acquisitions: Practice & Theory*[5] and *The Acquisitions Librarian,*[6] devoted exclusively to this topic; but also *Technicalities,*[7] *Serials Review,*[8] *The Serials Librarian,*[9] *Against the Grain,*[10] and *Cataloging & Classification Quarterly.*[11] *Library Software Review,*[12] and to a lesser extent, *Library Technology Reports,*[13] presented analyses of specific automated acquisitions packages. Bibliographies of acquisitions literature appeared in *RTSD Newsletter*[14] and its successor, *ALCTS Newsletter.*[15]

Several significant monographic publications in acquisitions were textbooks or manuals. These included *The Acquisition of Library Materials*[16] and its second edition, *Acquisitions Management and Collection Development in Libraries,*[17] published by the American Library Association (ALA); *Buying Books*[18] from Neal-Schuman and, most recently, *Understanding the Business of Library Acquisitions,*[19] also from ALA. Nevertheless, journal articles clearly predominated: entries for periodical articles comprised about three-quarters of the total listed under Acquisitions in the 1990 volume of *Library Literature.*

Technical services literature of the period reflected an increasingly precise usage of the term *acquisitions,* to refer to ordering, claiming, and receipt of library materials, rather than to their selection. The widespread agreement on the definition of acquisitions started to shift their emphasis from ownership to access. As access becomes our focus, what will acquisitions acquire? Will acquisitions encompass what most libraries now consider interinstitutional loan and document delivery? Will acquisitions literature of the next few years explore reorganization of technical services, with an expanded, document delivery-oriented acquisitions as the central component of library service?

I have frequently heard as well as read regrets that acquisitions literature has not produced a "text which has an underlying theoretical basis."[20] As one who has worked in most areas of technical services for many years and who has an interest in and passable understanding of the available theoretical underpinnings of bibliographic cataloging (for example), I have frankly been at a loss to guess what this underlying theoretical basis of acquisitions might be. The only possibility I can conceive of would relate to exploring and monitoring the publication and distribution of information, as elements and bellwethers of the economic and social system. The last 25 years have seen profound changes in publishing and communication of scientific and other scholarly information, including the growth of the information industry and an increasing commercialization which will have great impact on public-sector library service. I am struggling to comprehend these issues. Thus far, acquisitions literature has not much helped me. Instead, it has warned me of price increases, advised me on the selection of vendors, explained basic accounting procedures, and kept me apprised of developments in standard communication formats for transmission of orders and "business" data. These are useful strands of information, but they do not describe the whole cloth. An underlying theory surely would do so.

Anglo-American Cataloging/Cataloguing Rules

The extent of publication on this topic rises and falls with library concern about new and projected editions, versions, and revisions of the standard cataloging code used in the U.S. throughout the period under study. (Even the spelling of *Library Literature*'s heading reflects current code practice: the *u* appeared in the 1985 volume, a few years after AACR2 admittedly.) Some rule revisions and interpretations are not indexed in *Library Literature* (e.g., in *Cataloging Service Bulletin* and bibliographic utility publications), so total publication on this subject is greater than indexes indicate. Many monographs on this subject are handbooks, manuals, textbooks, etc., especially in the period immediately around publication of a new version. In Table 1.2, note the change in number of entries indexed in volumes for the quiescent years 1970-1973 (AACR1 appeared in 1967), then the jump during the high-anxiety years around the publication of AACR2 in late 1978,[21] then a drop with a very small resurgence in the years following publication of the 1988 revision.[22]

Another indicator of this basic publication pattern is the number of periodical titles which have one or more articles on AACR indexed in volumes of *Library Literature*. The 1980-1983 volumes indexed articles in many state and regional library publications, publications of special-interest library groups, and a wide range of general-coverage library journals. Articles indexed in the 1990 volume are from fewer titles, largely journals with a technical services focus: *Cataloging & Classification Quarterly, Library Resources & Technical Services, Serials Review*, etc.

The extensive publication surrounding cataloging codes is sometimes cited as evidence of the "unscholarly" nature of library literature.[23] This may be so, but does not much worry me in itself: the same objection might be made about the literature of any field of professional endeavor which applies regulations, laws, or other accepted standards. What does concern me is the apparent paucity of research before or after implementation of a major change, research to show what benefits might (or might not) be gained by the disruption and costs, as opposed to studies of the extent of disruption to expect, of which there are many. Also, in reviewing the literature surrounding AACR2, I was struck by the tendency not to recognize

TABLE 1.2. Anglo-American Cataloging/Cataloguing Rules

Library Lit. Vols.	Total No. Entries	No. Entries for Per. Articles	No. of Per. Titles
1970-71	25	12	8
1972-73	18	4	4
1974-75	53	40	17
1976-77	64	52	21
1978	27	24	13
1979	44	40	15
1980	73	70	30
1981	70	49	25
1982	62	48	27
1983	38	32	28
1984	28	17	12
1985	17	15	12
1986	33	19	12
1987	24	17	13
1988	17	14	13
1989	29	19	11
1990	21	15	10

the degree of change which full implementation of AACR1 would have required (to my mind, AACR1 remains the more significant departure), and the tendency to substitute assertion and wit for consistent analysis with regard to cataloging theory or for actual research. Thus, main entry–a term which unfortunately has meant both "principal and complete entry for an item in a catalog" and also "bibliographic identifier of a work, as expressed by author and title or by title alone"–must die and be reborn under other names (standard citation, etc.). There were, of course, exceptions to the disappointing level of discussion surrounding AACR2; an example is C. Sumner Spalding's "The Life and Death(?) of Corporate Authorship."[24]

The end of the period saw some evidence of a resurgence of interest in descriptive cataloging theory. *Foundations of Cataloging: A Sourcebook* made "outstanding contributions to the literature on cataloging theory of the last 150 years" widely available.[25] *The*

Conceptual Foundations of Descriptive Cataloging presented the proceedings of a conference[26] which suggested ways to recast underlying assumptions of bibliographic organization. Over the coming years, as the ways documents are published, distributed, and modified change, principles of bibliographic organization, as exemplified in our descriptive cataloging codes, will change and show continuity as well.

Authority Control

The *Library Literature* heading for this topic changed from "Cataloging–Authority files" (a subheading) to "Authority control" (a separate heading) in 1989 (see Table 1.3). This change reflected increased publishing activity and a shift in focus with regard to the topic, both no doubt stimulated by changes in the standard form of many access points associated with implementation of AACR2, and by growing experience with online catalogs.

In the earliest year of the period, "Bibliographic Dimensions in Information Control,"[27] by Seymour Lubetzky and R.M. Hayes, presented a discussion of the thinking behind name and title authority control–the need which authority control met–at a moment when the topic was virtually invisible. Over the next ten years, S. Michael Malinconico produced several influential articles; some were published in general library periodicals addressed to a wide professional audience.[28] Publication of the proceedings of the 1979 Library & Information Technology Association Institutes on authority control[29] also stimulated great interest in the topic. In 1989, a special issue of *Cataloging & Classification Quarterly,* entitled "Authority Control in the Online Environment,"[30] provided historical treatment and analysis of current practice; this title incidentally demonstrated the considerable development of the literature of authority control and the general acceptance of the importance of authority control which the literature may have done much to create.

MARC Formats for Bibliographic, Authority, and Holdings Data

During the last few decades, libraries' use of automation in cataloging, serials control, interlibrary loan, and online public catalog

TABLE 1.3. Authority Control

Library Lit. Vols.	Total No. Entries	No. Entries for Per. Articles	No. of Per. Titles
1970-71	0	0	0
1972-73	4	3	3
1974-75	1	1	1
1976-77	1	1	1
1978*	[1]	[1]	[1]
1979	4	4	3
1980	20	16	9
1981	13	10	7
1982	6	5	4
1983	15	13	8
1984	10	8	6
1985	21	17	10
1986	20	15	11
1987	17	17	10
1988	25	20	10
1989	25	20	10
1990	24	21	12

*No heading in this volume (the heading did appear in 1976-1977 and 1979); however, one item clearly qualified.

access has grown greatly. Central to that growth has been libraries' ability to share and exchange data, and thereby reduce costly duplication of effort. Central to sharing and exchange of library data has been the development of the MARC–Machine Readable Cataloging–formats for identification, storage, and communication of bibliographic, authority, and holdings data. MARC's history began with the MARC Pilot Project in 1966, just before the beginning of the period under study. The Pilot Project ended in 1968 with implementation of MARC II and distribution of LC cataloging records for books on magnetic tape. Though MARC began as a format for printed monographs, formats for serials, scores, maps, and other types of library materials soon appeared. With some national variations, use of MARC bibliographic format became international. The MARC formats became the "language" technical services librarians shared, much, perhaps, as the Dewey Decimal Classification had been the technical knowledge shared among an earlier period of professional history. MARC therefore appeared prominently and steadily in library literature throughout the period, with the most extensive publication activity in the mid-1970s, which saw MARC gain almost universal acceptance as a standard, and then again toward the end of the period, with use of MARC for archival materials, questions regarding possible licensing of USMARC by the Library of Congress, and projected integration of MARC bibliographic formats. *Library Literature*'s heading for MARC changed from "MARC project" to "MARC system" with the volume for 1985 (see Table 1.4).

Henriette D. Avram was the principal designer of MARC, as well as MARC's effective publicist. Her contributions to the literature of this subject are extensive and irreplaceable.[31] Another essential work for technical services librarians for their own work and for explaining cataloging's standard "grammar" to colleagues and support staff was Walt Crawford's *MARC for Library Use,* which appeared in two editions.[32] The USMARC documents of the Library of Congress, along with the various manuals of bibliographic utilities, constitute a considerable body of technical library literature.

Automation of Serials Control Processes

Automation of serials control processes is complex and time-consuming at the design, programming, and implementation stages (see Table 1.5). In addition, standards for serials holdings data have been long in development and slow to be accepted by libraries. One might assume from those two facts and the apparent relationship between wide agreement on standards and wide use of bibliographic databases and local online catalogs that literature on the automation of serials control processes might have appeared in significant volume only within the last decade. This is not the case: entries under the *Library Literature* heading "Automation for library processes–Serial records" appeared in every volume of the period, quite prominently in the 1974-1975 volume, as well as the 1988 and 1989 volumes. Nearly all entries were for journal/periodical articles. In part, the rather steady appearance of this subject in the literature appeared to reflect CONSER activity. After searching

TABLE 1.4. MARC Formats

Library Lit. Vols.	Total No. Entries	No. Entries for Per. Articles	No. of Per. Titles
1970-71	56	34	18
1972-73	69	40	19
1974-75	118	102	40
1976-77	85	75	35
1978	18	17	12
1979	24	22	10
1980	21	18	11
1981	19	14	10
1982	21	19	13
1983	28	27	19
1984	22	21	13
1985	21	19	11
1986	20	14	10
1987	28	22	16
1988	35	26	14
1989	41	39	16
1990	44	34	17

my memory as well as the citations, I concluded that computer-produced or online serials lists (either union lists or for a single institution) were a common do-it-yourself, nonstandard automation project in many libraries during the late 1960s and 1970s, and subsequently appeared in the literature in the "how-I-done-it-good" category of library journal articles. While such articles can be valuable, they are less so when they do not involve specific application of agreed-upon standard practices; then they recount endless rediscoveries of more or less round library wheels.

Most current automated serials control systems construct check-in and holdings records around the bibliographic record. Thus, serials cataloging is an important element in effective serials control and retrieval. Serials cataloging practices in the U.S. changed drastically during this period, and many libraries virtually recataloged their collections of currently-received serials publica-

TABLE 1.5. Automation of Serials Control Processes

Library Lit. Vols.	Total No. Entries	No. Entries for Per. Articles	No. of Per. Titles
1970-71	33	16	12
1972-73	34	24	14
1974-75	71	46	23
1976-77	46	41	22
1978	6	5	5
1979	15	15	9
1980	11	8	8
1981	20	20	11
1982	23	20	9
1983	21	18	8
1984	36	35	14
1985	23	22	11
1986	33	29	12
1987	40	35	12
1988	43	40	15
1989	48	47	16
1990	29	26	15

tions: AACR2 reduced entry under corporate bodies and specified creation of a new serial record for every "significant" title change in a serial publication's history. Again, to judge from the literature, libraries undertook this change and the commitment of specialized staff time required without significant study and demonstration of expected benefits, and without much apparent study of serial records in an online environment. Here was one place in library research in which a controlled experiment with selected patrons and staff interacting with online serials records might have been feasible and meaningful.

An early comparison and evaluation of possible methods of serials cataloging was Kathryn Luther Henderson's "Serial Cataloging Revisited–A Long Search for a Little Theory and a Lot of Cooperation."[33] This article, plus Professor Henderson's exhaustive (and exhausting) true-to-life serials cataloging exercises guaranteed that her students left library school with a sense of the possibilities for serials cataloging. Following adoption of AACR2 by the Library of Congress and OCLC (in bibliographic input standards for new records), other catalog librarians began to explore these possibilities as well. *The Serials Librarian* published a special issue on serials cataloging which has become required reading for technical services professionals.[34] Discussion on this issue continues.

Cataloging Costs: Time and Money

During the period under study, cataloging practice became more standardized. With proliferating rule interpretations, format documents, and requirements for input of new records into bibliographic utilities, cataloging became, arguably, more exacting, on a national basis if not in all libraries. A major reason during the 1970s for libraries to join a bibliographic utility was to cut the rate of increase of cataloging costs. But as libraries acquired online library systems, systems personnel, computer equipment that quickly grew obsolete, and all the other accouterments of automation, the cost of cataloging materials and maintaining the catalog as a whole seemed to loom as large as some academic libraries' backlogs of uncataloged materials. Cataloging costs were a universal object of administrative scrutiny, and a regular topic of library literature (see Table 1.6).

Unfortunately, library and even some technical services literature does not demonstrate a clear consensus concerning the catalog's purposes or intended audience. While cost is an important question, particularly in an era of shrinking real budgets, the first question must be cost of what. A prominent figure in librarianship once told me that the time my department spent working on the syndetic structure and consistency of access points in our online catalog was not useful, because "scholars don't search that way." Since users of this library were primarily undergraduates, I had assumed that the way scholars searched for materials in their own fields was not the only relevant consideration. To what extent are the library's bibliographic systems intended to aid in location of known items only? To what extent should these systems accommodate non-experts? The usual quinquennial calls for cataloging simplification generally do not address the non-expert user's need for multiple access points, natural-language entry into the system to guarantee retrieval, and

TABLE 1.6. Cataloging Costs: Time and Money

Library Lit. Vols.	Total No. Entries	No. Entries for Per. Articles	No. of Per. Titles
1970-71	16	11	9
1972-73	13	9	6
1974-75	10	8	8
1976-77	13	11	9
1978	3	3	3
1979	1	1	1
1980	2	1	1
1981	3	2	2
1982	0	0	0
1983	4	3	2
1984	3	2	2
1985	0	0	0
1986	8	7	7
1987	1	1	1
1988	5	5	3
1989	2	2	2
1990	1	1	1

controlled-vocabulary indexing to guarantee high recall. Simplified input will not necessarily result in ease and predictability of retrieval for users at varying levels of expertise. The literature on cataloging costs usually does not address this issue; most libraries skirt the issue with platitudes about serving everyone, whether or not the resources exist to do so. Soon a crisis in costs may force us to confront the issue.

Classification

Classification appeared as an important concern of U.S. librarians in two contexts during the period under study. At the beginning of the period, academic libraries of all sizes were investing vast amounts of staff time in reclassifying their collections from the Dewey Decimal Classification to the Library of Congress Classification. Most stated reasons for these projects involved expectation of reducing future costs for assigning call numbers, since the Library of Congress assigned full LC call numbers for most materials it cataloged, but only class numbers for the Dewey scheme. The literature surrounding this topic tended to focus on how-to: how to use the Library of Congress schedules, with which many technical services librarians were unfamiliar; how to plan the project; "how we done it good" once it was over, etc. There was some, but relatively little, discussion concerning the present uses of classification, the qualities of the two schemes as well as others, their respective usefulness in various situations, and potential uses of classification in automated library systems. In one paper toward the end of the heaviest period of reclassification, Gordon Stevenson stated that ". . . the most vigorous advocates of LCC have given us little more than opinion surveys, cost studies (which I cannot accept), and 'good news' from network organizers."[35] Stevenson pointed out the "self-evident potential" of DDC for online subject browsing, and the probable greater difficulties of using LCC, a less hierarchical and predictable scheme, for that purpose.[36]

During the 1980s, studies involving the use of classification as a tool for online subject retrieval began to appear more frequently in the literature. As a result of automation, U.S. librarians began to discover that classification was not necessarily and exclusively linked to shelf arrangement. Karen Markey's work in exploring the potential of classification systems, particularly DDC, resulted in several significant contributions.[37] By the end of the period, interest was sufficiently high for *CCQ* to publish papers from a symposium entitled "Classification as an Enhancement of Intellectual Access to Information in an Online Environment" as a special issue.[38]

Ironically, however, the same lack of understanding of the potential of classification and lack of knowledge of other countries' practices may stymie the development of online uses of classification. I have been dismayed in reading some of the literature to discover that there are prominent technical services librarians who may not know that a manual classified catalog ordinarily has a subject index, to enable users to enter the scheme easily, and, similarly, that effective use of classification as an online information retrieval tool must permit and facilitate entry by natural-language terms. Wider education on the concept of natural-language entry into a classification or controlled-vocabulary scheme might clarify longstanding discussions on the relative merits of natural-language vs. controlled vocabulary in searching.

The literature on classification was far more international in origin than that under any other heading I reviewed; many entries were for items in a language other than English, and English-language entries tended to originate in Great Britain. While *Library Literature* indexed vast numbers of articles and monographs on the subject of classification throughout the period, the volume of literature about this topic actually appears to have decreased (see Table 1.7).

Preservation of Library Materials

Preservation has become the growth industry of technical services literature. At the beginnng of the period, many technical services librarians (including this one) were using acidic glues, slapping on copious strips of vinyl repair tape, and sending periodicals out to be mutilated before oversewing–most of us quite ignorant of the damage we were doing. By the end of the period, an entirely different consciousness prevailed among librarians. The literature of preservation reflected and, to a large extent, may have affected this change.

While preservation-related literature appeared under many headings in *Library Literature* throughout the period, the bulk of relevant materials appeared under one access point which changed form twice. Its earliest incarnation was the subheading "Care and restoration" under the heading "Books." In the 1974-1975 volume, this index term became a heading in its own right–"Care and restoration of books, periodicals, etc."–a shift which facilitated more extensive and more specialized subdividing. Finally, in 1988, *Library Literature* changes its index term to match common professional usage of the previous 15 years: "Preservation of library materials."

Preservation literature showed a startling increase over the last two decades. It is an international and multilingual literature, as is its principal journal, *Restaurator.*[39] Its increase, however, must in part result from the subject's appearance in library periodicals of all types, including several U.S. state and regional library publications: *Oklahoma Librarian*[40] made a strong showing on this topic over several years.

Preservation literature of the past two decades has covered many

TABLE 1.7. Classification

Library Lit. Vols.	Total No. Entries	No. Entries for Per. Articles	No. of Per. Titles	No. of non-English entries
1970-71	176	100	47	24
1972-73	182	111	44	29
1974-75	232	175	55	60
1976-77	198	131	54	37
1978	84	43	25	11
1979	77	53	28	21
1980	93	69	30	20
1981	90	58	32	11
1982	77	56	31	7
1983	71	55	30	16
1984	53	47	25	24
1985	55	49	23	14
1986	101	76	30	28
1987	61	39	18	14
1988	52	40	27	7
1989	66	63	31	27
1990	87	78	24	23

topics, in particular the use of appropriate supplies and techniques for repair of library materials, binding practices, alkaline paper standards and publisher conformity, preservation microfilming, mass deacidification, and disaster planning and management. Two examples of the conservation-oriented repair manuals which appeared included *The Practical Guide to Book Repair and Conservation,* by Arthur Johnson,[41] and Jane Greenfield's *Books: Their Care and Repair,*[42] which was based on her earlier series of pamphlets. During this period, the Library Binding Institute issued its standards document in its fifth[43] through eighth[44] editions. Jan Merrill-Oldham and Paul Parisi wrote a *Guide to the Library Binding Institute Standard for Library Binding,*[45] which explained and illustrated principles of binding consistent with comfortable patron use, as well as with long-term preservation concerns. Of the many disaster planning documents of the period, a fine example came from the

Canadian Library Association: Claire England and Karen Evans' *Disaster Management for Libraries: Planning and Process.*[46] Lisa L. Fox's *A Core Collection in Preservation* provided an overview of literature on the subject toward the end of the period.[47] Literature of the coming decade will probably treat more extensively the preservation of literature only available in one of various machine-readable forms (see Table 1.8).

Technical Services

With the availability of LC MARC tapes, bibliographic utilities with contributed cataloging data, electronic order transmission to vendors, and computer-produced or online union lists, technical services became the first major area of library operation (possibly excepting circulation) to experience significant organizational impacts from automation. Staffing patterns changed; lines between acquisitions, serials, and cataloging units blurred. Lines between technical and public services wavered, and some libraries believed these lines should disappear. Technical services was the first major area of library operations to cope with the implications of national communications and data standards for local practices, and to feel the effects of extensive library-staff time spent at computer terminals. Technical services costs were an administrative concern throughout the period; scrutiny intensified as budget cuts loomed and materialized. To what extent did these upheavals stimulate discussion about technical services as an organizational unit, with special characteristics and problems, and with a particular future? To what extent did the literature reflect professional examination of technical services as a whole?

Entries in *Library Literature* suggest that the extent of published study and discussion was limited. Technical services management was the subject of articles in several publications and of a special issue of the *Journal of Library Administration;*[48] technical services costs and models for cost studies appeared; and a new journal of the period, *Technical Services Quarterly,*[49] presented an issue on the future of technical services.[50] Occasionally there were pieces with catchy titles which suggested that drastic changes in the basic organizational patterns of libraries would eliminate technical services *per se.* Few of these pieces dealt with the implications of the highly

TABLE 1.8. Preservation of Library Materials

Library Lit. Vols.	Total No. Entries	No. Entries for Per. Articles	No. of Per. Titles
1970-71	59	26	15
1972-73	50	22	9
1974-75	85	39	22
1976-77	86	39	18
1978	45	21	8
1979	61	22	8
1980	66	28	8
1981	50	21	4
1982	78	28	3
1983	65	34	7
1984	61	22	10
1985	76	33	11
1986	104	32	17
1987	87	36	3
1988	99	31	7
1989	122	44	14
1990	132	42	11

specialized and rapidly changing knowledge required of all levels of technical services employees.

Basic organizational changes may indeed be just around the corner for libraries. These will likely result from the shift from ownership to access, the increased commercialization of publishing and the growth of the information industry, and shrinking budgets for human services. If librarians continue to exist as an occupational group, they may all need the knowledge that technical services workers possess, in much the way that integrated library systems and large bibliographic databases have required circulation and interlibrary loan units to become more familiar with machine-readable bibliographic formats and their use for efficient operation. As the literature of most subject areas grows more extensive and becomes more highly specialized–just as the literature of technical services has done–can public services oriented around academic disciplines continue to exist in university libraries in a meaningful way? What if document delivery becomes part of acquisitions, and a major component in library services? Rather than moving technical services employees from their disbanded units into public services, would not most library operations become technical services? I hope that more technical services practitioners' thoughts on coming organizational changes in libraries will soon find their way into the literature (see Table 1.9).

Gifts "in Kind": Costs to Libraries

This topic was not one I found recurring in "Year's Work" articles. It is my personal interest, developed over years of observing staff time assigned to inventory, acknowledge, review, search, catalog (often originally), and process unsolicited gifts in kind. Was it only perception, or could I find verification that accepting gifts was expensive in labor? And were gifts indeed costly for public relations for a library to refuse? I decided to use this opportunity to check out the literature on the subject of gift costs.

"Books gifts" appeared to be the most relevant heading in *Library Literature,* but most entries under this heading concerned specific gifts to specific institutions. No *Library Literature* volumes for the period indexed more than 16 items under this heading; one volume had no entries, and five other volumes had five or fewer entries: a very small pool of literature. Another relevant heading was "Gifts, contributions, etc."; however, entries under this heading largely concerned fundraising and its attendant issues.

In 1980, Greenwood Press published a monographic treatment by Alfred H. Lane.[51] There is also an ARL SPEC Kit (though I generally find these less helpful than I hope they will be).[52] Gifts and exchanges rate a chapter in each of two editions of a standard acquisitions text[53] and of an important recent collection,[54] as well as a chapter in a recent overview of technical services.[55] But the journal literature on the topic is sparse; and examination showed it–despite promising titles and a chorus of "the library should control the gifts"–to be alarmingly upbeat. Worse, hard data was very scarce on the ground, so I could not confirm or debunk my prejudices with figures. As a starting point on this topic, perhaps librarians at several comparable institutions (e.g., middle-sized academic

TABLE 1.9. Technical Services

Library Lit. Vols.	Total No. Entries	No. Entries for Per. Articles	No. of Per. Titles
1970-71	25	15	10
1972-73	23	14	11
1974-75	19	11	10
1976-77	25	15	8
1978	7	4	4
1979	7	4	3
1980	8	6	5
1981	11	7	6
1982	6	5	4
1983	12	10	6
1984	9	7	5
1985	16	15	10
1986	6	4	3
1987	12	13	8
1988	20	10	8
1989	15	14	9
1990	17	13	9

libraries at state-supported universities) could compute their gift costs, following the recent "Guide to Cost Analysis of Acquisitions and Cataloging in Libraries."[56] They could compile their data, then pass the results to colleagues at comparable institutions which do not accept gifts in kind except for resale, for these colleagues' comments. An article sharing these data and observations, no matter what they were, would be a valuable addition to the current literature, for library administrators as well as technical services librarians.

SUGGESTIONS FOR STUDY

The fact that publishing in library and information science has increased dramatically during the past several decades is apparent from a cursory examination of the size of *Library Literature* volumes. The preceding discussion suggests that publishing in library technical services has also increased dramatically during the past 20 years. What is not obvious is whether library literature and technical services literature specifically have increased at a rate greater than that of scholarly or professional publishing in general. Research and production of scholarly work is increasing at an exponential rate.[57] The extent to which the rate of increase in publishing of technical services literature varies significantly from the rate for library literature generally or from the rate for other areas of scholarship (e.g., social sciences) would be an interesting focus of study.

A systematic exploration of the use of technical services literature in library practice–a methodologically sophisticated study with, perhaps, multiple means of gathering data, rather than the more generally encountered reductionist survey–might make for revealing reading, particularly if the study included the use of new forms of publishing/communications (already exemplified in *ALCTS Network News,* ACQNET, etc.) and its implications. Providing the profession with this information about its own behavior, apart from its intrinsic interest, could be useful in addressing issues in library education and professional development.

Another complex and interesting topic for study, previously suggested by Joe A. Hewitt,[58] would be the relationship between library research literature and library or specifically library technical services practice. Librarianship is a professional practice, not an academic discipline which exists primarily for the purpose of extending knowledge of its own field of inquiry. Its practice, however, would be more effective if it rested more firmly on a high-quality research base.[59] An accurate analysis of the present relationship between library research and practice could serve as a starting point for profession-wide discussions of what we would like that relationship to be, and of how we might accomplish a change, if we agree that a change is appropriate.

REFERENCE NOTES

1. Bernd Frohmann, "A Bibliometric Analysis of the Literature of Cataloging and Classification," *Library Research* 4 (1982): 359.

2. *Library Resources & Technical Services* 14-35 (1970-1991).

3. John J. Boll, "Professional Literature on Cataloging–Then and Now," *Library Resources & Technical Services* 29 (July/September 1985): 226-238.

4. *Library Literature: An Index to Library and Information Science,* 1970/1971-90 (New York: H. W. Wilson, 1972-1991).

5. *Library Acquisitions: Practice and Theory* 1- (1977-).

6. *The Acquisitions Librarian* 1- (1989-).

7. *Technicalities* 1- (1989-).

8. *Serials Review* 1- (1975-).

9. *The Serials Librarian* 1- (1976-).

10. *Against the Grain* 1- (1989-).

11. *Cataloging & Classification Quarterly* 1- (1980-).

12. *Library Software Review* 3- (1984-).

13. *Library Technology Reports* 1- (1981-).

14. James T. Diffenbaugh and Hope H. Yelick, "A Selected Bibliography of Library Acquisitions," *RTSD Newsletter* 13 (1988): 33-36.

15. James D. Diffenbaugh and Hope H. Yelick, rev. by Barbara C. Dean, "A Selected Bibliography of Library Acquisitions," *ALCTS Newsletter* 2 (1991): 43-47.

16. Stephen Ford, *The Acquisition of Library Materials* (Chicago: American Library Association, 1973).

17. Rose Mary Magrill and Doralyn J. Hickey, *Acquisitions Management and Collection Development in Libraries,* 2d ed. (Chicago: American Librarian Association, 1984).

18. Audrey Eaglen, *Buying Books: A How-to-Do-It Manual for Librarians* (New York: Neal-Schuman, 1989).

19. Karen A. Schmidt, ed., *Understanding the Business of Library Acquisitions* (Chicago: American Library Association, 1990).

20. Karen A. Schmidt, " 'Buying Good Pennyworths?' A Review of the Literature of Acquisitions in the Eighties," *Library Resources & Technical Services* 30 (October/December 1986): 336.

21. *Anglo-American Cataloguing Rules,* 2d ed. (Chicago: American Library Association, 1978). -Corrected 2d ed., 1979.

22. *Anglo-American Cataloguing Rules.* 2d ed. rev. (Chicago: American Library Association, 1988).

23. Bernd Frohmann, "A Bibliometric Analysis," 356.

24. C. Sumner Spalding, "The Life and Death(?) of Corporate Authorship," *Library Resources & Technical Services* 24 (Summer 1980): 195-208.

25. Michael Carpenter and Elaine Svenoius, ed., *Foundations of Cataloging: A Sourcebook* (Littleton, CO: Libraries Unlimited, 1985), xi.

26. Elaine Svenonius, ed., *The Conceptual Foundations of Descriptive Cataloging* (San Diego: Academic Press, 1989).

27. Seymour Lubetzky and R.M. Hayes, "Bibliographic Dimensions in Information Control," *American Documentation* 20 (July 1969): 436-441.

28. For example: S. Michael Malinconico, "Bibliographic Data Base Organization and Authority File Control," *Wilson Library Bulletin* 54 (September 1979): 36-45.

29. Mary W. Ghikas, ed., *Authority Control: The Key to Tomorrow's Catalog: Proceedings of the 1979 Library & Information Technology Association Institutes* (Phoenix, AZ: Oryx Press, 1982).

30. Barbara C. Tillett, ed., "Authority Control in the Online Environment: Considerations and Practices," *Cataloging & Classification Quarterly* 9, no. 3 (1989).

31. For example: Henriette D. Avram, *MARC, Its History and Implications* (Washington, DC: Library of Congress, 1975).

32. Walt Crawford, *MARC for Library Use: Understanding the USMARC Formats* (White Plains, NY: Knowledge Industry Publications, 1984); Walt Crawford, *MARC for Library Use: Understanding Integrated USMARC,* 2d ed. (Boston: G.K. Hall, 1989).

33. Kathryn Luther Henderson, "Serial Cataloging Revisited–A Long Search for a Little Theory and a Lot of Cooperation," in *Serial Publications in Large Libraries,* ed. Walter C. Allen (Urbana: University of Illinois Graduate School of Library Science, 1970), 48-49.

34. Jim E. Cole and Jackie Zajanc, eds., "Serials Cataloging: The State of the Art," *The Serials Librarian* 12, no. 1/2 (1987).

35. Gordon Stevenson, "The Library of Congress Classification Scheme and Its Relationship to Dewey," in *Major Classification Systems: The Dewey Centennial,* ed. Kathryn Luther Henderson (Urbana: University of Illinois Graduate School of Library Science, 1976), 97.

36. Ibid., p. 90.

37. For example: Karen Markey, "The Dewey Decimal Classification as a Library User's Tool in an Online Catalog," in *1984: Challenges to an Information Society: Proceedings of the 47th ASIS Annual Meeting, Philadelphia, Pennsylvania, October 21-25, 1984,* compiled by Barbara Flood, Joanne Witiak, and Thomas H. Hogan (White Plains, NY: Knowledge Industry Publications, 1984), 121-125.

38. Benjamin F. Speller, Jr., ed., "Classification as an Enhancement of Intellectual Access to Information in an Online Environment: Papers Presented as Part of the Second Annette Lewis Phinazee Symposium . . . ," *Cataloging & Classification Quarterly* 11, no. 1 (1990).

39. *Restaurator* 1- (1969-).

40. *Oklahoma Librarian* 1- (1950).

41. Arthur W. Johnson, *The Practical Guide to Book Repair and Conservation* (New York: Thames & Hudson, 1988).

42. Jane Greenfield, *Books: Their Care and Repair* (New York: H. W. Wilson, 1983).

43. *Library Binding Institute Standard for Library Binding.* 5th ed., rev. (Boston: Library Binding Institute, 1971).

44. Paul A. Parisi and Jan Merrill-Oldham, eds., *Library Binding Institute Standard for Library Binding,* 8th ed. (Rochester, NY: Library Binding Institute, 1986).

45. Jan Merrill-Oldham and Paul Parisi, *Guide to the Library Binding Institute Standard for Library Binding* (Chicago: American Library Association, 1990).

46. Claire England and Karen Evans, *Disaster Management for Libraries: Planning and Process* (Ottawa: Canadian Library Association, 1988).

47. Lisa L. Fox, for the Education Committee, Preservation of Library Materials Section, Resources and Technical Services Divison, ALA, *A Core Collection in Preservation* (Chicago: American Library Association, 1988).

48. *Journal of Library Administration* 1- (1980-).

49. *Technical Services Quarterly* 1- (1983-).

50. Peter Gellatly, ed., "Beyond '1984': The Future of Library Technical Services," *Technical Services Quarterly* 1, no. 1/2 (Fall/Winter 1983).

51. Alfred H. Lane, *Gifts and Exchanges* (Westport, CT: Greenwood Press, 1980).

52. Julieanne V. Nilson, *The Gifts and Exchange Function in ARL Libraries, SPEC Kit 117* (Washington, DC: Association of Research Libraries, 1985).

53. Ford, *The Acquisition of Library Materials,* 1955-1963; Magrill and Hickey, *Acquisitions Management,* 215-233.

54. Mae Clark, "Gifts and Exchanges," in Schmidt, *Understanding the Business of Acquisition,* 167-185.

55. Joseph W. Barker, "Gifts and Exchanges," in *Technical Services Today and Tomorrow,* comp. Michael Gorman (Englewood, CO: Libraries Unlimited, 1990), 23-37.

56. "Guide to Cost Analysis of Acquisitions and Cataloging in Libraries," prepared by ALCTS Technical Services Costs Committee *ALCTS Newsletter* 2 (1991): 49-52.

57. Eldred Smith, "Resolving the Acquisitions Dilemma: Into the Electronic Information Environment," *College & Research Libraries* 52 (May 1991): 235.

58. Joe A. Hewitt, "The Use of Research," *Library Resources & Technical Services* 27 (April/June 1983): 123.

59. Ibid., p. 131.

Chapter 2

From Catalog to OPAC:
A Look at 25 Years of Technical Services
in School Libraries

Kathleen L. Shannon
Mary Ellyn Gibbs

Having both been born in the very early years of the infamous baby boom, we have seen school libraries during the last quarter century from the varied perspectives of high school and undergraduate library patrons, of MLS students learning the mysteries of cataloging and other aspects of librarianship, of new graduates working with older colleagues whose ways did not always coincide with our own "newfangled" methods, and, more recently, as veterans of the high school library trenches who have ourselves had to cope with changes in the way libraries do things. The major changes in technical services can perhaps be grouped (and it is impossible to stop catalogers from grouping things!) under: (1) new rules and practices, (2) new types of materials to be handled, and (3) new types of equipment used to facilitate work in this area.

CATALOGING PRINCIPLES AND PRACTICES

The first really major change in cataloging practice during the past 25 years was the introduction in 1967 of the new *Anglo-American Cataloging Rules.* These replaced the 1949 *A.L.A. Cataloging Rules for Author and Title Entries* and the *Rules for Descriptive Cataloging in the Library of Congress,* that catalogers had used in tandem for 18 years.

The introduction to the 1949 *A.L.A. Rules* stated that,

> since promoting increased uniformity and standardization is an important purpose of the rules, few alternative rules have been suggested. It is recognized . . . that some . . . variations may be justifiable. . . . It should be emphasized, however, that such deviation should be made only to gain some distinct advantage, since libraries benefit most from the work of other libraries when all conform to standard practice.[1]

School librarians who were not bold enough to flout this rather stern declaration for uniformity, thus found themselves bound by cataloging rules more appropriate for large research collections than for those serving elementary and secondary students. Others ignored the A.L.A. rules altogether and continued with whatever systems were already in place in their libraries. Many school librarians *did* use the 1949 rules, but made their own exceptions, either because such complete, formal cataloging was inappropriate for their young patrons or because they themselves had neither the time nor the inclination to do such in-depth cataloging. (Let us admit here and now that cataloging is *not* a favorite task of many school librarians!)

The 1967 AACR provided a more flexible, realistic framework for cataloging in non-research libraries. The introduction to the new rules announced that,

> when the needs of research libraries and those of other libraries are irreconcilable, alternative rules have been provided for the use of the latter. Furthermore, considerable emphasis has been placed on . . . substituting headings that correspond more closely to the normal usage . . . for certain former headings that emphasized technical correctness to the point of pedantry.[2]

The new rules were thus much more helpful for schools and other non-research libraries that wanted a cataloging standard that would put them in line with the practices of larger institutions, yet without going to ridiculous extremes.

Many librarians are no more fond of change than they are of cataloging, and the new rules were certainly not greeted with universal enthusiasm, even among the school and other librarians whose needs they were designed to meet. Even for librarians who welcomed AACR, changing to the new rules meant a great deal of relearning. For those of us fortunate enough to have entered library school after 1967, the conversion was fairly painless. We simply learned AACR in our cataloging courses, and had to deal with the 1949 rules only insofar as we encountered them in the existing card catalog, and perhaps in working with older colleagues who were reluctant to let them go. Diligent cataloging professors did see to it that we knew enough about the 1949 rules to realize how lucky we were to have AACR instead, but we did not suffer the trauma of learning one set of rules and trying to apply it to the school library collection, only to then abandon it and be forced to learn an entirely new set of rules. For many of our colleagues, however, this was a necessary and often painful process, and represented a major change in their cataloging practices.

A change in cataloging practice that has occurred recently in many academic libraries, but that has *not* taken hold in elementary and secondary schools, is the shift from the Dewey Decimal Classification (DDC) to the Library of Congress (LC) classification system. While many colleges are adopting LC, with its more detailed breakdown of subject areas, school and public libraries have generally kept DDC or its abridged version, and seem to find this more than adequate for their patrons' needs. The 19th and 20th editions of DDC, that have appeared in the last quarter century, have contained substantial revisions in such major sections as the social sciences, history and geography, and music that have attempted to make those classifications more appropriate for modern libraries, and these revisions have required school librarians to do considerable amounts of reclassification in those portions of their collections. It is probable that various sections of the DDC will continue to be revised in the future, and that reclassification is consequently something that catalogers will need to do periodically.

Subject headings represent another aspect of library cataloging that is always in flux, but even more so in recent years due to rapid changes in every area of modern life from cooking and diets to nuclear weapons. The increasing speed of such change is reflected in the growing frequency with which the *Library of Congress Subject Headings* has needed revision. In the 65 years from 1909 to

1974, seven editions were published, while in the 15 years from 1975 to 1990, six new editions appeared, and new editions will henceforth be issued annually.

Keeping up with changes in subject headings, whether from LC, Sears, or some other source, is the bane of many overextended school librarians (even those who do not dislike cataloging in the first place). While we are always happy to see such pesky, obsolete headings as "European War," "Aeroplanes," and "Africa, South" disappear (thus eliminating several cross-references and much student frustration), there is no doubt that changing subject headings in the card catalog is tedious and time-consuming. (It is less of a problem with an online catalog that allows mass changes to be made.) We may perhaps be excused if we sometimes feel that the official updaters of subject headings (whom we suspect are *never* distracted from their work by 30 students all looking for a book on the same author or animal at the same time) demonstrate a rather cavalier and annoying inconsistency in the promptness with which they change headings. We floundered along with "European War" for 70 years, yet had used "Atomic" for less than half as long before "Nuclear" replaced it in many headings. We have also waited impatiently for new headings of great interest to our young patrons (such as "Rock music") to appear in the subject headings list, and have often gone ahead and used these before they became "official." Fortunately, the latter problem has diminished as the lists have been revised more frequently. School librarians have had to face the fact that, as computer capabilities allow faster and faster revision of subject heading lists, and as accelerating change creates the need for more and more new terminology, changing and adding subject headings in our catalogs has been increasingly necessary. As busy as we are with other activities and programs, we must take the time to keep up with this if we want our catalogs to be responsive to our young users' needs and interests.

Changing and updating aside, even getting books cataloged and processed for use in the first place can be an overwhelming task, especially when clerical help is scarce or nonexistent and when such seasonal activities as research papers and battle-of-the-books competitions are making their insistent demands on our time and energies. In the last 25 years, many schools have solved this problem by purchasing books already cataloged and processed from jobbers and publishers. This service has been a godsend for many school librarians, especially those who are the sole professionals in their buildings or districts and who feel they should spend their limited time working directly with students rather than on such behind-the-scenes detail work as technical services.

As increasing numbers of libraries have expressed an interest in purchasing prepared card sets and preprocessed books with labels, pockets and cards, and mylar jackets already attached, a wider variety of formats for these has become available, from the very simple for primary grade collections to complete MARC cataloging, either on MARC tapes or already printed on card stock. Computerization has allowed suppliers of cataloging and processing to provide each library with services tailored to its own specifications in terms of classification system, length of number, source of subject headings, annotations, and extent of description, collation, and notes.

Though it may seem a minor point to laypersons and to many of our nonschool colleagues, we should mention the impact of one lowly item, the mylar book jacket, on both technical and public services. These plastic protectors have totally changed the look of the school library by making it practical and desirable to leave the dust jackets on books. Shelves of drab buckram covers have thus given way to ranks of bright, attractive, and increasingly high-quality cover art that catches the eye of the young potential reader. Though this may be unimportant in academic and large public libraries, it makes it much easier for school librarians to sell their wares to often reluctant students, which is a major goal as we attempt to attract and develop lifelong readers and users of information. An added bonus is the protection that these jackets provide for the books, thereby reducing the need for time-consuming repairs. (A possible drawback for some school librarians is the fact that they can no longer base their displays on dust jackets pinned to bulletin boards, but this could also be a blessing, if it fans a spark of creativity somewhere!)

As prices for cataloging and preprocessing have become competitive enough for even small schools to afford, many school librarians have been able to spend more time working with students and teachers without sacrificing the professional quality of their technical services. For many, in fact, quality has improved, as they have become able for the first time to have standard unit card sets that bring their catalogs in line with those of larger libraries. Though prepared cataloging does present the slight drawback of having to accept someone else's choice of classification number and subject headings, on the whole it has been a boon to the school libraries that use it.

In the last 17 years, a new twist on prepared cataloging has developed that has caused some school libraries to revert to making their own card sets again. This is the advent of Cataloging in Publication (CIP), that provides complete Library of Congress cataloging data, including annotations for juvenile fiction, on the verso of a book's title page. There are now relatively few U.S.-published books without CIP, so that it has become practical for some schools that had been purchasing cataloging now simply to copy the CIP data onto cards (or into computers) themselves. A trained clerk or paraprofessional can often do this if one is available, provided that a librarian with a knowledge of cataloging checks the CIP data for errors (which are not uncommon and are sometimes major, e.g., a book on space exploration assigned to 639.4–"culture and harvest of mollusks"–rather than 629.4–"astronautics").

Another development concurrent with the advent of CIP that has increased the feasibility of using that data to produce in-house catalog records is the arrival of inexpensive, easy-to-use microcomputer programs such as Quik Card and Librarian's Helper for catalog card production. These programs use bibliographic information entered by keyboard to produce sets of finished unit cards, complete with accession information on the shelf list, annotations if desired, and all necessary added entries and subject headings. Labels for the spine, pocket, and book card can also be produced, eliminating the need to either type these or to purchase commercial processing. These card production programs, which usually cost only $200-$300, are available for both Apple and IBM computers. As more and more school libraries acquire microcomputers to handle management tasks, these programs are gaining popularity as an inexpensive way to produce in-house card sets and to process materials.

Centralized processing at the district level is yet another solution to the cataloging and processing problem that many school libraries have used in recent years. Under such a plan, a central office catalogs and processes materials for the individual school libraries in the district. This has the advantage of providing a modified form of in-house cataloging without requiring each library staff to spend time on this operation. Many districts have found this to be more efficient and economical than on-site cataloging in terms of both staff time and dollars (no need for multiple copies of cataloging tools, no duplication of effort, etc.).

Once a library has acquired cataloging for a given item, by whatever means, the task remains of getting the bibliographic information into the catalog. With an online system, the data are entered and the software "files" according to rules specified by the library. For the many schools that still use card catalogs, however, human beings must file the cards into the drawers (preferably *not* at the same time that students are trying to use the catalog). Some school libraries have found it effective, since students most often approach their collections by subject, to have a divided rather than a dictionary catalog, with subject cards filed separately from author and title cards. This approach somewhat simplifies filing in both portions of the catalog.

As with so many other aspects of technical services, filing rules have changed in the last two and a half decades. In 1968, the second edition of the *ALA Rules for Filing Catalog Cards* appeared, updating the 1942 edition and making provision for new types of entries that were not previously covered. The old rules had attempted to provide for diverse filing practices by including alternatives for 60 percent of the rules. By 1968, demand had grown for simpler filing rules, and the new code tried to follow, with minimal exceptions, a straight alphabetical order without regard for punctuation. These rules made life simpler for many school librarians, though they were certainly not perfect.

The 1968 rules were expressly intended for *card* filing, but as automated catalogs became more common, new rules were again needed to meet new requirements. Thus in 1980 the *ALA Filing Rules* appeared, abbreviated both in title and content (50 pages compared with 260 in 1968). The introduction to the new rules stated that "since the present rules are based to a much greater extent than their predecessors on the 'file-as-is' principle, and since the new rules are applicable to bibliographic displays in other than card formats, the work should be considered as new, and not as another edition."[3]

The major changes produced by this adherence to the file-as-is principle were: (1) names would now be interfiled with, rather than ahead of, other headings beginning with the same word; (2) abbreviations would be filed as-is rather than as if spelled out; and (3) numbers would be filed in numerical order before all alphabetical headings, rather than as if spelled.

While the new practices solved some problems (they were in some respects simpler for young patrons and were usable with automated systems), they created others, and the authors advised users that, in the interests of meeting local needs and of saving time and money, individual libraries might wish to retain some former practices. As might be expected, some school libraries have ignored the new rules altogether, some have adopted them wholeheartedly, and some have tried to work out reasonable compromises between old and new. For school librarians wishing to convert their card catalogs to the new filing guidelines, Christina B. Woll and Miriam C. Patton of El Paso, Texas, have outlined a successful incremental method.[4]

TYPES OF MATERIALS

Not only have changes in cataloging principles and practices had an impact on school libraries, but a second major change has affected the materials that school libraries catalog and process as well. Where the school library collection formerly consisted of a variety of hardback books, some magazines and newspapers, and perhaps some pamphlets, we now routinely handle paperback books, microforms, films, filmstrips, slides, kits, models, audio tapes, video cassettes, compact discs, and floppy disks. The need to organize these materials into a usable collection has created new cataloging rules and card formats that did not previously exist. School librarians responsible for cataloging these nontraditional materials have often found it helpful to take additional cataloging courses that emphasize nonprint materials. The 1967 AACR provided the first specific rules for such cataloging, and subsequent editions expanded on this coverage (the 1988 edition includes rules for various computer storage formats, laser disks, and videodiscs).

School librarians have not only had to learn how to catalog these new materials, but have also had to decide how and where to house and circulate them. Until the 1960s, audiovisual materials (usually consisting of relatively small collections of films, filmstrips, and phonorecords) were traditionally housed separately from the library collection. As nonprint information sources burst into the schools in the 1960s and 1970s, many school libraries began (often grudgingly) to make a place for nonprint items. The manner in which they did this ranged from separate but adjacent rooms for print and nonprint to special areas within the library for audiovisual resources to, in some cases, actual intershelving of book and nonbook materials. Though the majority of schools have stopped short of this last option (intershelving presents serious obstacles to efficient use of space, which is a must for most libraries), there are few today that do not at least have a small collection of nonprint resources and the accompanying hardware somewhere within their confines, and for many, nonprint materials represent a substantial part of their collection.

Paperback books, which first began to appear in many schools in the 1960s, presented special problems of their own. Debate raged in library circles over the desirability and propriety of including these low-priced, flimsy, popular books in the collection, and over how to treat them if they were included. Though many school librarians welcomed them as a means of catching student interest in reading, they were often considered a disposable item and therefore not worth cataloging. Many schools housed them on wire display racks, rather than on the regular shelves. As paperbacks gradually became a more accepted part of the collection (with many titles, both fiction and nonfiction now available *only* in paper), some school librarians decided that they would be used more effectively if they did appear in the catalog and were shelved with the hardbacks. By the 1990s, it is a rare school library that does not acquire paperbacks as a matter of course, and many treat them no differently than any other book, though some still house popular recreational titles, cataloged or not, on special display racks.

With the inclusion of more and more nontraditional materials in their collections, many schools have decided that the designation "library" is no longer adequate. Thus we now find a variety of new names that attempt to give a truer picture of the resources we offer, including library-media center or learning materials center (LMC), instructional materials center (IMC), learning resource center (LRC), and simply media center (MC). It should be noted that students and teachers do not seem as hung up about the name of the place as do those of us in the business, and many still refer to "the library" and "the librarian," regardless of what *we* decide to call ourselves and our domain!

AUTOMATION

The third major change that has affected many aspects of technical services in schools (indeed, in all libraries) is automation. As the massive mainframes of the 1960s have spawned ever more powerful and affordable mini- and microcomputers, we have become a nation increasingly reliant on and at home with these devices. Though many people, including a fair share of school librarians, still avoid computers like the plague, there are few schools left where the staff does not need to be "computer literate," given the students' eagerness to use this equipment and the computer's ability to take some of the drudgery out of such library detail work as cataloging and circulation.

Computers have made possible (and economically feasible, even for smaller schools) such wonders as automated circulation and inventory systems, online materials acquisition, online catalogs, in-house catalog card production, computerized control of serials, up-to-date union lists, and networking and resource sharing via modem. Though computers certainly play a part in the library's public services and programs, much of their impact has been in technical services, especially in the realm of bibliographic control. They have increased enormously the amount of shared cataloging in use, and are rapidly replacing the old reliable card catalog and published indexes in many schools. They eliminated a great deal of typing and filing–a definite boon to school librarians with insufficient clerical help, who used to have to do these chores themselves or leave them undone.

One perennial problem faced by schools using an online catalog is how to afford and make room for enough terminals so that the new automated version can serve roughly as many students at a time as could a multi-drawer card catalog. Administrators are often very eager to join the online bandwagon, but are appalled when the librarian explains how many terminals it will take to maintain previous levels of service in a busy school media center. (If terminals do not also have printers to provide hard copy, search time is increased as each student copies down the catalog information by hand.) When one or more entire classes try to look up materials simultaneously under the time constraints of the school schedule (a situation more or less unique to school libraries), a shortage of terminals can be disastrous. Some librarians, knowing they will not get enough hardware to provide effective online service, have opted to forego automation for the present, rather than frustrate young users with a poor system, or have kept the card catalog to backup and supplement the online catalog.

Computers have also made it possible to keep more accurate and extensive circulation records with less effort, and to inventory a larger portion of the collection in less time and with greater accuracy. This has had a positive impact on collection development by highlighting areas that need weeding or enhancing, and by helping guide acquisitions of new titles and replacement of older ones.

One problem faced by schools just launching into automation in any area of their library operations is the choice of which hardware and software to use, as well as what to automate first. Many schools have begun with automated circulation and later expanded to online catalogs. Automation is generally more successful when the library staff has a major role in the selection of the system to be used, since library operations, particularly in technical services, present unique problems and requirements that are unfamiliar to most laypersons. Most school libraries that had the choice have opted for mini- or microcomputer systems, rather than sharing time on a mainframe with other school operations such as accounting, personnel, and student records (library operations seldom take precedence when a mainframe is overloaded). Minis and micros allow the library to operate independently, avoiding the problem of downtime in circulation and catalog searches due to data overload.

Few school libraries exist today in which a CRT screen does not glow quietly somewhere, and in many schools, whole ranks of terminals stand ready to give students, teachers, and library staff access to powerful programs that provide information and help take much of the drudgery out of organizing it for use.

THE FUTURE

What is the future likely to bring to technical services in school libraries? None of us can say for certain, of course, but none of us doubts that change will continue, probably quite rapidly. There will almost certainly be further increases in the availability and use of shared cataloging, and thus more standardization of bibliographic records, along with less need for individual libraries to do a great deal of original cataloging.

As more schools go online with circulation and catalogs, the advantages of some systems over others will become more and more apparent, and the better ones will most likely squeeze the more marginal hardware and software out of the market. Further refinements and improvements will make the better systems more powerful and responsive to libraries' needs. Students are already experienced and enthusiastic computer users, and the day will soon arrive when teachers, including school librarians, will *have* to be equally at home with this new technology.

The expansion of CD-ROM information sources and various technologies linking audio, video, dataprocessing, and telecommunications systems will change the face of library operations and programs and open up possibilities that we are only beginning to glimpse at this time. These linkages are already beginning to put vast information resources at the fingertips of knowledgeable school librarians and their students and colleagues. This networking will most likely increase exponentially in the near future. It should be pointed out (and many commentators have done so recently) that, due to the archaic and inequitable methods still used by most states to fund education, there is a real danger that schools in many impoverished urban and rural areas will fall behind their more privileged counterparts in the acquisition and use of these new technologies and information networks. This could result in a segment of the school population (both faculty and students) becoming information have-nots, creating an even wider rift between these people and their more economically and technologically privileged peers–a rift that would most likely be lifelong.

School librarians of the future will need to be, not just preservers of past knowledge, but agents of change as well, creatively combining the best of the traditional with the best of the new. We will not be able to sit through two and three revisions of various manuals of our trade before reluctantly coming into line with our more up-to-date colleagues or drag our feet about accepting and using new methods and technologies. If we do, we will not only shortchange our students, who need to be prepared for the twenty-first century and all the changes it will bring; we will also effectively remove ourselves from the mainstream of education and from the central role we ought to play in all teaching that takes place in our schools.

Those school librarians who feel that the detail work of cataloging and other technical services is a bore and a waste of our professional time and talents need to realize that the masses of information we handle are useless if not organized. We must take advantage of the new technologies that make it possible to have quality, standardized records without spending a great deal of our own too-limited time creating these records ourselves. Perhaps some library school courses in technical services will come to emphasize where and how to acquire and use these services, rather than how to do original in-house cataloging.

Whatever the future brings, school librarians will need to embrace the new, not unquestionably or blindly, but with discernment and common sense, rather than cling to the past, if they wish to have well-organized, easily usable collections, and to play a vital central role in the lives of their schools.

REFERENCE NOTES

1. Clara Beetle, ed., *A.L.A. Cataloging Rules for Author and Title Entries* (Chicago: American Library Association, 1949), xxi.

2. American Library Association, *the Library of Congress, the Library Association, and the Canadian Library Association Anglo-American Cataloging Rules, ed. C. Sumner Spalding* (Chicago: American Library Association, 1967), 1.

3. *ALA Filing Rules* (Chicago: American Library Association, 1980), 1.

4. Christina B. Woll and Miriam C. Patton, *The School Librarian's Workshop* (Berkeley Heights, NJ: Library Learning Resources, September 1989), 6-7.

PART II:

ACQUISITIONS AND COLLECTION DEVELOPMENT

Chapter 3

Acquisitions and Collection Development

Marion Taylor Reid

One feature of the core courses provided new students in the Graduate School of Library Science curriculum at the University of Illinois in 1966 was a series of technical services laboratory sessions. These were designed to allow participants to experience procedures they would actually encounter on the job. During the acquisitions lab, each student was given a newly published title to search in the *American Book Publishing Record* and/or *Cumulative Book Index* and their supplements. Upon successfully completing his or her search, the student was allowed to leave . . . an attractive proposition, since this took place in a basement workroom of the main library on a Friday afternoon. It is amazing in retrospect that this author went into acquisitions work, since she was the very last student to complete this assignment in her section, finding the long-sought entry in the last possible issue of *Publishers Weekly.*

This exercise is out of place today in a world with OCLC's more than 23 million bibliographic entries available online. It represents one of many factors that make acquisitions very different from what it was 25 years ago. This chapter will describe changes in the last two and one-half decades in selection, funding, acquisitions tools, procurement methods, and staffing. It will also provide a brief look to the future. Focusing primarily on acquisitions trends in academic libraries in North America, it incorporates an overview of collection development.

SELECTION

In the last 25 years, selection has changed in the following areas:

- who is selecting
- how they are selecting
- how much they are acquiring
- what they are acquiring

Who Is Selecting

In the 1960s faculty commonly drove selection. The library materials budget was frequently divided into segments paralleling the academic areas of the institution and designated faculty members in each area determined how its segment was spent. Depending on the library organization, library staff responsible for communication with the faculty selectors were in acquisitions, reference, or a small bibliography unit. Those reviewing faculty orders occasionally supplemented them with orders for materials not covered by any academic area. In addition, librarians chose reference works and bibliographies.

In the 1960s library materials budgets were flush. Academic institutions were in a growth mode. Local support and federal funding were generous. Research library administrators began to hire subject specialists to coordinate collection development. Eventually the authority for library materials budget expenditure was moved from academic faculty to these subject specialists . . . or bibliographers . . . or selectors. Now, collection development has come into its own and in many libraries the coordinator of the collection development operation holds an administrative position reporting directly to the university librarian. In small academic libraries individuals are assigned the responsibility of coordinating collection development activities, even though in some places faculty members continue with primary selecting responsibilities for a specific portion of the library materials budget.

Terminology has varied during the transition.[1] "Collection development" and "collection management" is generally thought of as the building of the collection, whereas "collection management" is a broader term incorporating not only the building of the collection, but also weeding, circulation, and preservation aspects.

How They Are Selecting

Over the last two decades the growing cadre of collection development librarians have developed ways to analyze existing collections, to describe how they plan to add to those collections, and to seek ways to cooperate in collection development and preservation.

Collection development librarians created collection development policies to describe the directions in which they planned to build their collections. As budgets tightened, they analyzed their collections to identify strengths and gaps, and to provide data supporting rationale for future growth with limited funds. Some research library staffs undertook their own Collection Analysis Project, following the model developed by the Association of Research Libraries. Some librarians conducted use and user studies and bibliometric analyses to better determine their collection needs.[2]

During the 1970s two methods of collection description evolved: one quantitative and one with qualitative aspects. The quantitative method–the National Shelflist Count–was undertaken by members of the Chief Collection Development Officers of Large Research Libraries Discussion Group, a unit of the Association for Library Collections and Technical Services (ALCTS) (then known as the Resources & Technical Services Division [RTSD]) of the American Library Association. Those who chose to participate took careful measurement of their respective library's shelflist, by defined category. The resulting data was published by RTSD.

The qualitative method–the conspectus method–originated with collection development officers within the Research Libraries Group, who agreed to rate each of more than 5,000 subject segments of their collections on a scale of one (minimal level) to five (comprehensive level) in terms of existing collection strength and ongoing collecting commitment. Member libraries claimed "primary collecting responsibility" for those subjects for which they are pledged to continue to collect as the comprehensive level. The conspectus method was modified and adopted by smaller libraries in the Pacific Northwest so they could better cooperate in collection

development. In 1981 the Collection Development Task Force of
the Association of Research Libraries organized a project "to plan a
standard approach to cooperative collection development to ensure
that specialized research collections in ARL libraries would be
maintained as national resources."[3] The task force recommended
the conspectus as an assessment vehicle. The Association of Research Libraries and the Research Libraries Group continue to work
jointly on NCIP–the North American Collections Inventory Project.[4]

Collection development librarians have joined together in network groups and in other formations to go after the shrinking federal dollars which provide collection support. Frequently the cooperation disappeared when outside funding ended, but some
cooperative efforts continued after the federal dollars stopped. Notable cooperative collection development arrangements continue
among Duke University, the University of North Carolina, Chapel
Hill and North Carolina State University; between the University of
California, Berkeley and Stanford University; and among the nine
University of California campuses.

How Much They Are Acquiring

Libraries simply are not acquiring as great a percentage of materials available as they did 25 years ago. In 1965 the average price
for a U.S. hardcover book was $7.65, the preliminary average cost
for 1990 is about $39.90, or more than five times as much. In 1965
the average periodical price was $6.95, the 1990 average periodical
cost is $93.45, or more than 17 times as much!! Meanwhile, the
universe of what is available for purchase has increased. As an
example, the total numbers of hardcover trade books published in
the U.S. in 1967 was 16,257; the preliminary estimated number of
books published in 1990 is 23,468, an increase of 44 percent.[5]

The proportion of expenditures on books to serials has changed
dramatically. In the late 1960s a common rule of thumb for the
monographs/serials expenditure of the library materials budget was
$2.00 spent on books for every dollar spent on serials.[6] In
1975-1976 the Association of Research Library statistics first listed
monographs expenditures and serials expenditures separately. At

that time, the median split of ARL libraries' materials budgets was 55/45.[7] But in 1989-1990 that split changed to 40/60.[8] Results of the 1990 survey indicate that the majority of ARL libraries spend 50 to 74 percent of their budgets on serials.[9]

In 1976, when both outside and institutional funding for libraries was waning dramatically compared to what it had been, Daniel Gore's *Farewell to Alexandria* (Westport, CT: Greenwood Press) espoused the idea of a no-growth collection–a collection that remained static in size to solve the ever-expanding square footage need, but was annually culled of outdated materials that were replaced with new items. In keeping with this idea, "de-selection" was coined. However, librarians soon realized that, rather than having no collection growth, they would instead have slower collection growth. Advocacy of "no growth" ebbed and in 1977 the new journal *The De-Acquisitions Librarian* became *Collection Management* beginning with number three of its first volume.[10]

Even the great research libraries that several years ago still attempted to cover the globe through exhaustive acquisitions now realize that current funding levels force them to be selective rather than comprehensive. Their serials lists are not as long as they were; their in-depth collecting is not as expansive as it was.

What They Are Acquiring

The 1960s witnessed the blossoming of microforms and reprint acquisitions. As new institutions of higher education appeared and old ones expanded, microforms and reprint publishers grew along with them to capture a portion of their generous budgets. Microforms were touted as the technology of the future, along with the idea of carrying an entire microformat library in a briefcase. In 1972 the University of Toronto Press announced its intent to publish new books simultaneously in fiche and traditional book form.[11] Libraries bought microform collections and backruns of serials in microform, but researchers did not wholeheartedly take to this format. When both microform and hard copy are available, it is usually the hard copy that is used. It is hard to curl up with a microfiche reader!

In the late 1960s common complaints about reprint publishers were that they advertised titles with incomplete bibliographic information, that they advertised far in advance of publication–sometimes not producing the reprint unless their preliminary ads initiated a requisite number of orders, and that they changed their prices "without provocation." By 1970, 269 reprint publishers were identified.[12] The 1991 *Guide to Reprints* (Kent, CT: Guide to Reprints, Inc.) lists 470 reprint publishers.

When library materials budgets were fat 25 years ago, "freebies" added to the influx of materials. Libraries initiated gift and exchange arrangements without much thought on how the publications received fit in with their collection strengths. Government documents cost little or nothing; their low- or no-cost was taken for granted.

Today, both microforms and reprints are still available, but in much smaller quantities than the 1960s. Exchange arrangements are less numerous, with libraries seriously weighing their in-house and out-of-pocket costs against the value of what they are receiving. The Government Printing Office has raised prices, gone to microfilm, and greatly reduced "free and unhampered access to government data."[13] New formats have proliferated. CD-ROM indexes, which provide library users with citations to a plethora of journals, many of which the local library does not own, have resulted in increased demand on many libraries' interlibrary loan operations. CD-ROM products incorporating full-text of journal articles, such as University Microfilms International's ABI Inform, and services such as the Colorado Alliance of Research Libraries' UnCover2 that provides online full-text delivery, provide satisfying immediate access. As the technology proliferates, the need for technologically expert library staff members increases. Frequent enhancements and new products compound this need.

In this world of shrinking budgets and expanding publications and products, selectors are faced more and more with the question of access versus ownership. Acquisitions librarians have for many decades subscribed to a small number of indexes which required them to return superseded materials–a buying method that is more like leasing. Now, libraries are buying passwords to remote databases–in essence, entrees to specific information customized for a specific user. Library serials acquisitions are beginning to change from the buying of journals stored and loaned to patrons to the buying of journal articles for individual patron use.

FUNDING

The federal cash cow and highly supportive local funding situations that caused library materials budgets to mushroom in the 1960s began to disappear in the 1970s.

> Beginning in 1969 . . . librarians saw the beginning of large reductions in federal appropriations, presidential vetoes, and administrative impoundment. The problem was compounded by the threat of fund curtailment at the city and state levels, a threat which was fully realized by 1971 when many libraries were forced to cut back on hours, personnel, and book budgets.[14]

The percent increase between the median ARL library materials budgets in 1964-1965 and in 1989-1990 has more than kept up with the change in the consumer price index.[15] However, library literature since 1969 has bemoaned the loss of buying power in library materials budgets. How can this be? Quite a few factors contribute. Among them are:

- In the age of information explosion, the universe of what is available for purchase has multiplied.
- Although domestic book prices have slightly exceeded the consumer price index increase in the last 25 years, serials prices have increased astronomically.
- U.S. Postal rates have multiplied 15-fold.[16]
- Vendor discounts have declined.
- Serials vendors now charge for service and offer no discount.
- The value of the U.S. dollar has declined in the world market.
- Government documents cost considerably more.
- Not as many items are received on exchange or as gifts.

Library acquisitions funding levels simply cannot cover the publishing waterfront as they could in the mid-1960s.

TOOLS

Twenty-five years ago acquisitions staff relied on manual files and hard copies of book catalogs and bibliographies for their verification and searching needs. Frequently, acquisitions staff were responsible for identifying cataloging copy as a by-product of their searching duties. Library literature of the mid-1960s reflecting strong interest of librarians for developing more bibliographic tools (both to publish current cumulations of existing works and to create new bibliographies for the areas of the world not under bibliographic control) and for creating ways to share cataloging records. A series of projects begun in the 1960s and early 1970s have revolutionized the manner in which acquisitions staff verify the existence of titles they wish to order, the manner in which they identify potential cataloging copy, and the manner in which they search local files.

NPAC

In the 1960s most academic libraries purchased cardsets from the Library of Congress . . . a service which LC had begun in 1903. With the advent of the Library of Congress National Program for Acquisitions and Cataloging (NPAC), funded in 1965, LC offices established in other countries obtained a wide assortment of publications of other countries much more methodically and more rapidly than before.[17] With NPAC, the Library of Congress gave priority to cataloging these materials and supplied to each research library supporting the NPAC program a card for each title cataloged. Through NPAC, research library acquisitions departments were able to both verify titles and identify cataloging copy for many foreign materials more rapidly than ever before.

Standard Numbering

In 1968 the Standard Book Number was adopted by seven countries and endorsed by the International Organization for Standardization. Even though the U.S. was not one of those seven countries, the Library of Congress began including the SBN on cataloging cards.[18] Before the end of 1969 a few began to appear in PW's *Weekly Record*.[19] In 1970 the numbering system achieved international status and became known as the International Standard Book Number.[20] Publisher R. R. Bowker soon assumed the responsibility for assigning ISBN's for U.S. monographs and the Library of Congress began assigning ISSN's (International Standard Serials Numbers) for serials through the National Serials Data Program. Using ISBN's and ISSN's found in publisher's ads, reviews of and citations to new works has helped acquisitions staff differentiate among works—especially those with the same title and proceedings with complicated entries.

OCLC

In 1967 Frederick Kilgour went to Columbus, Ohio to spearhead the Ohio College Library Center (OCLC) project . . . a cooperative effort dedicated to keeping library processing costs down by sharing bibliographic records in an online environment. By 1991, OCLC, Inc. had an international membership of more than 11,000 libraries in some 40 countries. Its database included more than 23 million records including MARC tapes produced by the Library of Congress.[21]

MARC

In 1968 Library of Congress staff member Henriette Avram set out to create a uniform method of communicating bibliographic records in computer format. The resulting MARC (*MA*chine *R*eadable *C*ataloging) record, still evolving today, is the standard for bibliographic records in computer format.

CIP

In 1971 the Library of Congress initiated the Cataloging in Publication (CIP) program, whereby an LC cataloging record is published in the book which it describes. Each participating publisher provides LC with an advanced copy of each title. LC gives CIP books immediate cataloging priority and supplies each publisher with an incomplete cataloging copy, which the publisher in turn includes on the verso of the book's title page. As soon as the program was implemented, current American bibliographies began using CIP records for their bibliographic listing. CIP records are now loaded immediately into OCLC and other databases. CIP is a useful verification tool, for finding a CIP record allows an acquisitions staff member to know that even if the book is not published yet, it will appear in the very near future.[22]

Local Files

In the 1960s a select group of research libraries relied on mainframe computers for some order procedures. With the advent of OCLC and other networks, acquisitions librarians initially anticipated that acquisitions automation could take place in a network mode. However, today a majority of automated acquisitions systems represent a module of an individual integrated automated library system developed by a commercial vendor.

Access to bibliographic utilities (such as OCLC) whose databases offer bibliographic records in MARC format . . . replete with CIP records as soon as they are available, and ISBN's or ISSN's . . . allows acquisitions staff to verify a vast percentage of their orders through a simple computer search. These electronic bibliographic databases make the seemingly-endless searching described in the first paragraph of this chapter obsolete. In addition, the bibliographic records that they contain may be transferred into a library's automated system and used as a basis for the permanent local cataloging record. Long gone are the days of the 1960s when most acquisitions departments could get along with two electrical outlets: one for the shared electric calculator and one for the new state-of-the-art electric typewriter!

PROCUREMENT METHODS

For years, the most common method of ordering a book was to send abbreviated bibliographic information for a title to a vendor and requesting that a copy be sent. The *firm order* method, still common today, is supplemented by many other procurement methods, some cooperative, some commercial. Some other acquisitions methods used by academic libraries over the last 25 years are described here.

Farmington Plan

In 1942 Association of Research Libraries directors met in Farmington, Connecticut to design a cooperative procurement plan to acquire foreign materials in special subject areas to "assure that there should be in some collection in the country at least one copy of every current foreign publication of research value."[23] Selected vendors in those countries were designated to supply materials in specific subject areas to specific U.S. research libraries. A 1958 review of this project supported its existence and its secretariat was established by ARL in Washington, DC in 1962.[24] The plan was discontinued in 1972 due to increased use of blanket order arrangements, LC's NPAC program and reductions in many libraries' budgets.[25]

USBE

In 1948 the United States Book Exchange was created in Washington, DC as a "clearinghouse for the receipt, organization and redistribution of surplus and duplicate publications."[26] Eventually renamed the Universal Serials and Book Exchange, USBE began specializing in serials backruns and supplied them at low cost to members throughout the world. John Zubal revived USBE in 1990 and moved it to Cleveland, Ohio, where it continues today.[27]

PL-480

The 1954 Food for Peace Program (Public Law 480) provides the legal basis for a foreign country's supplying U.S. libraries with publications in exchange for U.S. surplus agricultural products.[28] U.S. research libraries actually began receiving PL-480 materials in the mid 1960s and by the end of that decade were receiving PL-480 items from more than 30 countries.[29] Although the program has been scaled back, it is still in operation today.

LACAP

In 1959 Stechert-Hafner in cooperation with the New York Public Library initiated the Latin American Cooperative Acquisitions Project.[30] By sending an agent to Latin America and eventually by establishing an office in Bogota, this program was successful in helping libraries obtain Latin American materials. The program ended in 1972.[31]

Approval Plans

In 1965 vendor Richard Abel began supplying ten Western universities with ". . . preselected titles from the lists of over 250 domestic publishers" and Flexowriter tape punched with LC card data for each book.[32] Thus began the *approval plan*–an arrangement with a vendor through which a library obtains on an ongoing basis and at substantial discount books in carefully defined subject areas. Upon receipt, librarians examine the materials and return for credit those which are not wanted. Literature describing the pros and cons of approval plans proliferated for more than a decade thereafter and four conferences focusing on this procurement method were held, the last taking place in 1979. Approval plans, which today are offered by many academic vendors, eliminate a lot of paperwork for acquisitions staff . . . and some provide bibliographic and accounting information in machine readable form to be loaded directly into the library's local automated system.

Processing Centers

In the late 1960s processing centers appeared in several locations. These agencies, which acquired and cataloged materials for a group of libraries, were created in order to keep unit costs down. With the advent of alternatives to shared cataloging, very few of these centers exist for academic libraries now. Today they are most commonly found in school districts.

This section would be incomplete without comment on the National Periodicals Center, a proposed procurement method that was never implemented. In 1978 a Council on Library Resources plan proposed a ". . . centralized collection of periodical titles directly accessible to libraries throughout the nation with back-up referral libraries for provision of titles not held in the NPC."[33] The National Periodicals Center plan was endorsed by ARL and the Association of American Universities and funding to the tune of $1.5 million per year for fiscal years 1981 through 1985 was provided through HEA Title II-D. However, in 1979 the National Commission for Libraries and Information Science commissioned Arthur D. Little, Inc. to analyze the NPC proposal. The Little report concluded that "due to on-line interlibrary loan and private document delivery systems, periodical access would be improved by 1985, even without an NPC."[34]

STAFFING

Changes in acquisitions staffing in the past 25 years can be summarized under three headings: who is doing what, what they are doing, and the acquisitions community.

Who Is Doing What

In the mid-1960s there were proportionally more professionals working in acquisitions. The then common position of assistant head of acquisitions provided excellent training opportunities for librarians to learn the business of acquisitions. Today there are few assistant acquisitions head positions. That fact, combined with the problem of fewer master's degrees in library and information science being granted than a decade ago, produces the current dilemma of where to find qualified people for acquisitions head positions.

What They Are Doing

With the advent of automation, acquisitions librarians have gained automation expertise. In addition, they have been forced to redesign and reevaluate workflow and design or analyze screen formats and computer-produced forms. Time spent on automation has been time not spent on other duties, now transferred to the portfolios of high-level support staff. Acquisitions paraprofessionals have assumed more responsibility not only because their librarian bosses have become automation managers, but also because their use of automated systems demands that they understand how acquisitions procedures relate to other areas of the library. In a machine environment, their actions have more long-term effect than they did in a manual file setting, since a bibliographic record selected by an acquisitions staff member at the point of order or receipt is very likely to be the one edited for the permanent bibliographic record in the library's local system. As acquisitions support staff are trained in more cataloging details, the demarcation between acquisitions functions and cataloging functions is becoming blurred. In some acquisitions departments, support staff are handling copy cataloging tasks in tandem with book receipt tasks.

The Acquisitions Community

Automation and networking have brought librarians from all sizes of academic libraries together to work on cooperative projects and in user groups. Organizational participation opportunities have proliferated. In the 1990/1991 *ALA Handbook of Organization* under its new name, the Association for Library Collections and Technical Services (ALCTS) listed 40 units related to acquisitions and collection development. In addition, groups with a focus on acquisitions can be found in other divisions of the American Library Association, such as the Association for College and Research Libraries and the Reference and Adult Services Division. The ALCTS groups create relevant guidelines and standards; they all sponsor programs at the ALA annual conference and in regional settings. Since 1965, acquisitions literature has proliferated, with quite a few titles dedicated to various aspects of the specialty. One indicator of the expanding literature is the number of articles cited in the *LRTS* acquisitions year's work articles. The article for 1990 lists[35] 103 citations, almost four times as many as the 26 cited in the article for 1965.[36] Today, two electronic newsletters, *ALCTS Network News* or *AN2,* and the *Newsletter on Serials Pricing Issues,* and two electronic discussion groups–"ACQNET" and "SERIALST"–put acquisitions librarians with access to Bitnet or Internet in an immediate information exchange with a wide arena of colleagues. The national community of acquisitions librarians is much closer than it was 25 years ago.

A LOOK TO THE FUTURE

In 1965 Dougherty said, "We might as well resign ourselves that many problems confronting us today will likely be the same ones someone will report on 25 years hence; maybe, some will be closer to solutions; others, possibly, will have become more critical."[37] He and McKinney, in their summary of acquisitions activities from 1956 to 1966 looked briefly to the future with "the four Cs": computers, communication, cooperation, and cash.[38] Certainly acquisitions activities since 1965 could be categorized into those four Cs; and they most likely could be for the next 25 years as well.

Here are a few predictions:

- The focus on access rather than ownership will cause some acquisitions departments to be more closely allied organizationally with interlibrary loan and document delivery operations.
- Nonbook formats will continue to proliferate, but the book will remain very much in vogue. The proliferation of nonbook formats will more frequently raise questions such as: should a library buy the same work in multiple formats? Which format(s) should be retained permanently?
- Collections will grow more slowly as more resources are spent to purchase information for specific end-users. Acquisitions will deal more with access and less with ownership. Libraries will buy more information customized for and given to a specific end-user and fewer books to hold in perpetuity. This change will raise preservation issues: Who will preserve for the long-term journals held by few? Who will retain for the archival record different iterations of electronic data, that can be altered so frequently? As technology changes, who will convert data so it can be accessed through new formats?
- The National Research Education Network will reshape the organization and distribution of educational information. The highly-touted scholars' workstation will become reality in

more libraries, but there will be many alternate ways to obtain information.

- Electronic journal production sponsored by universities and scholarly societies will gain a niche in serials publishing in an effort to keep spiraling serials costs lower than they would be otherwise.
- Funding for library materials and information will continue to be less rather than more. What Bruer observed in 1974 will continue: Librarians will focus on "how to get the most out of what is available" rather than turning their attention to "how little there is."[39]
- As library materials buying power diminishes more libraries will combine the collection development function with another function, such as references or acquisitions.[40]
- Collection development librarians will determine what to buy and what to buy access to. They will learn the details of how to obtain information for specific end-users (e.g., how to obtain database passwords, how to lease films and videos).
- Now that automated acquisitions systems are functioning pretty well, their enhancements will concentrate more on the convenience of the end-user.[41]
- In the era of declining purchasing power, acquisitions staff will look for the most effective, least expensive verification tools, some opting for dialing in access to other libraries' catalogs over searching a network database.
- Recruiting efforts will be initiated to encourage more people to go into acquisitions work. More acquisitions training and continuing education opportunities will be made available to help compensate for the declining pool of prospective acquisitions department heads. More individuals with business expertise rather than a library degree will be put in these positions.
- Acquisitions librarians will more clearly define the subdiscipline of acquisitions, using such vehicles as the fairly new ALCTS Acquisitions Administrators Discussion Group. Two examples of stimuli in this search for professionalism are Ross Atkinson's seminal piece on the acquisitions librarian as change agent[42] and Joyce Ogburn's 1991 "ACQNET" pieces on the tenets of acquisitions.

REFERENCE NOTES

1. Michael J. Bruer, "Resources in 1974," *Library Resources & Technical Services* 19:229-230 (1975).

2. Frederick C. Lynden, "Resources in 1977," *Library Resources & Technical Services* 22:312 (1978); Frederick C. Lynden, "Resources in 1978," *Library Resources & Technical Services* 23:220-224 (1979); and Rose Mary Magrill, "Collection Development and Preservation in 1979," *Library Resources & Technical Services* 24:256-258 (1980).

3. David Farrell, "The NCIP Option for Coordinated Collection Management," *Library Resources & Technical Services* 30:51 (1986).

4. Telephone conversation of February 6, 1992 with Jutta Reed-Scott, Association of Research Libraries.

5. *The Bowker Annual of Library and Book Trade Information.* New York: R. R. Bowker, 1966 p. 91, 102, and 105. *The Bowker Annual of Library and Book Trade Information.* New York: R. R. Bowker, 1991, p. 401 and 429.

6. Herbert S. White, "Strategies and Alternatives in Dealing with the Serials Management Budget," In *Serials Collection Development: Choices and Strategies,* ed. Sul H. Lee. Ann Arbor, MI: The Pierian Press, 1981, p. 32.

7. *ARL Statistics 1975-1976: A Compilation of Statistics from the One Hundred and Five Members of the Association of Research Libraries:* comp. by Suzanne Franke. Washington, DC: Association of Research Libraries, 1976, p. 15.

8. *ARL Statistics 1989-90: A Compilation of Statistics from the One Hundred and Nineteen Members of the Association of Research Libraries:* comp. by Sarah M. Pritchard and Eileen Finer. Washington, DC: Association of Research Libraries, 1991, p. 30-31.

9. Jane Treadwell and Lee Ketcham, "The Serials Marketplace," *Library Journal* 116:84 (1991).

10. Michael J. Bruer, "Resources in 1975," *Library Resources & Technical Services* 20:201-203 (1976); Michael J. Bruer, "Resources in 1976," *Library Resources & Technical Services* 21:237 (1977); and Frederick C. Lynden, "Resources in 1977," *Library Resources & Technical Services* 22:314 (1978).

11. Michael J. Bruer, "Acquisitions in 1972," *Library Resources & Technical Services* 18:176 (1974).

12. Abigail Dahl-Hansen and Richard M. Dougherty, "Acquisitions Trend–1968," *Library Resources & Technical Services* 13:374 (1969) and Ashby J. Fristoe and Rose E. Myers, "Acquisitions in 1970," *Library Resources & Technical Services* 15:136 (1971).

13. Michael Gorman, "The Academic Library in the Year 2001: Dream or Nightmare or Something in Between?" *The Journal of Academic Librarianship* 17:8 (1991).

14. Michael J. Bruer, "Acquisitions in 1972," *Library Resources & Technical Services* 18:171-181 (1974).

15. The median ARL library materials budget increased more than 7-fold between 1964-1965 and 1989-1990, whereas the consumer price index increased only

four-fold during this period. Consumer price information is taken from *Business Statistics,* 1961-88 p. 24 and from *Survey of Current Business,* September 1991, p. S5.

16. In 1966 the library rate was four cents for the first pound and one cent for the second. By 1991 it was 65 cents for the first pound and 24 cents for each pound thereafter (*Bowker Annual* 1966, p. 189 and 1991 U.S. Postal rates).

17. Richard M. Dougherty, "Acquisitions–1965 in Review," *Library Resources & Technical Services* 10:165-172 (1966).

18. Abigail Dahl-Hansen and Richard M. Dougherty, "Acquisition Trends–1968," *Library Resources & Technical Services* 13:373-379 (1969).

19. Ashby J. Fristoe and Rose E. Myers, "Acquisitions in 1969," *Library Resources & Technical Services* 14:165-173 (1970).

20. Ashby J. Fristoe and Rose E. Myers, "Acquisitions in 1970," *Library Resources & Technical Services* 15:132-142 (1971).

21. Tom Gaughan, "The Corporate Culture of OCLC," *American Libraries* 22:894-896 (1991).

22. Robert R. Newlen, "Read the Fine Print: The Power of CIP," *Library Journal* 116:38-42 (1991).

23. Herbert Goldhor (Ed). *Selection and Acquisition Procedures in Medium-Sized and Large Libraries.* Urbana IL: University of Illinois, 1963, p. 97.

24. Helen M. Welch, "The Year's Work in Acquisitions and Resources," *Library Resources & Technical Services* 3:79 (1959); and Dorothy Bevis "Acquisitions and Resources; Highlights of 1962," *Library Resources & Technical Services* 7:142-155 (1963).

25. Michael J. Bruer, "Acquisitions in 1972," *Library Resources & Technical Services* 18:171-181 (1974).

26. Helen Rovelstad, "Economics of the Universal Serials and Book Exchange (USBE)," *Interlending Review* 7:98-101 (1979).

27. Phone conversation of November 12, 1991 with John Zubal.

28. Herbert Goldhor (Ed). *Selection and Acquisition Procedures in Medium-Sized and Large Libraries.* Urbana IL: University of Illinois, 1963, p. 2.

29. Marietta Chicorel, "Highlights in Acquisitions," *Library Resources & Technical Services* 8:112-125 (1964).

30. Helen M. Welch, "The Year's Work in Acquisitions and Resources," *Library Resources & Technical Services* 4:101-108 (1960).

31. Michael J. Bruer, "Acquisitions in 1972," *Library Resources & Technical Services* 18:171-181 (1974).

32. Richard M. Dougherty, "Acquisitions–1965 in Review," *Library Resources & Technical Services* 10:165-172 (1966).

33. Frederick C. Lynden, "Resources in 1978," *Library Resources & Technical Services* 23:213-245 (1979).

34. Rose Mary Magrill, "Collection Development and Preservation in 1979," *Library Resources & Technical Services* 24:247-273 (1980).

35. Karen A. Schmidt, "Please, Sir, I Want Some More: A Review of the Literature of Acquisitions, 1990," *Library Resources & Technical Services* 35:245-254 (1991).

36. Richard M. Dougherty, "Acquisitions–1965 in Review," *Library Resources & Technical Services* 10:165-172 (1966).

37. Richard M. Dougherty, "Year's work in Acquisitions," *Library Resources & Technical Services* 9:149 (1965).

38. Richard M. Dougherty and Abigail McKinney, "Ten Years of Progress in Acquisitions: 1956-66," *Library Resources & Technical Services* 11:289-301 (1967).

39. Michael J. Bruer, "Acquisitions in 1973," *Library Resources & Technical Services* 18:240 (1974).

40. Conversation of January 26, 1992 with Charles A. Hamaker, Assistant Director for Collection Development, Louisiana State University Libraries.

41. Conversation of July 19, 1991 with Joseph W. Barker, Head, Acquisitions Department, The Library, University of California, Berkeley.

42. Ross Atkinson, "The Acquisitions Librarian as Change Agent in the Transition to the Electronic Library," *Library Resources & Technical Services* 36:7-20 (1992).

PART III:
CATALOGS

Chapter 4

A History of the Online Catalog in North America

Larry Millsap

> Anyone who computerizes at this point in time is hitching his
> wagon to a falling star. The honeymoon is over, if our seduc-
> tion by computer can be so termed. . . . Computerizing library
> operations at present and projected costs, and with foreseeable
> results, is intellectually and fiscally irresponsible and manage-
> rially incompetent.[1]

Thus fulminated Ellsworth Mason in "The Great Gas Bubble
Prick't" in 1971. The online catalog required a convergence of
computing power and mass storage available at a low enough price
that a library could afford it, software that permitted efficient manipulation of large files, and the files themselves, representing all or
a significant part of a library's collection in a usable format. None
of these essential elements was available in 1971, and Mason was a
prominent voice discouraging their pursuit. However, many failed
to heed his advice and libraries continued to automate. Despite
some false steps, occasionally very expensive ones, the star of
automation that was going to transform the library was just beginning to rise.

The goal of library automation in the 1960s was the development
of a total integrated system for a single library.[2] Some libraries
began very early to work on such systems. Newly founded Florida
Atlantic University generated a great deal of publicity from its plans
for a totally computerized library in 1963. Using an IBM 1401
computer, the library planned to produce a book catalog plus print-

outs of book orders, overdue notices, a daily circulation list to be posted at different places in the stacks to tell readers which items were in circulation, a current serials list produced three times a week showing arrivals of current journals, and an annual serials holdings list.[3] A complete set of locate tags was developed for entry of bibliographic information. In order to have enough characters to represent items in a research collection, it was also necessary to modify the standard IBM print chain, which at that time consisted of 26 uppercase letters, ten numerals, and 12 special characters.[4] The IBM 1401 had 4K of main memory.[5] Unfortunately Florida Atlantic's aspirations were ahead of available technology, and the project was abandoned.[6] The University of California, Santa Cruz, another institution founded in the 1960s, successfully achieved its smaller goal of using computer technology to avoid the need for a card catalog. At Santa Cruz, a large database of records in a "simplified" MARC format (e.g., tag 100 was used for all 1XX fields) was built from that which book catalogs and later COM catalogs were produced, but a local online catalog was never introduced.[7] One early system that embodied many goals of automated systems was BELLREL, the Bell Laboratories' Library Real-Time Loan System, which became operational in March 1968. BELLREL was an online circulation system that linked the three largest Bell libraries to a central computer. Bell was able to focus on the "immediate and long-range gains for the library as an information system" rather than the gross costs of an online system.[8]

Kenneth John Bierman surveyed the state of automated alternatives to the card catalog in 1974 and 1975. Reasons that were given by ten or more libraries for their interest in automation were (1) to provide access to the complete and up-to-date catalog from multiple places, (2) to provide more and improved access points and search capabilities, (3) to expand the availability of increased resource sharing, (4) to eliminate or reduce the inconsistencies and inaccuracies of card catalogs and their in hospitality to change, (5) to reduce the increasing problems and costs of maintaining card catalogs, and (6) to deal with pressures and influences for change (most especially from the Library of Congress). The kinds of changes that the Library of Congress was planning and that were going to cause major difficulties in large card catalogs were the abandonment of superimposition, revision of romanization policies, and major revisions of the subject heading lists. Ohio State University had two other reasons to automate the catalog:

> (1) Americans have been conditioned to expect very fast response, and electronic catalogs are the only way to provide fast response; and (2) if librarianship is best served by smaller units of service, then library activities must be decentralized, including decentralized access to the most up-to-date and accurate library records.[9]

Among the ways libraries were beginning to automate were by converting to book catalogs, by converting to online catalogs, or by beginning integrated automated processing systems. Since the MARC II format had been accepted in 1967,[10] it was no longer necessary for a library that wanted to automate to develop the format locally though of course some did. Also the power of computers was steadily increasing as was the performance to price ratio. However the development of the software was still up to the individual library.

In 1974 there were two other libraries with large collections in addition to the University of California, Santa Cruz, that had book catalogs produced from machine-readable records; these were the Los Angeles Public Library and the New York Public Library. At that time, all three of those libraries were planning to change to microform in the near future because of cost and time factors. Bierman also identified nine intermediate size libraries with book catalogs, among them Bell Telephone Labs.[11] While most libraries did not yet consider online catalogs a viable alternative because of cost, some libraries were beginning to develop them. Rochester Institute of Technology was converting its 150,000 titles into a locally developed online system and the Aerospace Corporation Library in California had 80,000 titles online. IBM had a few libraries holding fewer than 20,000 titles with online catalogs.[12] Ohio State University had brief records available online as a by-product of LCS, its circulation system.

Of the libraries that began work on integrated systems in the late 1960s and early 1970s, three became particularly prominent. At Stanford University BALLOTS (Bibliographic Automation of

Large Library Operations using a Time-sharing System) was begun as an online acquisitions system in 1967. BALLOTS supported acquisition and cataloging operations from 1972 although operational costs were excessively high.[13] Northwestern began developing NOTIS (Northwestern Total Library Information System) as a technical processing system in 1970. The University of Toronto had a partially operational online system. UTLAS (University of Toronto Library Automation System) had been used to produce a book catalog for its science library. Toronto was also experimenting with a partial online catalog. Online systems were also under development at the University of Chicago and Syracuse University.[14]

The type of access provided in these early systems was limited. The Aerospace Corporation and Syracuse had no subject access; at Syracuse and Stanford the systems were generally for processing use, though public use terminals were being planned. Northwestern's system was for technical processing but plans existed to add author/title and title/author indexes that would permit the system to serve as a public catalog. At Ohio State, locations and status (in circulation, at bindery, etc.) were shown.[15]

The portion of the collections of larger libraries represented in their online catalogs varied greatly. At Syracuse and Ohio State the entire collection was available though access points were limited for much material. At Stanford and Northwestern recently cataloged materials were available; also at Stanford the entire collection of the undergraduate library was online.[16] The University of Toronto used a non-MARC format to convert about 1.25 million records. "This presented some interesting problems when it became necessary to merge these records into a composite data base with records from several other sources . . . "[17]

OCLC led the way in providing a reasonably priced method of building a database of MARC records. Established in 1967 and operational online in 1971, OCLC was the "first large, multiparticipant, computerized, online, shared cataloging and union catalog system . . . "[18] OCLC began its existence as the Ohio College Library Center; its operation was supported by the state of Ohio and by 50 institutions in Ohio. Before the end of its second year of operation, institutions outside Ohio were making "vociferous demands" for participation and OCLC's success seemed assured.[19] In

1981 the acronym was retained but the name was changed to Online Computer Library Center. Although many libraries used the system at first as a means of obtaining cataloging cards, by the 1980s it was more important as a source of MARC records. Several libraries in Bierman's survey were planning to use OCLC as their local catalog within five years. Such use was going to be dependent on the availability of subject access, improved author/title access, and accessibility of complete local data, including variations in the bibliographic data plus local call number and location.[20]

In 1978 the Research Libraries Group was formed and chose BALLOTS as its processing system. BALLOTS was renamed RLIN (Research Libraries Information Network) and became the prestige source of records. RLIN was much praised as the "system of the future."[21] An advantage of RLIN over OCLC was that RLIN maintained the local record online. This ceased to be a significant advantage after it became apparent that OCLC and RLIN were not going to serve as local catalogs themselves but would be the source of MARC records for catalogs, in fact "bibliographic utilities." RLIN's subject searching capability was also less of an advantage in a bibliographic utility. The debate over the quality of records in the RLIN database versus OCLC raged for about ten years. Finally the chief difference became size and price, and it had long been apparent that OCLC had a larger database and was less expensive.[22] Even Stanford was using it for cataloging by 1990.

De Gennaro predicted that the importance of OCLC's shared cataloging would diminish as the Library of Congress and other national libraries increased the currency and scope of their MARC output.[23] In fact by 1990 LC-created MARC records in OCLC accounted for only about 16 percent of the total records,[24] and in 1991 the Library of Congress began planning to use the OCLC and RLIN databases to reduce its backlogs.[25] Another source of MARC records became available in the mid-1980s. The Library Corporation offered Bibliofile, and Library Systems and Services offered MINI MARC; both were CD-ROM data files.[26]

In 1986 members of the Association of Research Libraries were surveyed to provide information on conversion of their catalog records to machine-readable form. At that time 14 libraries had completed retrospective conversion, 72 were planning to undertake it, and 13 had no plans for any significant work before 1988. Four libraries did not complete the survey.[27] By 1986 there were many sources of copy of both current cataloging and for retrospective conversion projects. Libraries could use their own staff and search OCLC, RLIN, or a variety of other databases directly. It was also possible to have an outside agency do the conversion based on the library's shelflist. OCLC, RLIN, Washington Library Network (WLN), and UTLAS offered conversion services as did the Amigos and Solinet networks of OCLC. By 1990 OCLC staff had converted 48 million bibliographic records for libraries.[28] Autographics, Brodart, and the Computer Company were commercial vendors offering conversion services. Blackwell, Inforonics, General Research Corporation, Marcive, and PACfile were commercial vendors that offered batch conversion services.[29] For those services the library had to enter a search key on a floppy disk; then the search keys were run against a database of MARC records. Another database that provided an important resource for recon projects was REMARC. This project was undertaken by the Carrollton Press. The 5.2 million records in the Library of Congress shelflist were converted to machine-readable form. While some title fields were truncated and other files were truncated or omitted, the file was used by many libraries in their conversion efforts.[30]

In 1975, De Gennaro declared that the era of localized library automation had effectively come to an end. The availability of networks such as OCLC and turnkey systems from commercial vendors made it feasible for only the largest libraries to develop, maintain, and operate local systems.[31] Some large libraries continued to do just that. Local systems were developed at the Los Angeles (Orion) and Berkeley (GLADIS) campuses of the University of California and at Virginia Tech (VTLS), and the University of California Systemwide Division of Library Automation developed the online union catalog MELVYL. In 1982 a report compiled jointly by OCLC and RLG identified 20 libraries with operational or "almost operational" online catalogs. Fourteen were developed in-house, two were GEAC, and there was one each from CLSI, ULISYS, DataPhase, and Computer CAT.[32] However, the greatest development after 1975 was in commercial turnkey systems.

The turnkey systems began in the 1970s usually as circulation systems. Four of these systems were installed in 1973; 73 in 1977; and 284 by 1981.[33] By the end of 1990 there were 1,877 systems installed in the United States and 2,745 worldwide.[34] As the number of vendors and thus competition increased, additional modules were added to complement the circulation systems. By 1981, CL Systems, Inc. (CLSI), Data Research Associates, and Universal Library Systems (ULISYS) were offering operational online catalogs. Several other vendors had online catalogs in development or planned.[35] Since the circulation systems did not contain full bibliographic records, an online catalog using a circulation database did not ordinarily have full access. The problem that libraries most often encountered when they installed a catalog module to a circulation system was that the computer did not have enough main memory or secondary storage capacity to accommodate the additional requirements of the catalog.[36]

Rather than having the OCLC cataloging subsystem serve as a local online catalog as had seemed an early possibility to some, OCLC began marketing a stand-alone system in 1983. After several attempts to find the right way of providing a local system in 1983, OCLC selected the Integrated Library System developed at the National Library of Medicine and marketed it under the name LC\2000.[37] Also in 1983 Carlyle Systems began offering a turnkey online catalog and planned to introduce its circulation system the following year. Innovative Interfaces, which began by providing a "black box" interface between OCLC and CLSI, developed acquisition and serials control systems.[38] Later an online catalog was offered. Often the original system components worked better than those that were added on. Carlyle was a vendor that was almost completely overwhelmed by financial difficulty and problems concerning the release of a fully functional circulation component.[39] The idea of linked systems rather than total systems from one vendor became popular. Vendors also sometimes found it advantageous to combine forces. For example in 1991, CLSI was selling the Innovative Interfaces acquisition module in conjunction with its own online catalog and circulation system.

There was another significant event in the turnkey market in 1983. Paul Sybrowsky, the president of Computer Translation Inc. (CTI) was asked to resign after CTI was purchased by the Government Systems Group. Sybrowsky and a number of other CTI employees formed Dynix. By 1990, Dynix had installed more library systems than any other vendor.[40] In addition to commercially developed systems, the systems developed by libraries began to be marketed in the late 1970s and early 1980s. NOTIS and VTLS were the most successful and had a large number of installations. By 1990 there were 145 VTLS installations and 133 NOTIS installations in the United States. Among the other systems that were offered for a time were Maggie's Place, developed at Pikes Peak Library, and Rosemary's Baby, developed at Midlands (Michigan) Public Library.[41]

While the development of a system within a library meant a considerable expenditure, buying a turnkey system was not entirely without risk. CTI support for installed systems disappeared after 1983. The Boulder Public Library sued DataPhase for lack of performance in 1983.[42] DataPhase recovered from its problems, and the suit was dropped the next year.[43] However, the company again ran into difficulty when it tried to develop ALIS II and went bankrupt. After the failure of DataPhase, many of the former customers turned to OCLC local systems division for support.[44] By 1986 Decicom and BLIS had also failed. Except for DataPhase, these companies were considered high risk because they had installations in fewer than 20 sites. BLIS was large in scale if not in number of sites. It was being installed at Brown University, Columbia, Indiana University, the University of Cincinnati, the University of California, San Diego, and Metropolitan Toronto Public Reference Library.[45]

By 1985 the basic functionality that we had come to expect was available from the major turnkey vendors. CLSI, Dynix, OCLC, and VTLS all supported all types of records in all kinds of formats. They each provided call number, author, title, series, and subject access. Keyword approach, Boolean logic, and the possibility of combining indexes were available.[46] Thus most of the goals of a "second generation" online catalog had been achieved.[47]

Some vendors developed a means of achieving the aims of a second generation catalog on a smaller scale of technology. In 1985 Brodart introduced LePac, a CD-ROM based catalog. Autographics, General Research Corporation, Library Corporation, Marcive, and other vendors also introduced CD-ROM products. CD-ROM catalogs were considered by some to represent the dawn of affordable library automation; others considered them the equivalent of microfiche and a distraction from the only real solution to library needs: an integrated online system.[48] While CD-ROM did not have the currency of actual online catalogs, the cost was much lower. This permitted institutions and groups of institutions with small resources to have online catalogs and union catalogs. The problem of the data being out-of-date as soon as the disk was produced was solved to some extent by some vendors. They processed and made available new records and indexes that a library could copy to a hard disk on a PC where it is logically chained to the original file.[49]

Much of the progress in library automation until the late 1980s was in the application of technology to improve operations and service effectiveness, such as tracking book loans, sharing catalog data, and generating bibliographies. The library user is interested in library technology to satisfy personal information needs more completely.[50] Progress then began to be made in meeting those aims in "third generation" catalogs. Included in the features Hildreth identified as characteristics of third generation catalogs were integration of free text and controlled vocabulary search approaches, individualized, tailored displays, expanded access via subject-enriched bibliographic records or linkages to multiple databases, and abstracting and indexing information.[51] By 1991 there had been more activity in the area of augmenting access to databases than in enhancing searching abilities. Additional bibliographic databases as well as dictionaries and encyclopedias were mounted on the catalog, and users were passed through networks to other catalogs or databases. Arizona State University had loaded many indexes onto its library system: *Applied Science and Technology Index, Business Periodicals Index, General Sciences Index, Humanities Index, Education Index, Social Sciences Index, UnCover,* and *Article Access.* The Colorado Alliance of Research Libraries (CARL) had loaded *Grolier Encyclopedia, Roget's Thesaurus, American Heritage Dictionary,* and the *Denver Business Journal.*[52] MEDLINE was loaded on MELVYL in 1987; Current Contents, in 1990. In the 1991/1992 academic year, Information Access Corporation's (IAC) *National Newspaper Index, Computer Database,* and *Expanded Academic*

Index were to be loaded on MELVYL. IAC had also agreed to make the full text files of approximately 40 percent of the publications in *Computer Database* and *Expanded Academic Index* available.[53]

On MELVYL in 1991 there were more than 20 other catalogs that could be accessed. In addition to American university libraries, access was provided to the *Institute Tecnologico y de Estudios Superiores de Monterrey,* in Monterrey, Mexico, and to the JANET network in Great Britain.[54] Such a myriad of possibilities can be overwhelming. Buckland saw automation as a means of separating bibliography from library records. He defines *bibliography* as the whole apparatus of access to records of all kinds and in all media. Bibliography is concerned with the work while library records must be specific to individual copies.[55] Buckland believed a better configuration would be large bibliographies available online with links to local libraries operating records, e.g., circulation, acquisitions, serials. Rather than searching a series of separate catalogs, a user would conduct a general search of what existed. Then the links would tell where the item was physically available. Many items could be available in electronic form online. Buckland then believed we could expect that "the catalog would merge back into the mainstream of bibliography."[56] Kilgour believed that by the end of the century we would move "beyond bibliography," that "time and technology have conjoined to make desirable and possible the evolution of libraries beyond their 19th century foundation in bibliography into institutions providing information per se."[57]

If indeed the catalog merges back into the mainstream of bibliography and the library moves beyond bibliography, perhaps the history of the next 25 years of online access will begin with the obituary of the online catalog.

REFERENCE NOTES

1. Ellsworth Mason, "The Great Gas Bubble Prick't, or, Computers Revealed–by a Gentleman of Quality," *College and Research Libraries* 32(3): 192-193 (1971).

2. Richard De Gennaro, "Library Automation: Changing Patterns and New Direction," *Library Journal* 101:177 (1976).

3. Edward Heiliger, "Florida Atlantic University, New Libraries on New Campuses," *College and Research Libraries* 25(3):184 (1964).

4. Jean M. Perreault, "The Computerized Book Catalog at Florida Atlantic University," *College and Research Libraries* 25(3):196 (1964).

5. Franklin M. Fisher , James W. McKie, and Richard B. Mancke, *IBM and the U.S. Data Processing Industry: An Economic Histor.* New York: Praeger, (1983), 130.

6. De Gennaro, "Library Automation," *Library Journal* 101:176 (1976).

7. Allan J. Dyson and Larry Millsap, "Automation at UCSC," *DLA Bulletin* 3(2):4-5 (1983).

8. R. A. Kennedy, "Bell Laboratories' Library Real-Time Loan System (BELLREL)," *Journal of Library Automation* 1(2):129 (1968).

9. Kenneth John Bierman, "Automated Alternatives to Card Catalogs: The Current State of Planning and Implementation," *Journal of Library Automation* 8:279 (1975).

10. De Gennaro, "Library Automation," *Library Journal* 101:179 (1976).

11. Bierman, "Automated Alternatives to Card Catalogs," *Journal of Library Automation* 8:282 (1975).

12. Bierman, "Automated Alternatives to Card Catalogs," *Journal of Library Automation* 8:283 (1975).

13. "Stanford University's BALLOTS System," *Journal of Library Automation* 8(1):31-32 (1975).

14. Bierman, "Automated Alternatives to Card Catalogs," *Journal of Library Automation* 8:289 (1975).

15. Bierman, "Automated Alternatives to Card Catalogs," *Journal of Library Automation* 8:288 (1975).

16. Bierman, "Automated Alternatives to Card Catalogs," *Journal of Library Automation* 8:289 (1975).

17. R. J. Braithwaite, "Automation of the Catalog: the Transition from Cards to Computers," in *Problems and Failures in Library Automation*, ed. F. W. Lancaster. Urbana-Champaign: University of Illinois Graduate School of Library Science (1979) 61.

18. Frederick G. Kilgour, "OCLC Grows Up," *American Libraries* 10(6):362 (1979).

19. Kilgour, "OCLC Grows Up," *American Libraries* 10(6):362 (1979).

20. Bierman, "Automated Alternatives to Card Catalogs," *Journal of Library Automation* 8:283-284 (1975).

21. Jean Slemmons Stratford, "OCLC and RLIN" *College and Research Libraries* 45(2):126 (1984).

22. Slemmons Stratford, "OCLC and RLIN," *College and Research Libraries* 45(2):125-126 (1984).

23. De Gennaro, "Library Automation," *Library Journal* 101:181 (1976).

24. "Bibliographic Records in the OLUC by Source of Cataloging," *OCLC Pacific Network News Update* 52:1 (1990).

25. "Copy Cataloging at the Library of Congress," *Cataloging Service Bulletin* 51:8 (1991).

26. Judy McQueen and Richard W. Boss, "Sources of Machine-Readable Cataloging and Retrospective Conversion," *Library Technology Reports* 21(6):616 (1985).

27. Jutta Reed-Scott, "Questionnaire on Retrospective Conversion: Preliminary Analysis of Results," *Retrospective Conversion*, Washington DC, Office of Management Studies, Association of Research Libraries (1987).

28. Nita Dean, "Retrospective Conversion Series, They're Fast and Accurate," *OCLC Newsletter* 184:15 (1990).

29. McQueen and Boss, "Sources of Machine-Readable Cataloging," *Library Technology Reports* 21(6):614 (1985).

30. Richard De Gennaro, "Libraries & Networks in Transition: Problems and Prospects for the 1980's," *Library Journal* 106(10):1048 (1981).

31. Richard De Gennaro, "Library Automation, the Second Decade," *Journal of Library Automation* 8(1):4 (1975).

32. Joseph R. Matthews, "One Public Access Catalogs: Assessing the Potential," *Library Journal* 107(11):1068 (1982B).

33. Joseph R. Matthews, "Competition & Change: The 1983 Automated Library System Marketplace," *Library Journal* 109(8):855 (1984).

34. Frank R. Bridge, "Automated System Marketplace," *Library Journal* 116(6):51 (1991).

35. Joseph R. Matthews, "The Automated Circulation System Marketplace: Active and Heading Up," *Library Journal* 107(3)235 (1982A).

36. Deanna Marcum and Richard Boss, "Information Technology," *Wilson Library Bulletin* 55(7):519 (1981).

37. Matthews, "Competition & Change," *Library Journal* 109(8):853 (1984).

38. Matthews, "Competition & Change," *Library Journal* 109(8):853 (1984).

39. Robert A. Walton and Frank R. Bridge, "Automated System Marketplace 1988: Focused on Fulfilling Commitments," *Library Journal* 114(6):43-44 (1989).

40. Frank R. Bridge, "Automated System Marketplace 1991," *Library Journal* 116(6):51 (1991).

41. Matthews, "Competition & Change," *Library Journal* 109(8):857 (1984).

42. Matthews, "Competition & Change," *Library Journal* 109(8):854-855 (1984).

43. Joseph R. Matthews, "Unrelenting Change: The 1984 Automated Library System Marketplace," *Library Journal* 110(6)33 (1985).

44. Robert A. Walton and Frank R. Bridge, "Automated System Marketplace 1987: Maturity and Competition," *Library Journal* 113(6):42 (1988).

45. "BLIS Problems/Lessons to be Learned," *Library Systems Newsletter* 6(8):57-60 (1986).

46. Joseph R. Matthews, *Directory of Automated Library Systems*. New York: Neal Schuman, (1985) 56-83.

47. Charles R. Hildreth, "Pursuing the Ideal: Generations of Online Catalogs," *Online Catalogs/Online Reference, Converging Trends*, eds. Brian Aveney and Brett Butler. Chicago: American Library Association (1984) 41.

48. Karl Beiser, "CD-ROM Catalogs: The State of the Art," *Wilson Library Bulletin,* 63(3):25 (1988).

49. Beiser, "CD-ROM Catalogs," *Wilson Library Bulletin* 63(3):26 (1988).

50. Jon Drabenstott, "Beyond the Online Catalog: Great Potential and Profound Change," *Library Hi Tech* 21:108 (1988).

51. Hildreth, "Pursuing the Ideal: Generations of Online Catalogs," *Online Catalogs/Online Reference, Converging Trends,* eds. Brian Aveney and Brett Butler. Chicago: American Library Association (1984) 41.

52. William Gray Potter, "Expanding the Online Catalog," *Information Technology and Libraries* 8(2):100 (1989).

53. "New Databases Joining the MELVYL System," *DLA Bulletin* 10(3):28 (1990).

54. Laine Farley, "MELVYL System Update," *DLA Bulletin* 10(3) (1990).

55. Michael K. Buckland, "Bibliography, Library Records, and the Redefinition of the Library Catalog," *Library Resources & Technical Services* 32(4):299-300 (1988).

56. Buckland, "Bibliography, Library Records, and the Redefinition of the Library Catalog," *Library Resources & Technical Services* 32(4):308-309 (1988).

57. Frederick G. Kilgour, "EIDOS and the Transformation of Libraries," *Library Journal* 112(16):46 (1987).

Chapter 5

Automating Access to Bibliographic Information

Debora Shaw

INTRODUCTION

Today even the casual library user is impressed with the number and variety of computer-based systems that supply bibliographic information in the well-equipped library. Online catalogs, CD-ROM (compact disc–read only memory) search systems, and end-user searching are becoming expected, if not essential, means of access to library materials. When access was through printed sources we seemed willing to allow each index to adopt its own approach for organization, and access to, the primary literature it covered. The sometimes staggering differences among the underlying databases had become apparent now that we have access to computer-based resources through nearly identical terminals and microcomputers.

This assortment of computer-based bibliographic tools is a consequence of the variety of organizations responsible for providing access to the primary literature. Libraries have taken the lead in book cataloging, while professional societies and commercial ventures emphasize their respective portions of the journal and report literature. Given the different orientations of these organizations, there is a surprising degree of similarity in the automated systems. The development of automated information handling was affected first by rapid changes in computer capacities and costs–later by improved understanding of how the technology could be applied to information-handling problems. The automation of bibliographic information can be viewed in four stages: early developments, diffusion into libraries, current efforts at further integration, and looking beyond bibliographic access.

EARLY DEVELOPMENTS

In the beginning there was no commonly held idea of what a computer-based retrieval system would be, how it should be created, or how people would use it. Early efforts were in a sense by-products of using computers to produce paper access tools. For example, when the Library of Congress contemplated automation in the early 1960s, functions considered included cataloging, searching, indexing, and document retrieval. At this time the Council on Library Resources provided support "for a study of the possible methods of converting data on LC cards to machine-readable form for the purpose of printing bibliographical products by computer."[1] The eventual development of MARC (MAchine-Readable Cataloging) was unusual in many ways, such as the decision at the outset to include all data on the LC printed cards in the machine-readable record, and to augment this with additional information for machine manipulation and retrieval. The Library of Congress recognized and accepted its central role in the MARC development process, which led to a standard for cataloging information which is widely accepted and even acclaimed.

In contrast, bibliographic databases for the journal and report literature developed in response to needs of particular constituencies, often with the assumption that the machine-readable files would not be used by anyone other than the creators. Hayes and Becker prepared an inventory of databases available in the late 1960s. They noted, "many of the files were created for specific purposes and were tailored to meet the special needs of the parent organization. Therefore, they have been designed without regard to a capability for easy readability for other purposes."[2] And, "record formats (fixed or variable), from one file to another are virtually unrelated."[3] Of the 48 databases identified in the survey, 34 (70 percent) were machine-readable versions of print products; the descriptions often mention that the files were created for typesetting printed indexes.

The journal and report databases from abstracting and indexing (A&I) services that were designed for computer manipulation offered a wide range of subject coding and retrieval techniques. Automatic indexing and use of key works were explored as ways to reduce the human effort in providing subject access.[4] Uniterms, descriptors, and semantic coding using links and roles were new ways of representing, retrieving, and manipulating information.[5] Boolean logic was introduced as a way to coordinate individual key works, uniterms, or descriptors. These techniques from the basis of post-coordinate indexing, which allows the searcher to bring together concepts of the search request rather than relying on terms pre-coordinated by the subject indexer.

DIFFUSION INTO LIBRARIES

The 1970 University of Illinois Clinic on Library Applications of Data Processing, organized by Kathryn Luther Henderson, focused on MARC uses and users. In his introduction to the conference Spaulding observed, "the number of libraries now utilizing the MARC tapes is small and may remain so for awhile."[6] At the same meeting Griffin reported on a survey of MARC users. He believed that the 13 respondents who indicated they were using the MARC tapes accounted for most of the actual users as of 1969. The most frequent uses of MARC were:[7]

book selection	5 now doing, 5 plan to do
acquisitions	4 now doing, 12 plan to do
catalog cards	3 now doing, 21 plan to do
book catalogs	3 now doing, 20 plan to do

More exotic or unusual applications were not in wide practice. Two institutions reported SDI (selective dissemination of information) uses, and there were three mentions of plans for database applications and information retrieval. Clearly the early users of MARC approached the computer as a way to handle traditional library functions. Avram's paper for the Clinic discussed the concept of a "data utility" noting that MARC had been designed as a generalized system to support a complete automation program. She described the MARC files as "maintained in a single standardized format, i.e., the records within each file are self-defining and the data elements in each record are represented in a common structure." This approach increased the likelihood for development of a data utility: "a data-oriented, computer-based centralized service, with emphasis toward generalized applications on a centrally maintained set of data files for access by a variety of users."[8]

The few MARC pioneers were soon joined by other libraries. The emergence of the Ohio College Library Center (OCLC, later Online Computer Library Center) demonstrated the promise of the data utility approach, exploiting online capabilities, centralizing computer expertise and processing power to support many libraries in their use of MARC records.[9] Hagler and Simmons note that, "within a very short time the machine-readable bibliographic database, centrally stored and maintained but cooperatively created, [became] a basic tool of librarianship."[10]

OCLC and a handful of similar organizations such as RLIN (Research Libraries Information Network) and WLN (Washington Library Network, later Western Library Network) emerged as "bibliographic utilities," common sources for MARC records. OCLC was also a leader in cooperative cataloging, with member libraries contributing their own original work to the online union catalog; the number of member-contributed records soon exceeded the number of records created by the Library of Congress.[11] For most OCLC users the system was simply a better way of producing catalog cards, but that rather narrow view changed gradually as the percentage of libraries' holdings represented on the OCLC "archive tapes" increased and as computer technology, especially the minicomputer, brought control of local automated systems into the library.

Major commitments to automation entered many library budgets with the availability of minicomputer-based circulation systems.[12] Often the introduction of automation meant a change in attitude toward circulation; instead of recording the absence of specific books from the library, the entire collection was seen as an "inventory" with some items "in stock" (on the shelves) and other unavailable because they were in circulation.[13] Having virtually the entire collection in a single database, however brief the records and however limited the access, opened the way for new kinds of searches. The basic circulation functions were augmented with more search features, the brief inventory records were expanded and the online catalog emerged. Enhancing brief circulation records or creating new ones to support online catalog functions was not an easy process; the trails of "retrospective conversion" gripped libraries throughout the 1970s and well into the 1980s, and still face many research libraries. There was general consensus that "full MARC" was what was needed to support online catalog functions. Interestingly, the online catalog systems that emerged have not made much use of the additional information that MARC Designers had included to augment the cataloging record for machine manipulation and retrieval.

Advances in telecommunications and disk storage that made bibliographic utilities feasible also helped improve access to the A&I databases. Online searching developed as time-sharing systems could support multiple users with reasonable response times. In 1971 Cuadra estimated there were 150 online search systems, at least 20 designed specifically for bibliographic retrieval.[14] Lancaster and Fayen, in 1973, described 29 online systems including DIALOG, ORBIT, and the New York Times Information Bank, which were the first widely used commercial search services.[15]

Online searching was accepted readily in many libraries. In a sense the technology might be new, but the underlying philosophy was not, since most librarians had long relied on outside sources, abstracting and indexing services, for bibliographic control of the journal and report literature. Within a remarkably short time librarians learned the computer skills and search strategies to exploit these new resources, but the major hurdle for many, especially in public and academic libraries, was the cost of online searching.[16] Questions of how to reconcile "free" library service with what seem to be huge and unpredictable costs for individualized service have yet to be resolved.

CURRENT EFFORTS AT FURTHER INTEGRATION

Current developments in the online catalog realm include search methods adapted from the world of online searching. Many online catalogs have evolved from circulation control systems with limited

access for known-item searching; next came the "online card catalog" which replicated the author, title, and subject heading access
of the paper-based counterpart. Today keyword searching using
Boolean operators is expected in the-to-date online catalog. We also
see increased attention to making the librarians' tools helpful to the
searcher: authority control and subject heading lists can be integrated into the catalog.

Online catalogs have attempted to reach the masses as well. The
trails of interface design have been confronted in the marketplace,
with touch screens, functions, keys, and command mode searching
put to the text by library users. Remote access to library catalogs is
encouraged, with academic libraries making the online catalog accessible on the campus network and public libraries supporting
dial-up ports for home and business use. Discussions of the Internet
and NREN (National Research and Education Network) include
online catalogs as resources which will be accessible on the "information highway."[17]

The online searching world encountered two challenges in the
1980s: CD-ROM and databases distributed on tape from producers
directly to libraries. Both approaches provide contact between the
database producer and the subscribing library, unlike online searching where the search service stood as an intermediary between the
parties. Also unlike online searching, the costs of distributed databases, while significant in relation to library budgets, are at least
known before the service is offered. Computer technology has finally evolved to support locally mounted databases of reasonable
size for several users. Libraries usually still rely on outside agencies
to prepare the databases and the search systems; however, the machines to support the searching are controlled (CD-ROM) or shared
(as with a campus computer system) by the library. Some search
services have responded by entering the market as CD-ROM producers (DIALOG) or by leasing their search software for local use
(BRS). Online catalog producers are also seeking a niche in this
market by supporting bibliographic as well as cataloging files on
the same system (NOTIS).

To date most library users still encounter the online catalog and
the databases of journal citations as separate, often quite distinct
information sources. Integration of search results from A&I data-

bases with online catalog holdings information is still in the experimental stage.[18] It is possible that, just as online circulation systems evolved into online catalogs, online catalogs and bibliographic databases will eventually merge into a consolidated source for access to the collection. Hayes and Becker stress the similarity of catalogs and indexes in providing bibliographic descriptions, intellectual access, intellectual organization, physical access, selective dissemination of information, and administrative control of information resources.[19] Perhaps the day is approaching when access mechanisms can help encourage this integration.

LOOKING BEYOND BIBLIOGRAPHIC ACCESS

While "full MARC" has become the goal for online catalog databases, various suggestions have been made for the enhancement of these resources with additional access points and descriptive information. Indeed, the typical OCLC cataloging record with an average of 1.4 subject heading[20] and infrequent contents or summary notes is rather meager when compared with a record from an A&I database with its abstract and long list of descriptors.[21] Cataloging of children's materials is the only area where librarians have consistently provided annotations with the bibliographic record. Atherton's work demonstrates that including tables of contents with the bibliographic descriptions of books would improve retrieval.[22] Others have suggested allowing catalog users to supplement catalog entries with their own comments and evaluations.[23/24]

With all this interest in augmenting catalog records the time may come when retrieval systems make significantly more use of information already in the MARC format–the "fixed field" and other coded information that was included in the format as an aid for computer-based retrieval systems. For over 20 years catalogers have coded for presence of biographical information, nature of contents (book reviews, bibliographies, etc.), types of illustrative material, intellectual level, geographic area treated, as well as language and date of publication and other attributes. Classification codes also have potential as a means of improving access.[25] Operational online catalogs seldom make use of this information; surely it should be explored even as we consider yet more retrospective conversion projects to augment catalog records with other kinds of information.

The revolution that led to computer-based production of printed catalog cards and indexes also has affected book and journal publication. Full text databases are making major inroads in the database/ search service world, and retrieval systems offer specialized features to improve access such as proximity searching and ranking of documents by number of times search terms occur. Hjerppe presents a vision of the online catalog in this brave new world of multimedia.[26] A related development is the optical storage of document images, which overcomes the restriction to text–graphic images and even sound can be retrieved and presented to the user.[27]

As catalogs and other information sources become larger and more complex we will need retrieval systems that are at once simpler and more sophisticated. Subject access in major online catalogs can produce enormous retrieval sets, especially when systems support keyword access.[28] Lynch suggests that the interfaces for online catalogs include capabilities for improving search results. Incorporating the expertise of experienced searchers on how and when to broaden or narrow a search.[29] Ranking of retrieved items in order of estimated relevance could also help reduce the frustrations of drinking from a fire hose. While ranked output is available on a few systems, it is not yet expected by users of computer-based systems. The problems of increasing complexity in library retrieval systems may be ameliorated somewhat by expert systems techniques.[30]

CONCLUSIONS

In 1975 the Information Science and Automation Division of the American Library Association sponsored an institute on "The Nature and Future of the Catalog." Visions of what the online catalog would bring included remote access catalogs, improved access points and search capabilities, union catalogs, reduced inconsistencies in access points, reduced problems and cost of maintenance, and means of coping with pressures for change.[31]

Many of these goals are within sight today. Remote access and union catalogs have brought us face to face with the need for improved document delivery. Improved search capabilities have forced us to consider the issues of human-computer interaction and how naive or infrequent searchers can best make use of the sophisticated systems at their fingertips. The problems of inconsistencies in data entry have been somewhat alleviated by keyword searching, and the gradual recognition that main entries are less meaningful in a computer-based catalog where alternative forms are equally searchable. On the other hand, computer indexing of every word in a file brings to light typographical errors that are less obvious in the card file.[32] Maintenance problems still exist, though they are more often expressed in terms of disk space and software upgrades. And pressures for change have led to increased cooperation with other information handling units in our institutions–the library-computing center alliance has been established and recognized without the creation of chief information officers.

Our 1990s assessment of the nature and future of the catalog reflects the complexity of creating a coherent source of information from varied roots. The different histories of the databases seem at times designed to frustrate our efforts. Thus, while we recognize and understand the background, we also aspire to a more comprehensive and coherent retrieval tool, recalling the adage "the future is longer than the past."

REFERENCE NOTES

1. Henriette D. Avram, "Machine-Readable Cataloging (MARC) Program," *Encyclopedia of Library and Information Science,* eds. Allen Kent, Harold Lancour, and Jay E. Daily (New York: M. Dekker, 1975), vol. 16, p. 381.

2. Robert M. Hayes and Joseph Becker, *Handbook of Data Processing for Libraries* (New York: Willey-Becker-Hayes, 1970), p. 830.

3. Hayes and Becker, *Handbook of Data Processing for Libraries*, p. 831.

4. Lauren B. Doyle, *Information Retrieval and Processing* (Los Angeles: Melville Publishing Co., 1975).

5. Irene S. Farkas-Conn, *From Documentation to Information Science* (Westport, CT: Greenwood Press, 1990).

6. Carl Spaulding, "Foreword: The Meaning of MARC," *Proceedings of the 1970 Clinic on Library Applications of Data Processing: MARC Uses and Users,* ed. Kathryn Luther Henderson (Urbana, IL: Graduate School of Library Science, University of Illinois, 1971), p. viii.

7. Hillis Griffin, "MARC Users: A Study of the Distribution of MARC Tapes and the Subscribers to MARC" *Proceedings of the 1970 Clinic on Library Applications of Data Processing: MARC Uses and Users,* ed. Kathryn Luther Hen-

derson (Urbana, IL: Graduate School of Library Science, University of Illinois, 1971), p. 32.

8. Henriette D. Avram, "The Evolving MARC System: The Concept of a Data Utility," *Proceedings of the 1970 Clinic on Library Applications of Data Processing: MARC Uses and Users,* ed. Kathryn Luther Henderson (Urbana, IL: Graduate School of Library Science, University of Illinois, 1971), p. 2.

9. Kathleen L. Maciuszko, *OCLC, a Decade of Development,* 1967-1977 (Littleton, CO: Libraries Unlimited, 1984).

10. Ronald Hagler and Peter Simmons, *The Bibliographic Record and Information Technology* (Chicago: American Library Association, 1982), p. 277.

11. "A New Perspective on the Database," *OCLC Newsletter* no. 190 (March-April 1991): 20-29. 1991.

12. Audrey N. Grosch, *Minicomputers in Libraries, 1981-82: The Era of Distributed Systems* (White Plains, NY: Knowledge Industry Publications, 1981).

13. Barbara Evans Markuson, "Granting Amnesty and Other Fascinating Aspects of Automated Circulation: A Review of Recent Developments for Non-Experts," *American Libraries* 9, no. 4 (April 1987): 205-211.

14. Carlos Cuadra, "On-Line Systems: Promise and Pitfalls," *Journal of the American Society for Information Science* 22, no. 2 (March-April 1971):107-114.

15. F. Wilfrid Lancaster and Emily Gallup Fayen, *Information Retrieval On-Line* (Los Angeles: Melville Publishing Co., 1973).

16. John Budd, "The Terminal and the Terminus: The Prospect of Free Bibliographic Searching," *RQ 21* no. 4 (Summer 1982): 373-378.

17. Ralph Alberico, "The Development of an Information Superhighway," *Computers in Libraries* 10, no. 1 (January 1990): 33-35.

18. Linda C. Smith, "Toward Integration of Online Resources," *Annual Review of OCLC Research* (July 1989-June 1990): 55-57.

19. Hayes and Becker, *Handbook of Data Processing for Libraries,* p. 587-596.

20. Edward T. O'Neill and Rao Aluri. "Library of Congress Subject Heading Patterns in OCLC Monographic Records," *Library Resources & Technical Services* 25, no. 1 (January-March 1981): 78.

21. John K. Duke, "Access and Automation: The Catalog Record in the Age of Automation," *The Conceptual Foundations of Descriptive Cataloging,* ed. Elaine Svenonius (San Diego: Academic Press, 1989), p. 117-128.

22. Pauline Atherton, *Books Are for Use: Final Report of the Subject Access Project to the Council on Library Resources* (Syracuse, NY: School of Information Studies, Syracuse University, 1978).

23. Raymond DeBuse, "So That's a Book . . . Advancing Technology and the Library," *Information Technology and Libraries* 7, no. 1 (March 1988): 7-18.

24. Michael E. D. Koenig, "Linking Library Users: A Cultural Change in Librarianship," *American Libraries* 21, no. 9 (October 1990): 844-849.

25. Karen Markey Drabenstott, Anh N. Demeyer, Jeffrey Gerckens, and Daryl T. Poe, "Analysis of a Bibliographic Database Enhanced with a Library Classification," *Library Resources & Technical Services* 34, no. 2 (April 1990): 179-198.

26. Roland Hjerppe, "HYPERCAT at LIBLAB in Sweden: A Progress Report," *The Online Catalog: Developments and Directions,* ed. Charles R. Hildreth (London, England: The Library Association, 1989), p. 177-209.

27. Carl Franklin, "Hypertext Gets Practical," *Online '89: Proceedings of the Online Inc. Conference* (Weston CT: Online Inc., 1989), p. 70-73.

28. Simone Klugman, "Failures in Subject Retrieval," *Cataloging & Classification Quarterly* 10, no. 1/2 (1989): 9-35.

29. Clifford A. Lynch, "The Use of Heuristics in User Interfaces for Online Information Retrieval Systems," *ASIS '87: Information, The Transformation of Society: Proceedings of the American Society for Information Science 50th Annual Meeting,* ed. Ching-Chih Chen (Medford, NJ: Learned Information for the American Society for Information Science, 1987), p. 148-151.

30. Ralph Alberico and Mary Micco, *Expert Systems for Reference and Information Retrieval* (Westport, CT: Meckler, 1990).

31. Kenneth Bierman, "The Future of Catalogs in North American Libraries," *The Nature and Future of the Catalog,* eds. M. J. Freedman and S.M. Malinconico, (Phoenix, AZ: Oryx Press, 1979), p. 115.

32. "The Dirty Database Test," *American Libraries* 22, no. 3 (March 1991): 197.

Chapter 6

Authority Control

Robert H. Burger

INTRODUCTION

How has authority control come to have the importance that it does today? Did we just wake up in the past 15 years to a sleeping giant of a problem that has plagued us for several decades? With all the attention on authority control in recent years do we really need another examination simply entitled "Authority Control?" Do we have an authority control article glut? Perhaps. For example, in 1982 Tillett has counted 411 citations to articles on authority control, only 13 of which were published prior to 1960.[1] In a 1989 review of recent authority control literature Taylor wrote: "So much has been written on the subject in recent years that it has been necessary to limit the scope of this review."[2] Indeed, with such an outpouring of information about authority control, what could be written that is new without more research? Probably nothing. My purpose, therefore, is not to reveal anything new about authority control *per se*, nor to produce anything resembling a literature review, but to assess the development of authority control thinking and practice, especially over the past quarter century.

I make no pretense that this is anything but an idiosyncratic examination. How could it be otherwise? I have only been active in librarianship for 16 of those years and became a librarian just when authority control started to become interesting. I know events prior to that time only from reading and anecdote. My examination will be divided into three chronological parts, each of which overlap slightly. The first part will briefly cover 1894 to 1965, the second part 1965 to 1978, and the third part 1977 to 1990. Based on what is brought forth for examination, I will try to see into the dimly lit future and predict some kind of action that lies ahead.

1894 (CUTTER) TO 1965

As Auld in his 80-year review of authority control revealed, Cutter first formally discussed an authority list,[3] suggesting that "a cataloger's author list, kept alphabetically,"[4] should be established. Cataloging rules from 1908 up to the present AACR2Rev (Anglo-American Cataloguing Rules, 2nd edition, Revised) have either suggested or mandated the making of cross references from the forms of personal and corporate names chosen as entries but did not specify the mechanism in the library by which these references were to be made and maintained. It was assumed that libraries would take care of this themselves in a manner that was most convenient and efficient.

The dominant technology of this preliminary period was the card catalog, even though printed book catalogs and microfiche catalogs did exist. With such technology there were only two choices available for the construction of an authority file. First, a separate authority file was constructed, most likely in the cataloger's work section. Catalogers would check forms of names against this file to ensure consistency. They would add forms different from the authorized form to the main entry for that name in the authority file as a record of the variations of the name; a separate card with that new variation would also be made in the authority file as a reference to the authorized form.

Makers of this type of file surely faced decisions concerning whether to make a card for each name in the dictionary catalog or only for those names with references. If they chose the second option, then the cataloger would also have to check the dictionary catalog in order to be sure that the form of name chosen for the entry did not conflict with the form in the dictionary catalog. That is, the cataloger had to ensure that a newly chosen form of name was not itself a variation of a name already established. The University of North Carolina at Chapel Hill, for example, established an authority file in this manner. Generally speaking, additional cross references from variant forms of names may or may not have been given guidance in the system that the library adopted.

The inefficiency of this type of arrangement and the difficulty of use by patrons led other libraries to chose a different type of authority file. Here, the dictionary catalog itself became the authority file. In this configuration, the cataloger would not have to check a separate authority file and the dictionary catalog, but just the dictionary catalog itself. Cross references were made on cards to lead both the cataloger and patron to the authorized form. A record of the cross references made was typed on the back of the first card made for that author or corporate body. This type of system shortened the work of the cataloger and helped the patron at the same time. The University of Illinois at Urbana-Champaign adopted this system.[5] There are always variations on themes and the location of the authority file was no different. The Library of Congress used the best of both systems. Its authority file was interfiled with the official catalog, on separate yellow stock, with the cross references recorded on this card.

I have taken the time and effort to describe these two systems in some detail because I believe that they exhibit several themes, some of which are self-evident, but often overlooked, that I would like to explore in the course of this chapter. First, authority control has always been part of descriptive cataloging. Authority control enables the catalog to carry out the findings and gathering functions. In Helen Schmierer's words:

1. the library catalog should enable a user to ascertain if the library has a particular item and
2. the library catalog should show what items the library has that share a common characteristic.[6]

Second, authority control has been constrained by the technology of the catalog. Prior to automation of the card catalog, the concept and practice of authority control was dominated by a syndetic structure of records. After automation developed we moved to the present syndetic structure of entries.[7]

The pre-machine technology catalogs existing up to the postwar era primarily took the form of cards or books. Bibliographic records in such catalogs were created individually and connected or linked to other records in the catalog. This was done because the only individual element by which to connect bibliographic information was the individual bibliographic record. There was essentially one file, and within this file, records, not entries, were linked. The linkage took place by collocation (records filed together) within the catalog or by means of notes on catalog records specifying that the record for which the note was written was linked in some way to another record.

In a machine system, linkage of entries, instead of records can be carried out. This system does not preclude the linkage of records to other records, but such linkage is often accomplished through the linkage of entries common to both records and not among the records themselves.[8]

The technology used to construct library catalogs greatly influenced both the theory and practice of authority control, as I will show below.

The third evident theme is that catalogers have consistently tried to effect authority control in the most efficient and cost effective manner possible. Catalogers love the elegant complexity of the catalog, but they also generally do not like to waste time and effort. They would rather look something up in one place rather than two. The structure and extent of the authority record and the physical placement of the authority file is continuously influenced by this desire.

Fourth, there has not been an authority record code, like AACR2Rev for bibliographic records, although informal discussion of a code continues among librarians. As we move from the focus on individual institutional authority files to national level authority files, such as those available on OCLC and RLIN, the push for a code for authority records gains more force. This is in part influenced by the movement towards cooperation and the desire for efficiency and cost effectiveness.

Fifth, and finally, the user of the catalog usually has taken a back seat to our efficient and cost effective methods. My only argument in support of this generalization is that our focus has been primarily on the mechanics of authority control to effect maximum access. We could hardly be faulted for this since access is the main goal of the catalog. But with our automated catalogs we have been too quick to find an elegant solution that solved all the problems as we saw them but ignored, or relegated to secondary status, problems that confronted the user.[9] Let us turn now to the examination of developments from 1965 to the present to see how these themes have played themselves out.

1965 TO 1978

There are four key developments that willy-nilly influenced the theory and practice of authority control from 1965 to 1978. These are the development of the MARC format, the establishment of OCLC, the adoption and revision of the Anglo-American Cataloging Rules (hereafter AACR), and the influence of the Library of Congress in the setting of the national bibliographic standards.

MARC Format

The MARC format was a technological innovation that had a great impact on the development of authority control. The library world was certainly not a leader in the automation of document retrieval. By the time MARC came along others had already applied it to the retrieval of technical reports and other scientific literature and the National Library of Medicine had used it for some time in the MEDLARS program for retrieval of medical literature. Prior to MARC, early pioneers in library automation, such as Columbia, Harvard, Yale, and Florida Atlantic universities had paved the way for the MARC project.[10]

Whatever importance the MARC project had in general for the advancement of bibliographic control and the improved efficiency of handling large amounts of bibliographic records, its relevance for both the theory and practice of authority control was immense. Theoretically it enabled librarians to perceive a bibliographic record as a collection of elements that could be isolated from some master or unit record and individually manipulated. Practically this made global changes in bibliographic systems possible and supported new ideas for retrieval system design. This is not to say that such a perception was not engendered by the rise in computer literacy in general, but simply that the MARC format for bibliographic records forced anyone working with bibliographic records to become familiar with the format, its fields, and its structure. This led to both fertile and futile discussions about various possibilities and visions of different types of systems. It became a catalyst for change.

The MARC family grew towards the end of the period in question. In 1976 the preliminary edition of the MARC authorities format was established. This was public recognition that libraries actually used authority records and files. At its inception only the Library of Congress produced records in this format. It was a cumbersome, but highly innovative tool used to record the chosen form of heading and the attendant *see* and *see also* references. The presence of an authority control number enabled systems using these records to update them with record changes and record additions issued by the Library of Congress. Although the system used to effect such changes was cumbersome at best, the future editions of the authority format rectified this situation. The introduction of the format further supported the notion of the independence of headings from the bibliographic record in a way that the separate authority file, using card technology, never did.

OCLC

The establishment of the Ohio College Library Center, subsequently OCLC, Inc. also has been cited as a catalyst for change. But as far as authority control was concerned, it had during this period an important, but decidedly secondary role. Its importance lay in the possibilities of efficiency and in signaling the necessity for uniform choice of the forms of entry. One wag had called OCLC during this period the Kmart of bibliographic data, implying, I assume, the existence of low quality, or differing quality of data found there. As an extension of NUC, however, it had a dizzying effect. With NUC, contributing libraries had to conform to Library of Congress headings. If a NUC contribution was received that did not conform, it was changed so that the finding and gathering functions of the printed NUC would not be compromised. With OCLC, however, the library world finally witnessed what most had already probably intuited. Not all libraries interpreted the rules for form of entry in the same way. Hence the Kmart effect was manifest in OCLC.

The bibliographic utility could ask for compliance with the existing cataloging rules, but the trouble was, there was latitude built into the rules and often expediency and the demands of one's own institution won out over fealty to the national good. As a result, the use of OCLC often entailed an enormous local outlay of time and trouble to "correct" headings (as well as other elements of the record) in order to comply with local usage. This was counter to the original intent of OCLC founder Fred Kilgour, who had hoped that his cooperative venture would make cataloging more efficient.

In some libraries, studies found that it took as long, if not longer sometimes, to catalog items from OCLC, simply because of the corrections deemed necessary. After a while some catalog department heads forbade original catalogers from even touching OCLC copy and set up strict guidelines for support staff for those elements that could be changed.

Anglo-American Cataloging Rules (AACR)

AACR was published in 1967 and during the next decade was gradually revised, sometimes chapter by chapter, to eventuate in AACR2 at the end of the period in question in 1978. Just like its predecessors, AACR gave no guidelines for the making of authority records. Its language for choosing forms of entries was often rife with exceptions and the Library of Congress itself stymied its impact with its policy of superimposition.

Library of Congress

The Library of Congress had the ability to do this because of its sheer ability to turn out cataloging copy faster and in greater quantity than anyone else. Libraries had become dependent on Library of Congress printed cards that were distributed nationally. Libraries generally accepted, without change, the headings appearing on these cards. Once OCLC expanded nationally in the early 1970s there was an historically ingrained habit of using and waiting for LC copy. One thing any Library could be sure of was the consistency of LC headings. For many members of OCLC, member copy usually had a low priority for use, librarians preferring instead to wait until LC copy showed up on the system. This attitude gradually changed in the early to mid 1980s, after the introduction of AACR2.

The Library of Congress's policy of superimposition–the adopting of a new cataloging code while leaving headings established under previous codes unrevised–reinforced the hegemony of LC in the establishment of forms of names. The reason was clear and simple. A library could establish a form of name easily enough without LC guidance and have cards made for the library catalog. If by chance the Library of Congress would also subsequently establish that name, but in a different form, the effort required to change the card was immense and tedious.

For those unfamiliar with this high-tech process, it went something like this. Once a heading established by an individual library was no longer in the form established by LC, or had to be changed for some other reason, the catalog maintenance crew or individual catalogers had to pull any card in the catalog that had the offending form on it. The cards were then brought back to the clerk's desk, the old heading erased (often with a motorized electric eraser that looked like an oversized dentist's drill), the new, corrected heading typed on and the card refiled in the catalog. No wonder the ability to do global changes from a terminal was greeted so enthusiastically by librarians!

This period from 1965 to 1978 (from the inception of the MARC Pilot Project in 1966 to the publication of AACR2 in 1978) was an immensely formative one for authority control. From 1978 to 1990 more subtle, but perhaps more far-reaching changes were in store.

1978 TO 1990

This period is generally characterized by four events of phenomena. The first is the establishment of NACO (Name Authority Cooperative), the second is the publication of AACR2Rev, the third is the introduction of the Linked Systems Project (LSP) and the last, not an isolated event, but more a phenomenon, is the increase in empirical research on authority records and files.

NACO (Name Authority Cooperative)

Up until 1977 the only institution that was producing authority records that were used nationally was the Library of Congress.

Once the preliminary edition of the Authorities Format was issued, it soon became apparent that the Library of Congress alone could not keep up with the pace of constructing new headings and the making of authority records for them. Therefore it stated the Name Authority Cooperative (NACO) that was designed initially to enlist the contributions of authority records from the Government Printing Office (GPO). This project entailed not only a mechanism for receiving and processing GPO's contributions, but ensuring that GPO followed the same standards for authority record construction as did the Library of Congress. In order to do this it had to add an additional chapter to the Library of Congress cataloging manual, an in-house tool that prescribed practices for the entire range of cataloging activities, from the record construction to evaluation of personnel. This chapter, N-1, along with several chapters in the Z section of the manual that prescribed how the authority record was to be constructed and gave guidance on citing sources of citation and other elements of the authority record, were now shared with GPO.

This was the first time since the 1940s that guidance for authority records was issued beyond the Library of Congress. At that earlier time the Library of Congress started a program called Cooperative Cataloging. Under this program selected libraries were asked to submit bibliographic records to the Library of Congress for inclusion in the National Union Catalog. These libraries also had to prepare authority cards on special yellow stock. Guidance was also given for the format of the information appearing on the cards.[11]

Guidance was no longer sufficient in the computer age, however, uniform authority records required training and explicit standards. Catalogers from the Government Printing Office were sent to the Library of Congress for training in name authority record construction, using Library of Congress standards as reflected in the Library of Congress cataloging manual. NACO was born. The project worked so well that other libraries, starting with the Texas State Library in 1979, joined NACO.[12] At last count there were over 80 contributing libraries to this cooperative authority record construction venture.

In spite of some difficulties in participating in this project,[13] NACO became an extremely successful program. Beyond its practical success, however, it is even more important for the development of authority control in that it established a code, still considered an internal LC standard, for the construction of authority records. Chapters Z-1, Z-2, Z-7, and Z-8 of the LC Cataloging Manual set forth rules and procedures for completing the authority record form, and for changing and deleting records. The "code," however, was used hand in hand with AACR2.

The publication of AACR2 in 1978 and its revised edition in 1988 was an important event for descriptive cataloging, and an especially important event for authority control. There was much controversy over interpretation of rules and the effects of changed headings on catalogs. With more bibliographic data available nationally through the primary utilities, OCLC, RLIN, and WLN, many were aware of the importance of uniform interpretation of individual rules. In the age of the card catalog, many libraries had developed local policies to deal with the problem of interpretation. The Library of Congress had issued its own interpretations since 1978 in the *Cataloging Service Bulletin.* Before the advent of the utilities, however, where idiosyncratic interpretation of a rule could mean more work for other libraries, these LC interpretations could mean more work for other libraries, these LC interpretations were helpful, but not crucial. Libraries could choose to follow or ignore them, given the exigencies of their local situation. This changed with the utilities. Now LC Rule Interpretations became increasingly important not only because they would determine the form of heading on LC records, which in many libraries could account for up to 80 percent or more of their cataloging copy, but because other libraries were also contributing records to these national databases. The NACO participants had to follow the LC RIs. Other libraries, not involved in this cooperative project, also followed suit. The Library of Congress, you will remember, was immune from the anxieties of other libraries concerning member copy. They did not use the primary utilities at all in their cataloging. This practice is, however, gradually changing. Increasingly, then the Library of Congress, through its rule interpretations of AACR and its own internal code for the formation of authority records, came to dominate authority record construction. The Linked Systems Project (LSP) reinforced this domination.

Linked Systems Project (LSP)

The Linked Systems Project (LSP)[14] is a means to electronically link three individual databases to create a national data pool. The three databases are the Library of Congress MUMS database, OCLC, and RLIN.[15] Through telecommunication links anyone having access to any one of the three databases could also search the other databases and have records contributed to one database become part of the other two. The relevance to authority control comes in because the first use of LSP was to submit authority records to NACO, who having once authenticated them, would distribute them to the utilities as part of a subscription to authority records through the Cataloging Distribution Service. This procedure streamlined the NACO process and reinforced not only LC's control over the making of authority records, but also the importance of a standard code for authority records. The implied, eventual goal, you see, is to allow non-NACO libraries to contribute authority records to a common database. This cannot be done unless the procedures are codified and interpretation of the rules is as uniform as possible.

Empirical Research

Once many libraries got in the act of making authority records and even more in the act of constructing authority records for their own OPACs, several researchers started to question many of the practices involved in the time-consuming task of authority record construction. After all, if well-designed computer programs could eliminate the need for certain types of cross references, then why bother taking all that trouble to make those references in the first place? Taylor,[16] herself one of these researchers, has accurately and evenhandedly summarized the various types of studies that have come out over the past decade. These findings also led to further theoretical developments in authority control procedures and record structure that need not be resummarized here. The point I wish to make is that it was not until certain practical advances had been made in the technology of catalogs and the rules and procedures for authority record construction had been, for all intents and purposes, codified by the Library of Congress, that researchers began to examine further what these developments had brought forth. Were practices that had been warranted under the old card catalog technology now unwarranted with the widespread use of computers? I expect this type of research to continue and to intensify.

THE FUTURE

Where do we go from here in authority control and what developments should we expect in the next five to ten years? I believe that certain trends will continue. For example, we will continue to refine and improve the technology of our catalogs. This will bring with it demands from our patrons for easier use. We will be forced to design new and better interfaces for our catalogs. These changes will give rise to some development in our concepts and practice of authority control.

What will these changes be? I have no idea. Like anyone who is not prescient, all I can do is to predict what is just before my eyes. One example of a new development in authority control is the increasing emphasis on multiscript languages. There is talk of including vernacular non-roman script fields in authority records, just as there are in bibliographic records.

With rising labor costs, there will be more emphasis on efficiency and cost-effective procedures. Computerized systems lend themselves to more direct and sometimes easier evaluation techniques. I expect we should see an increase in this kind of activity. Costs will also push the need for global catalogs, and with global catalogs will come the demand for more and more standardization. The introduction of artificial intelligence techniques will eventually spill over into authority work.[17]

Finally, my greatest concern is that the user will be forgotten in all of this. Along with our fascination for the elegant, efficient, cost-effective system, we may be leaving many users in patron-limbo, where they lack the knowledge, to use our newest creation. To counter this trend, I think it is imperative that we not only look at the technical and organizational aspects of our work as we progress to new and better systems. We also need to keep an eye on the cultural aspects of our work and the way that we, using technology as participants of bureaucracies try to bend people to our way of doing things because it is more convenient, or more efficient, rather than forming systems that serve people and their needs. My worry is that this concern will either be ignored because it is not technologically flashy, nor cost-effective. If it is ignored, we will all be the losers.

REFERENCE NOTES

1. Barbara B. Tillett, "Automated Authority Files and Authority Control: A Survey of the Literature," seminar paper, Graduate School of Library and Information Science, University of California, Los Angeles, June 1982; with corrections and additions, October 1982. Cited by Taylor (see ref. note 2)

2. Arlene Taylor, "Research and Theoretical Considerations in Authority Control," *Cataloging and Classification Quarterly* 9, no. 3 (1989): 29-56.

3. Larry Auld, "Authority Control: An Eighty-Year Review," *Library Resources and Technical Services,* 26 (October/December 1982):319-330.

4. Ibid, p. 320.

5. A more complete description of these card-based systems may be found in my book *Authority Work,* Littleton, CO: Libraries Unlimited, 1985.

6. Helen F. Schmierer, "The Relationship of Authority Control to the Library Catalog," *Illinois Libraries* 62 (September 1980): 599-603.

7. Ritvers Bregzis, "The Syndetic Structure of the Catalog," in *Authority Control: The Key to Tomorrow's Catalog,* ed. Mary W. Ghikas Phoenix, AZ:Oryx Press, 1979, p. 19-35.

8. Robert H. Burger, *Authority Work: The Creation, Use, Maintenance, and Evaluation of Authority Records and Files,* Littleton, CO: Libraries Unlimited, Inc., 1985, p.7.

9. Arlene Taylor, "Research and Theoretical Considerations in Authority Control," p. 35-36.

10. Barbara Evans Markuson, "Bibliographic Systems, 1945-1976," *Library Trends* 25 (July 1976):311-328.

11. Library of Congress, Descriptive Cataloging Division, *Cooperative Cataloging Manual for the Use of Contributing Libraries,* Washington, DC: Government Printing Office, 1944.

12. Judith G. Fenly and Sarah D. Irvine, "The Name Authority Co-op (NACO) Project at the Library of Congress: Present and Future," *Cataloging and Classification Quarterly* 7, no. 2 (Winter 1986): 7-18.

13. Robert H. Burger, "NACO at the University of Illinois at U-C: A Narrative Case Study," *Cataloging and Classification Quarterly* 7, no. 2 (Winter 1986): 19-28.

14. For a good introduction to LSP see *The Linked Systems Project: A Networking Tool for Libraries,* compiled and edited by Judith G. Fenly and Beacher Wiggins. Dublin, Ohio: OCLC Online Computer Library Center, Inc., 1988.

15. WLN was originally a member of this group. However, since their internal authority format software did not contain a field in which to store the authority control number, they have not been part of the current phase of LSP.

16. Arlene Taylor, "Research and Theoretical Considerations in Authority Control," pp. 29-56.

17. Roy Meador III and Glenn R. Wittig, "Expert Systems for Automatic Cataloging Based on AACR2: A Survey of Research," *Information Technology and Libraries,* 7 no. 2 (June 1988):166-172.

PART IV:
CATALOGING

Chapter 7

Death of a Cataloging Code: Seymour Lubetzky's Code of Cataloging Rules and the Question of Institutions

Edgar A. Jones

This chapter is about the politics of catalog code revision. It centers on the treatment of "institutions"– a class of corporate body that under the 1949 American Library Association (ALA) code had been entered in catalogs under the name of an associated place– locality or jurisdiction–but would, under a proposed revision of that code, be entered directly under their own names. In a broader sense, this chapter is also about another type of institution, our major research libraries–as key players in the process of code revision itself.

The mid-twentieth century was a time of heated debate over the nature and content of our cataloging rules. The American version of the code agreed to in 1908 by ALA and the (British) Library Association had grown ever more complex, culminating in 1941 in the publication of an extremely elaborate successor code. The elaboration of the 1908 code originated in the Library of Congress (LC) where it was felt that catalogers needed more guidance when confronting difficult or unusual situations. As other American research libraries became increasingly locked into LC practice through cooperative cataloging programs, access to these internal LC elaboration's became ever more crucial to the integrity of their own catalogs. The eventual result was the 1941 code (published in final form in 1949, and referred to hereafter as the 1949 code).

The process of code elaboration was unfolding at the same time as librarians were demanding that practical steps be taken to simplify cataloging procedures, which were seen to be causing larger and larger backlogs. Library administrators were beginning to question the direction in which cataloging rules were heading. "The Crisis in Cataloging," a 1941 article by Andrew Osborn, sounded the clarion call to reform of the increasingly "legalistic" code. Osborn was associate librarian of Harvard University and had served as a member of an advisory committee to the Librarian of Congress, the unpublished findings of which were reflected in his article.[1]

The stage might have seemed set for a stand-off between library administrators, arguing economics, and catalogers, arguing law. This did not happen. Although catalogers were not primarily concerned with economy in cataloging, they were, like Osborn, interested in a rational code based on clear principles, and it was hoped, perhaps naively, that economy in cataloging would naturally follow from this. Thus was constituted the "uneasy alliance" between the two groups that was to continue for almost 20 years before foundering on the rock of the "institutions."[2]

Reform was occurring both in the domain of organizational structure, with the separation of the functions of descriptive cataloging and subject cataloging at LC, and the domain of the catalog code itself.[3] The rules for bibliographic description were widely viewed as being overly detailed. LC assigned Seymour Lubetzky, recently arrived from UCLA and already possessing a reputation for clear-headedness, to analyze these rules. Lubetzky's analysis was highly critical, and boldly included principles to underlie any future revision. He defended these principles before an advisory committee of outside experts, and they were ultimately reflected in LC's revision of the relevant section of the 1941 rules, published in 1949 and known as the Green Book.

The Green Book was acclaimed widely for its logic and clarity, and was adopted by ALA as its own. The rest of the 1941 code–the rules on choice and form of access points (known at the time as rules of entry)–was republished separately, substantially intact, also in 1949 (the "Red Book"). Its reception was less than favorable, and agitation commenced almost immediately for a thoroughgoing revision.

Movement on reform in this area began with corporate names. In 1951, ALA's Board on Cataloging Policy and Research asked Librarian of Congress Luther Evans to have Lubetzky undertake a study of the rules for corporate name headings. Lubetzky threw himself into the task, producing at the end of two years a report–*Cataloging Rules and Principles*–which, while it may not have agreed with the views of all members of the board, satisfied their desire for intensive analysis. Lubetzky had managed to get his mandate expanded from a narrow focus on corporate names into a general evaluation of the ALA rules for entry, something he had been advocating privately at least since his chairmanship of a special LC committee on the future of its catalog. Again, Lubetzky proposed principles to underlie future revision, including that which would serve as the cornerstone of his later work: the "authorship principle," which he applied not just to works of individuals, but also to works of corporate bodies (a concept since rejected in Anglo-American practice). Lubetzky felt cataloging could be greatly simplified if this principle were applied across the board: that a work whose "author" was known would be entered under that author, and otherwise under title. In terms of the form of name to be used, he argued for the form used in the author's works, augmented only to avoid ambiguity. Lubetzky tried to disarm critics in advance by including a "question and answer" section in his report.[4]

While the board accepted Lubetzky's report, one member–John Cronin–felt it had been remiss in so doing. Cronin, director of LC's Processing Department, oversaw the largest cataloging operation in the country and wielded considerable influence both inside and outside LC. He would loom as an *eminence grise* in the later stages of the debate on "institutions," and would be an active defender of an elaborate catalog code. For the time being, however, the general response among catalogers was favorable to Lubetzky and his principles.[5]

Although saying the 1949 ALA code lacked principles, the principles were obscured frequently by the mass of detail. Items were cataloged according to the category of publication (e.g., encyclopedia) rather than the type of authorship exhibited (e.g., work of changing authorship). Likewise full legal names were preferred to forms actually used by authors in their works, a process that often involved considerable detective work and occasionally resulted in a heading very different from the name actually used by an author. And for corporate bodies in certain categories–so-called "institutions"–artificial entries were constructed using jurisdiction or locality as the entry element (e.g., Michigan University; Paris. *Bibliotheque nationale*).

Librarians had grown used to these rules, with all their complexities, and to some Lubetzky's simplified approach represented an untested and dangerous departure from custom. Many librarians were still attempting to patch the first leak in the dam: an early LC decision to stop seeking full legal names of individuals when the form used in their works would be unique to the catalog (the so-called "no conflict" principle). Now Lubetzky proposed to throw wide the floodgates by extending this practice to corporate names as well, and by severely circumscribing the practice of entering such names under place.

If some librarians were distressed, catalogers seemed exhilarated. A program on the Lubetzky report at the 1953 ALA conference went under the banner "ALA Rules for Entry: The Proposed Revolution!" And Marie Prevost's treatment of the Lubetzky report in the April 1954 *Journal of Cataloging and Classification* fell just short of reverential.

Although Lubetzky was on the staff of the Library of Congress (as Consultant on Bibliographic and Cataloging Policy, under Cronin), LC's official position was ambiguous from the start. As the formal structure of code revision was being put in place, LC presented a six-page list of "proposals" suggesting how to proceed. While the document, prepared by Richard Angell, acting chief of the Descriptive Cataloging Division, did not represent the official position of the Library of Congress, its distribution was approved by then acting Librarian, Verner Clapp. Lubetzky took strong issue with it, feeling it undercut the design he had put forward in his report. But in the end it was this document that formed the basis of the code revision committee's "Statement of Objectives and Principles for Catalog Code Revision."[6]

Despite appearances, however, Lubetzky's association with code revision was not being curtailed. Early in 1955, in a move that caused some confusion, LC assigned him to draft, for its own internal use, a separate revision of the 1949 ALA rules. Benjamin Custer, president of the Cataloging and Classification Division, wrote the new Librarian of Congress, L. Quincy Mumford, questioning why such a work was being undertaken. It was the belief of Willis Wright, chair of the ALA steering committee on code revision, that Lubetzky had been given the assignment for want of anything better for him to do. Wright was insistent that whatever document Lubetzky produced be treated on the same basis as any other submission to the code revision committee. At LC, Lubetzky was quietly reassigned to another task.[7]

ALA's work on code revision was organized into two ad hoc committees. A steering committee managed the day-to-day work of code revision and refined questions on policy and individual rules for discussion and vote by a larger general committee drawing on a broader representation. In addition the executive and policy and research committees of the Cataloging and Classification Division would as time passed become more and more involved in policy issues.

An early action of the steering committee was to select an editor for the revised code. The editor assumed his duties in September 1956. It was Seymour Lubetzky. In the scheme of things, he would be the source of the draft rules for consideration by the steering committee. His goal in the post was "to reconstruct our entire code on the basis of the best principles embodied in the various codes which have been evolved since Panizzi's rules." Despite Paul Dunkin's having styled him "Cutter Redivivus," Lubetzky would claim descent on a line passing from Panizzi through Jewett. His life project was upon him.[8]

DEINSTITUTIONALIZATION

Early on Lubetzky encountered problems with the rules for corporate names that he himself had proposed in 1953. At that time he had suggested that if a name did not "identify" a given body, the body would be entered under the name of the locality or jurisdiction with which it was associated. In his critique he had admitted that "this principle lacks a sharp criterion . . . [and] in the absence of such a criterion the decision would in many cases have to be arbitrary," but he still thought the method useful. However, while he had thus eliminated "type of body" as a criterion for entering corporate names under place, his substitution of the equally vague "type of name" was arguably not much better. After reading a 1956 report by the IFLA Working Group on the Coordination of Cataloging Principles that recommended entry directly under name for all corporate bodies, he abandoned his "type of name" concept in favor of the IFLA recommendation. Although Lubetzky anticipated the change would be controversial, he drew encouragement from having been able to persuade the section heads of LC's Descriptive Cataloging Division of its merits.[9]

Reaction to Lubetzky's decision among members of the steering committee and elsewhere was likewise generally positive, though some members demurred. Ruth MacDonald of the National Library of Medicine worried about the cost of the change–a concern that would dog the code to its end–while Paul Kebabian, chief cataloger at the New York Public Library, reported that some of his colleagues felt a confusing mass of entries would accumulate under common words such as "University." Bernice Field, head of the cataloging department at Yale, would argue against the draft rule to the end, and was most articulate in pressing her case. While she found Lubetzky's aim laudable, she felt certain that users of the catalog, often lacking the exact form of name under which to search, would be hopelessly lost, and that the Library of Congress and other libraries with very large catalogs would be faced with an impossible amount of recataloging.[10]

Early on the steering committee had taken a decision not to consider economic effects of implementation until after completion of the draft code. But Field felt the implications of this particular rule were too great to postpone discussion. She was in a minority on the committee. Sumner Spalding, then chief of LC's Descriptive Cataloging Division, argued for tabling discussion, and this was done. At the upcoming code revision institute at Stanford University where Field would bring her criticisms before a more general public, Lucille Morsch, Spalding's superior at LC, would likewise argue against premature debate.[11]

The 1958 Stanford Institute, held in conjunction with the ALA conference in San Francisco, was the first of two public hearings on cataloging code revision, the second of which would take place in 1960 at McGill University in Montreal. The institute was designed both to inform the nearly 200 attendees about progress being made in code revision and to solicit their input to the code revision process. Attendees received in advance copies of the *Code of Cataloging Rules* (*CCR,* Lubetzky's partial draft code) and 11 working papers dealing with particular questions. Each of the institute's sessions was organized around one or two of these papers, the author(s) of which would present a summary, followed by a question-and-answer period. Wright served as moderator.

Some 181 persons attended the Stanford Institute. As might be expected, ARL institutions were heavily represented (79 attendees), with the balance made up of library school faculty, local librarians, and a scattering of other interested persons, including 12 foreign librarians.

Laura Colvin, of the Simmons College library school, addressed the question "Entry of All Institutions under Name rather than Place." Lubetzky, present to defend his proposed revolution, explained the reasons for abandoning entry under place, noting that, beyond the general problem of defining satisfactorily a "distinctive" name, when otherwise nondistinctive names included the name of a locality or jurisdiction (e.g., Bank of England) the problems were especially intractable. But his arguments did not seem to sway the audience. Expressing what seems to have been the majority opinion, Richard Angell, now chief of the LC Subject Cataloging Division, argued that, if necessary, a satisfactory definition of "distinctive name" could be arrived at by consensus.[12]

On this and other matters, the steering committee came away from Stanford with more questions than answers. Their time, however, now became divided between code revision proper and developing an American position for a planned International Conference on Cataloguing Principles. On his part, Lubetzky proceeded with new chapters of *CCR,* leaving the chapter on corporate authorship as it was.

The questions raised at Stanford were ultimately addressed by the code revision committee a year and a half later, at its meeting of January 28, 1960. The audience response at Stanford apparently made little impact. To the question of whether some corporate bodies should be entered under place, the minutes record "unopposed agreement" that they should not. The questions, prepared by Lubetzky, had been considered by the steering committee at their meeting of December 5 and 6, 1959 and were forwarded to the full committee for formal vote. The meeting was quite brief, and Paul Kebabian, for one, felt the questions had not been considered adequately. He proposed at its spring meeting that the Cataloging Policy and Research Committee, take a stand "on some of the basic, yet controversial points of the proposed *Code,*" but a decision was postponed until after the McGill institute.[13]

The code revision committee's action on corporate names was also beginning to provoke a more active resistance elsewhere. At Yale, Bernice Field alarmed her colleague Roy Watkins, the chief reference librarian, with a recounting of the proceedings. Watkins wrote to Katharine Harris, president of the ALA Reference Services Division, demanding action. She in turn wrote to Wright asking that a paper be included at the McGill institute by an author representing the "reference point of view." Wright agreed, and Watkins was asked to write the paper.[14]

THE GATHERING STORM

By the time of the McGill institute in June 1960, many thought the controversy surrounding corporate entry was somehow diminishing. In his paper on corporate names prepared for the institute, Arnold Trotier, associate director for the technical departments at the University of Illinois, gave a much more cursory overview than had Colvin at Stanford. He handled the question by quoting two paragraphs of a letter from Wright pointing out the more glaring shortcomings of the existing rules, and by invoking the now-familiar steering committee policy of deferring debate on costs.[15]

It appears from the discussion that followed that many participants remained uneasy with Lubetzky's proposed uniform treatment, but for each argument advanced against it there was a well-worn counter-argument. Roy Watkins brought up the problem of large files of entries developing under such words as "university," to which Audrey Smith (Free Library of Philadelphia) replied that Colvin's Stanford paper had shown the new rules would, overall, *decrease* such concentration, now centered under place names. Sue Haskins (Harvard) objected that Lubetzky's treatment would disperse entries for civic institutions throughout the catalog, but others countered that assembling such entries in one place, though useful, was the function of subject headings rather than name headings.[16]

Watkins, in his paper, attacked *CCR* on all fronts, including the idea of trying to develop the best possible code without considering the amount of recataloging that might be entailed. "It is too late in the history of the world to start with a *tabula rasa,*" he argued. "There must be an accommodation with the past." He claimed that *CCR* would change useful practices and be too costly to implement. The question of "administrative implications" was broached for the first time in a paper by Maurice Tauber, of the Columbia Library School, and Robert Kingery, of the New York Public Library. Primarily a literature review, their paper showed a paucity of research so far on the likely effects the draft code would have on existing catalogs. In the area of corporate names, they found "meager comment" but cited an unpublished paper by Johannes Dewton, assistant chief of LC's Union Catalog Division, that predicted the effect of the change in practice for corporate entry would be "quantitatively [sic] enormous." In their own research, Tauber and Kingery determined that apprehension about *CCR* concentrated for the most part in research libraries. They called for more studies to help administrators reach informed decisions.[17]

The call for studies was not new. In subsequent discussion, Margaret Ayrault, head of cataloging at the University of Michigan and a member of the Cataloging Policy and Research Committee, noted that the code revision committee "had originally been charged with an obligation to see that studies were made in certain areas." This was true, and in fact the committee had issued detailed calls for studies as early as 1954, but without effect. The only substantive study, an experiment at LC in applying *CCR* to a subset of its current cataloging, had had mixed results. The dearth of studies may have been due to nothing more than a reluctance by libraries to divert scarce staff and money to see them through; this was certainly the attitude at Harvard. But Lubetzky felt studies, even if there were willing guinea pigs, would be a waste of time, that anyone unable to see the superiority of the draft code would not be convinced by experiments. Despite the unpromising prospects, Ayrault later convinced the policy committee to propose itself to the code revision committee as a suitable body to review whatever studies might be forthcoming, and optimistically proposed setting aside a two-day meeting for the task.[18]

Apparently, misreading events was an occupational hazard at the institute. Jens Nyholm, librarian of Northwestern University, came away feeling that opposition to the draft rule on corporate names had diminished considerably since Stanford, despite a straw vote showing that much of the support for the draft rule among institute attendees was extremely shallow. (While only one person disapproved of the draft rule, 66 of the 129 approving conditioned their approval on its impact being lessened.)[19]

But if some thought things were looking up at McGill, the code revision effort was about to receive a shock that no amount of optimism could absorb. On August 9 Lubetzky resigned his position at the Library of Congress to take a teaching position with the UCLA library school, fulfilling a long-held desire. He would remain editor of the draft code on a part-time basis until a successor could be selected. With Lubetzky's resignation, the contract between LC and ALA governing code revision came to an end. Spalding, the LC representative on the steering committee, tried to assure the executive committee that, despite this, LC retained an interest in revision and would continue to conduct studies and to make its staff available. The committee would seek ongoing funding from the Council on Library Resources.[20]

Studies at LC did continue, and Wright hoped the results would be available for the January 1961 meeting of the Association of Research Libraries, to be devoted to the "administrative implications" of the draft code. If Tauber and Kingery were correct that disquiet with the new code was concentrated in research libraries, the ARL meeting would be revealing. John Cronin, director of LC's Processing Department, tried at one point to forestall the meeting, feeling that more investigations were needed outside LC, but plans were already too far advanced.[21]

The meeting was similar in organization to the earlier code revision institutes. Three reports were made to the association. Tauber and Kingery prepared a paper on the administrative implications of the draft code; Wyllis Wright reported on code revision and on a small study he had performed with the cooperation of some ARL libraries; and finally, Sumner Spalding discussed a proposal on how the Library of Congress might adjust its catalogs to accommodate entries based on *CCR*.[22]

Tauber and Kingery broadly endorsed *CCR,* though they recommended that entry under place be retained for nondistinctive names, as Lubetzky had originally proposed in his 1953 critique. Cronin was unimpressed with the paper, feeling it was "a summarization of the commentary of Paul Dunkin which was printed as a part of the Montreal draft of the code."[23]

In his own paper, Wright reported on a limited experiment in application of *CCR* carried out in 18 ARL libraries. He noted that the draft rule on corporate names had resulted in different entries from the ALA rules in 40 percent of cases, making it "undoubtedly the rule which will cause the greatest amount of changes in the present catalogs."[24]

Spalding's paper followed logically from this, describing how the Library of Congress proposed to adjust its catalogs to the new rules. While the proposal assumed the present LC catalogs would be frozen, it also assumed that "split files of works by the same author (presently cataloged works under the old rules and newly cataloged works under the new)" would not be permitted. LC proposed to adjust entries on cards in its own catalogs to accommodate the new rules, but not to make these revised cards available to other libraries, which would be left to fend for themselves. The paper was initially accompanied by an outline of "Major Choices to be Made on Adoption of [the] New Cataloging Code." The outline did not at first include the choice of "superimposition"–applying the new rules of entry only to newly established headings–but a revision issued just prior to the ARL meeting did, though the word was not used, and the proposal itself was cloaked in rather obscure language.[25]

Spalding was not comfortable with the idea of "superimposition." It had been around, though without a name, since Lubetzky's 1953 critique, where in the Q and A section it had been proposed as a way to get around costs of change. And Lubetzky continued to stand by it. Although Spalding had included it in his outline of choices for LC, he felt that in several cases, such as the rule for corporate names, "it would cause serious trouble."[26]

Reaction to Spalding's talk at the ARL meeting was confused. Stanley West of the University of Florida observed that, among the earlier speakers, "almost everyone agreed the rules would be an improvement over the existing rules, and then when we have got to talking about money, it seems it becomes more and more complicated primarily because of the cost of changing the catalogs of the large research libraries." Donald Coney of Berkeley felt *CCR* represented an "elegant ideal: that would live or die on the decision of the Library of Congress as to how far it was willing to go, 'if anywhere.' "[27]

With the hour growing late, Lubetzky was asked "to give his impressions of this meeting, keeping in mind especially the administrative implications." He provided what he called "a few footnotes which I hope you will find pertinent." He likened the present conflict to that experienced by the German cataloging profession over retention of the practice "grammatical" filing (an analogy he had made earlier at McGill), whereby titles were filed in the catalog according to a complex philological analysis of the relationships between the various words, a method which was not only complicated for the cataloger but of dubious value to the user. Failure to replace that method was not without cost, and failure to reform the ALA rules would likewise not be without cost. "The question, in the words of a a colleague of mine, is that of a leaky faucet. In the long run it may be not only annoying but also more costly not to replace it."[28]

The negative tenor of the ARL meeting alarmed those catalogers present (directors have been invited to bring along their heads of technical services). Margaret Ayrault feared that another meeting like it would be disastrous for the draft code. At the ALA conference taking place at the same time, the code revision committee discussed the need to establish a "channel of communication with administrator," while the executive committee decided to establish a board of consultants, on which numerous interested parties, including ARL, would be represented.

But the opposition was now coalescing. On May 1, 1961 they

fired a volley from the pages of *Library Journal,* where editor Eric Moon joined them in trying to rally the profession.[29]

Two articles appeared in that issue of *LJ,* one by Roy Watkins along the lines of his earlier working paper for the McGill institute, the other by Johannes Dewton, whose often lengthy writings on the code–made available to members of the relevant ALA committees through the medium of John Cronin–had previously been available only as multilithed copies. Dewton's article was accompanied by an official LC disclaimer, but the position taken by Dewton–that *CCR* was too philosophical and not "elaborate" enough to ensure the uniformity necessary for cooperative cataloging; that, because it "starts from scratch, [it] ignores existing card catalogs, and diminishes the value of existing card distribution services and existing printed catalogs"–was identical to that already taken in private by John Cronin. For those opposed to the code, Dewton became a rallying point.[30]

At the steering committee of May 27, 1961, the need to counter the *LJ* articles took precedence over all else. Dunkin, Lubetzky, and Spalding had already composed rebuttals, and, perhaps naively, given the tenor of Eric Moon's editorial, the steering committee hoped these rebuttals would appear in *LJ* before the ALA Cleveland conference in July. (They did not appear until September.)[31]

Also at the steering committee meeting, Spalding introduced the question of "superimposition," observing dispassionately that, "if indeed the new rules could be adopted for new headings with only very minimal change of old headings and if this would not produce a badly disordered catalog, then the great and perhaps critical difficulties attending the problem of changing older entries would melt away." The strongest support for superimposition came from the two extremes on the question of corporate entry, Field and Trotier; and after some discussion a consensus emerged in favor of the idea. The minutes record, however, that several members, including Spalding, "expressed variously feelings of disappointment and disillusionment if the code revision effort should come to no more than this." The consensus also obscured the fact that there was still substantial support on the committee–Field, Vann, Dunkin, and Wright–for permitting some form of entry under place, a position which even Lubetzky said he would be willing to go along with if it were stated outright as an "administrative necessity," though he "could not go along with a specious rationalization."[32]

It might be that studies would have helped crystallize the situation, but this is not at all clear. Four studies made available at the 1961 ALA conference in Cleveland were of poor quality. The policy committee made arrangements for studies to be abstracted in Marian Sanner's "Studies and Surveys in Progress" column in *Library Resources and Technical Services,* but the column was then discontinued and the Cleveland papers were the first and last to be listed there.[33]

Studies at the Library of Congress seemed to be the only ones of much use. In the summer 1961 issue of *LRTS,* which was devoted in its entirety to the draft code, Spalding reported on one such study, though cautioning other libraries against trying to translate its results into a local context. In the context of LC, it appeared that adoption of the draft code would result in changes to at least 3.67 percent of the cards in the public catalog (nearly half a million cards). Margaret Beckman reported in the same issue that, while early adoption of *CCR* at the University of Waterloo, Ontario, was resulting in changes to 15 percent of the LC cards received, this was more than offset by "the constant logical relating of all catalog rules to Mr. Lubetzky's principles [which had] made cataloging at the same time more scientific and more satisfying." In the same issue, one could find between and beyond these extremes, Paul Dunkin adopting a philosophical approach to the difficulties of implementation, and Harvard's Sue Haskins declaring over the honeymoon between proponents of the draft code and those concerned with the cost of implementation.[34]

If the honeymoon was indeed over, it was not just critics of *CCR* that were growing hard-nosed. At their Cleveland meeting, the full code revision committee, considering several proposals that would have permitted some entry of corporate names under place, found that each proposal in turn involved "such difficulties in application or such illogic in results as to be unacceptable." Ruth Eisenhart found "[t]he temper of the Committee . . . not favorable to exceptions of any kind."[35]

COUNTERREVOLUTION

At the July 1961 meeting of the Association of Research Libraries, Jens Nyholm reported on the results of the May code revision committee meeting. He felt that, in contrast to the code revision committee's preoccupation with philosophical questions, ARL should concern itself purely with "accepting the code or modifying it for adoption under practical conditions." To this end, he thought it would be useful to have a member of the code revision committee on any ARL committee that might look at the code. ARL was being asked to form such a committee by Quincy Mumford "to confer with the Library of Congress on the problems associated with the adoption of the code." Although ARL would resolve that its committee have "a reasonable coloration of catalogers or heads of technical services," the committee as finally constituted included neither. Nor did it include Nyholm's suggested representative of the code revision committee. This did not augur well for an approach sympathetic to the draft code.[36]

The committee's members were Nyholm himself; Frederick Wagman, director of the University of Michigan Library; and Harald Ostvold, chief of the reference department at the New York Public Library. This was not as bad as it appeared on the surface, for both Wagman and Nyholm had earlier worked with Lubetzky. As head of the processing department at LC, it had been Wagman who had appointed Lubetzky to draw up his 1953 critique of the ALA code, and it had been Nyholm at UCLA who had first brought Lubetzky into cataloging and served as his mentor in the early years. Time had passed, and both had left technical services for administration, but an affinity persisted.[37]

A more important relationship for Wagman, however was with the head of his department, Margaret Ayrault, who as the incoming chair of the Cataloging Policy and Research Committee would be in a position to influence code revision. Ayrault's sympathies were already with Cronin (Wagman's own successor at LC), and her efforts to draw the policy committee into as close a relationship as possible with the ARL committee would create a powerful combination against the supporters of the draft code.[38]

Not all policy committee members shared Ayrault's enthusiasm for cooperating with ARL. Paul Kebabian feared the ARL committee would be too much concerned with implementation and not enough with the reform of the cataloging code. Marian Sanner hoped the policy committee would be able to use its influence in support of the draft code, while Jeannette Hitchcock, Ayrault's predecessor as chair, worried that things were moving too quickly, with a meeting planned with the ARL committee before the members of the policy committee had discussed matters among themselves.[39]

At the same time, Roy Watkins was trying unsuccessfully to mold his RSD committee into a more potent force. At its Cleveland meeting, the committee boldly decided to approach CLR for money to hold a conference of reference librarians "to formulate a position on the controversial aspects of the draft code" and also for money "to cover the expenses of two RSD observers to attend the [Paris] IFLA Conference in October." CLR was not interested. In his answer to Watkins' request, Verner Clapp, citing CLR's already heavy involvement in code revision, felt that supporting RSD's venture would appear to be encouraging internecine conflicts within ALA. Internecine conflicts would have to proceed without outside funding. Watkins felt he had been misled at an earlier meeting with Clapp into thinking the latter would be more receptive.[40]

On November 8 and 9, 1961, as the code revision committee took steps to provide as much opportunity as possible for ARL to make its point of view known, the policy committee met with the ARL committee at the Library of Congress. The members of the ARL committee had already had some discussions among themselves. Nyholm, although impressed with Lubetzky's code, felt the requirements of cooperative cataloging mandated a code that lent itself more to standardization, and any suggestions Dewton might have from the NUC perspective would be useful in this regard. He was not against the draft code, however. While he thought studies of the code's impact would be superfluous–it was already clear most libraries would not want to spend the funds necessary to adjust their catalogs to its requirements–he hoped it would be economical to make such adjustments in a cooperative context, perhaps through revision and redistribution of exiting NUC entries in the National Union Catalog.[41]

Ostvold was less friendly to *CCR*. He was particularly opposed to the elimination of entry under place for institutions, primarily, it seems, because users were already used to thinking in terms of geographic location. He thought Nyholm's NUC proposal coercive, forcing libraries to adopt the code by the backdoor of cooperative cataloging programs. In this, Ostvold had stumbled upon the enormous power of cooperative cataloging to tilt the balance in favor of the draft code as well as against it. Nyholm's proposal had had the potential of destroying one of the most compelling arguments then being offered by opponents of *CCR:* that it would undermine cooperative cataloging because no single library could be able to afford to change its catalog. His proposal would figure prominently at the subsequent meeting with the policy committee.[42]

At that meeting, Angell and Spalding were present from LC (as well as Cronin on the policy committee). The two committees learned the results of the Paris cataloging conference, which was widely regarded as a triumph for the principles of *CCR.* Ostvold was impressed, feeling that he would have to reconsider his position in light of international support for the draft code. Ayrault assured him, however, that while the results of the conference should be taken into consideration, "an international code is a long way off."[43]

Among the areas of agreement at Paris, representing a *rapprochement* between the German and Anglo-American traditions, was one of the stickiest: corporate entry, where, inter alia, the delegates accepted entry under name, as originally proposed by the IFLA working group in 1956. Although this was also the American position, Spalding observed that the American delegation had made no effort to influence the conference.[44]

Cronin and Angell then brought the discussion to the nature of the draft code, in the process continuing a debate that seemed still unsettled at LC: was it better than the ALA code? Angell found the basis of the draft code–bibliographic condition–superior to the "instances and various criteria" of the ALA code. Cronin, long skeptical of the merits of Lubetzky's code, asked what the advantage of such a code might be. Angell and Spalding both felt that, in the cataloging process, the draft code would be more efficient and more economical, and that benefits to the reader would be maintained "*only* in so far as the provisions of the Code are applied."[45]

Both Wagman and the policy committee seem to have believed that the policy committee would have some role in final approval of the draft code. In fact, only the executive committee would have such a role. Wagman suggested a formula be developed to allow individual libraries to estimate the local cost of adopting the draft code, but in the ensuing discussion a consensus emerged that cost studies were "not very useful." Remarkably, it was also agreed that the draft was still too incomplete to initiate studies of its application. Those libraries that had contacted the policy committee with proposals for studies were now to be told the time was not yet ripe.[46]

Meeting alone subsequently, the ARL committee decided to propose a "corps of people who could be relieved of their present duties temporarily" to visit representative ARL libraries and estimate the likely impact of the draft code on their catalogs. They would also investigate, along the lines of Nyholm's proposal, "the possibility of financial support to enable the Library of Congress to either reprint cards or print a list of revised headings."[47]

An alternate to Nyholm's proposal would, of course, have been superimposition, but there is no evidence the subject was ever discussed in committee. Wagman was unalterably opposed to the idea, on the grounds that it would have unspecified bad effects on branch library catalogs, of which Michigan had many.[48]

Wagman presented an interim report to ARL in January. At that time he observed that positive movement was taking place in a number of areas where the Library of Congress was having trouble with *CCR*. In particular, Wright had indicated to him that compromise on the rule for institutions should be possible. The British were known to favor some sort of entry under place, and CLR was making future funding of code revision contingent, among other things, on cooperation with the British. In a letter to Nyholm he revealed an additional spur to compromise, that many of the nation's largest libraries would not adopt the code if it involved radical changes. In particular, he identified Harvard, Yale, and the New York Public Library (in independent listings, Roy Watkins and John Cronin both added Wagman's own institution, the University of Michigan).[49]

With CLR attaching conditions (including an 18-month deadline) to its continued funding of code revision, all eyes were on the January 1962 meeting of the code revision committee. The meeting turned out to be anticlimactic, with the committee accepting the CLR conditions without objection. The Paris "Statement of Principles" was also accepted, along with a steering committee recommendation that Spalding be appointed to replace Lubetzky.[50]

Much of the remainder of the meeting was devoted to a new attack on *CCR:* a December 1961 paper by Dewton in which he suggested the Paris "Statement of Principles" was more consonant with the 1949 rules of entry than with *CCR.* Lubetzky found the assertion so outrageous–a "libertine manipulation of facts and quotations, directed at the unwary under the implied sponsorship of the Library of Congress"–as to demand an immediate response. The committee duly issued a response rejecting Dewton's contention and attached a "draft policy statement" strongly reaffirming the philosophical underpinning of the draft code and tacitly rejecting the idea of making exceptions on purely economic grounds.[51]

The committee's response went largely unnoticed. Roy Watkins took Dewton's arguments very seriously indeed and drafted a letter on behalf of his committee recommending to Wright that further work on *CCR* be abandoned in favor of a revised 1949 code. The letter was to have been presented at the code revision committee meeting, but the RSD representative on that committee, Isabel Howell, decided against it. Support for Watkins' initiative on the RSD committee was lukewarm, though they did feel that the time had arrived for the Reference Services Division to take a stand on the draft code, particularly with respect to corporate entry. In their midwinter report, they proposed to draft a statement for approval by the RSD board. The board and the workings of bureaucracy ensured that the formulation of that statement would be delayed until no longer relevant.[52]

The conditions attached to the CLR funding of code revision produced a flurry of activity, if not controversy, at midwinter. The executive committee endorsed the choice of Spalding, appointed Lubetzky to the steering committee, and proposed that LC appoint someone to replace Spalding on relinquishing Spalding to the editorship.[53]

The Librarian of Congress initially agreed to release Spalding, though in his official reply to the committee's request, drafted by Cronin, he noted that LC's interest was in the development of a "3rd edition of the ALA Code" to meet the needs of research libraries, and expressed his hope that the new code "will be based on both practical and realistic rather than purely theoretical considerations." He also disclosed his intention of convening a meeting of the ARL committee at LC, the outcome of which "should be of material assistance to the ALA Committee in its fashioning of a workable Code."[54]

LC also hoped to be of material assistance by making Lucille Morsch its choice for replacing Spalding on the steering committee. Since 1953 Morsch had been deputy chief assistant librarian, and she now succeeded Spalding as chief of the Descriptive Cataloging Division. In 1941 she had been the first incumbent of that position, at which time she had thrown in her lot with the conservatives on the staff. Morsch would be an "instructed member," that is, one who would speak not for herself but for the official point of view of the Library. Speaking to the policy committee at its spring meeting, Cronin said this step had become necessary because, with Lubetzky, "points made at meetings of section heads of the Descriptive Cataloging Division, during reviews of the Draft Code, were not taken into consideration.[55]

Cronin also announced that he was personally making an "intensive analysis" of the Paris Statement of Principles for the Librarian of Congress. Echoing Dewton, he asserted that the Paris statement was "nothing but a rearrangement of the ALA rules, except in cases where the ALA rules call for change."[56]

Cronin went on to attack the "author principle" that formed the very essence of Lubetzky's approach, claiming that the principles in Lubetzky's 1953 critique had been accepted by the library community without ever having been properly debated. He said that after he reported to the Librarian, it would be up to Mumford to make a decision, which would be conveyed to the ARL committee. Cronin expected LC would say "that it cannot make some of the changes and it needs an elaborate code to work with." Superimposition would not be recommended. Events were moving to a climax.[57]

The meeting between the ARL committee and staff members of the Library of Congress took place on May 25, 1962, less than a month before the ALA Miami Beach conference. LC's position was already known to the ARL committee, and it was simply a question of putting it in a form that could be voted on by ARL. Spalding had prepared a compromise proposal for the rule on corporate names, couched in the framework of the Paris "Statement of Principles." Spalding hoped it would be possible to "say that we are observing the Paris principles and write a draft code that would leave much of the 1949 code as it is." That is in fact what his compromise proposal did. The text, when read against the simple principles forming the Paris statement, is jarringly "elaborate" (see Appendix).[58]

Although LC put forward the compromise proposal, it developed in discussion that LC was also toying with the idea of "riding with the present rules." As Spalding explained it, "a new [code] could be issued that would not be changed from the old, or a compromise could be made that would reduce the number of estimated changes to about one-third."[59]

The members of the ARL committee were substantially in agreement with "Dr. Wagman's and L.C.'s views" (in the words of the minutes). A tentative decision to sound out ARL libraries on the points in question was discarded in favor of a committee recommendation that ARL support the LC compromise proposal. ARL directors were to come to the Miami Beach meeting prepared to vote the committee's report up or down.[60]

LC had been "unable" to release Spalding until it had met with the ARL committee. In a letter to Paul Dunkin dated June 6, Mumford reported on the results of that meeting, and expressed his hope that ARL would accept its committee's report, since "I know you are anxious to see resumption of further work on the code."[61]

ARL adopted the report and accompanying resolution unanimously. On a motion by Wagman, the resolution, which recommended that the code revision committee accept the LC position on three points and strive to reach a compromise on the fourth (corporate entry), was amended to further recommend the "sufficiently detailed" code that Cronin wanted.[62]

The next day, the code revision committee accepted the compromise proposal, since known as the "Miami Compromise." Spalding, assisted by Wright and Morsch, reworked his draft into a tentative rule, which was accepted "unanimously but not very enthusiastically" by the committee. The draft rule would now begin an odyssey between the committee and LC that would eventually clarify its intent and its extent.[63]

AFTERMATH

Spalding began his term as editor on September 1, 1962. He would continue until the completion of the revised code in 1966. In the January 1, 1963 issue of *Library Journal,* Lubetzky denounced the Miami compromise, claiming that it undermined the foundations of international agreement on cataloging principles and that it was based on an assumption that had not been properly examined or debated.[64]

At the July 1963 meeting of the steering committee, Lucille Morsch, LC's "instructed" member, announced that the Library of Congress would, after all, be adopting a policy of superimposition. The implications of this were profound–superimposition would eliminate the argument of cost that had formed the whole basis of the Miami Compromise–but the timing of her announcement appeared to have had the desired effect: the committee was too weary to raise objections, at least for the present.

At the next day's meeting, however, seemingly winding up the session, Wright asked whether there were "any other problems" regarding the chapter on corporate entry. Paul Kebabian responded by asking whether, in light of Morsch's announcement of the previous day, the committee "should reconsider the whole area of the compromise proposal." The question was put to a vote, and a bare majority (7-6) was mustered in its favor. The committee reopened debate, though people's hearts do not seem to have been in it. Once again, Ayrault advanced the argument that entry under place was defensible on its own merits, regardless of economic effects. Spalding, on the other hand, acknowledged that adopting a policy of superimposition, which he had so long opposed, changed "the whole frame of reference." Wright claimed the exceptional nature of the two rules (descendants of Spalding's original compromise rule) meant libraries could ignore them at will, but Morsch countered that the two rules were *not* exceptions. Two British observers present for the meeting stated that the two rules would not be acceptable to the British, who would attempt to draw up an alternative. At that, Spalding proposed tabling the two rules until the British alternative was available. It seemed the battle might be joined once again.[65]

Such was not to be the case, however, for the "frame of reference" had indeed changed. The basis of the draft code was no longer Lubetzky's principles but those of the Paris conference (similar though they might be), and, more important, the conditions attached to the CLR funding. Progress on code revision now required cooperation with the Library of Congress and cooperation with the British. There might be a chance of resuscitating the Lubetzky rule by playing one off against the other, but that was the only chance, and a remote one at that. As it turned out, the British proposal proved much too vague for acceptance, resting as it did on something called "everyday usage," that would have worked well for many British institutions (producing entries like "Oxford University" for the body calling itself the "University of Oxford") but would not have done much for American bodies (no one really called the University of Michigan "Michigan University"). The tabled LC compromise rules were accepted into what would become the North American Text of the *Anglo-American Cataloging Rules,* though a footnote was added stating the reason for their inclusion in the code.[66]

Entry under place for new headings was finally discontinued by LC in 1974; superimposition was discontinued with the implementation of AACR2 in 1981.[67]

It is difficult to identify, even at this distance, all the consequences of the Miami Compromise, especially as these were so quickly overwhelmed by those of superimposition. Among the greatest was the introduction into machine catalogs of a cataloging principle–entry under place for institutions–that had been found wanting in manual catalogs nearly a quarter-century earlier. AACR1 might have been a model cataloging code, bravely facing the future, like the German code then under development; instead it was a hobbled code, trying to placate the past.[68]

Could it have been avoided? Perhaps. But there can be little doubt that personal opinion was divided on the utility of entry under place, exclusive of cost. It was not just divided between administrators and catalogers. It was divided on almost every committee that dealt with the question. As long as it remained a question of opinion, however, those arguing the cost angle would find ready allies at one end of that opinion.

While it is true that studies of cost and application of the code would have been of limited value until the code was more complete, it should have been possible, through user surveys, to test the hypothesis underlying the draft rule on form of corporate entry–that users of the catalog were more likely to seek an "institution" under its name than under the name of a place associated with it. An answer to this question would have replaced a debate that had been based entirely on conflicting personal impressions with a consensus based on a set of objective data.

Part of the problem, however, lay in the opposition of John Cronin to the draft code in general. He used any and all means available to undermine it. Even in seeming victory, long after the Miami Compromise, Spalding's assumption of the editorship, and superimposition, he remained adamantly opposed to the draft code.[69]

Might superimposition have been the answer, as Lubetzky had originally proposed? History seemed to say no. Although such a policy on its own would have preserved the integrity of Lubetzky's code, it would also have minimized its impact on library catalogs (as was in fact the case from 1967 to 1980). This was its primary attraction to those concerned with cost, its primary drawback to those concerned with rational catalogs. In the end, Lubetzky would triumph, at least in the question of the form of corporate name, but it would have to wait until 1981 and the implementation of AACR2, where in contrast the application of his "authorship principle" to corporate bodies would be discontinued. In this light, the action of LC and ARL must now appear akin to that of Canute commanding back the tide. This is not said simply with the benefit of hindsight. Many saw it clearly at the time. Frederick Wagman, later to be chair of the ARL committee, gave one of the most effective defenses of the draft code against compromises based on questions of "economy" in a paper read at the 1955 ALA Philadelphia conference, at a time when code revision was just getting off the ground. It serves as a fitting close to this discussion.

Despite the fact that it is difficult to relate the Catalog Code Revision Committee's third Consideration to the rights of the catalog user, I feel it necessary to make some mention of this Consideration before I conclude. "Code revision," the Committee states "should proceed without regard to the amount of recataloging of materials at present in the catalog which may be involved." This reflects a courageous and praiseworthy acceptance of a doctrine that should be one of the cardinal tenets of our profession.

The collections of our general research libraries are a cultural deposit of the records of the past, but our methods of bibliographical control must be as modern and efficient as we can make them, uninfluenced by false tradition, guided only by a clear conception of our objectives and by the answers to the question, what are the simplest and most efficient methods of achieving them. Delay in correcting the deficiencies, the cultural lag, in our catalogs because of short-term considerations of economy will earn us the contempt of our successors.[70]

APPENDIX

SECTION 9.4 OF ICCP STATEMENT OF PRINCIPLES AND MODIFICATIONS NEEDED TO ACCOMMODATE TERMS OF THE MIAMI COMPROMISE

From the Statement of Principles adopted by the International Conference on Cataloguing Principles, Paris, October 1961 [footnote in original]:

9.4 The uniform heading for works entered under the name of a corporate body should be the name by which the body is most frequently identified in its publications, except that

    9.41 if variant forms of the name are frequently found in the publications, the uniform heading should be the official form of name;

    9.42 if there are official names in several languages, the heading should be the name in whichever of these languages is best adapted to the needs of the users of the catalogue;

    9.43 if the corporate body is generally known by a conventional name, this conventional name (in one of the languages normally used in the catalogue) should be the uniform heading;

9.44 for states and other territorial authorities the uniform heading should be the currently used form of the name of the territory concerned in the language best adapted to the needs of the users of the catalogue;

9.45 if the corporate body has used in successive periods different names which cannot be regarded as minor variations of one name, the heading for each work should be the name at the time of its publication, the different names being connected by references;[8]

9.46 a further identifying characteristic should be added, if necessary, to distinguish the corporate body from others of the same name.

How proposed "compromise" would have fit into framework of Paris principles (from minutes of "Meeting on Catalog Code Revision," Library of Congress, 25 May 1962) [asterisk in original]:

9.4 The uniform heading for a corporate body should be its name, except that

9.41 U.S. and Canadian national, state, provincial, county and other non-municipal government institutions are entered under the appropriate jurisdiction followed, after a period, by the name* unless the name begins with a proper noun or phrase (other than the name of the controlling jurisdiction) in which case entry is under name;

9.42 Such other institutions as are specified below are entered under the name of the municipality of their location followed, after a period, by their name*

9.421 Churches, cathedrals, monasteries, abbeys, convents, temples, mosques and the like;

9.422 Public schools below the college level;

9.423 Institutions of higher learning that are particularized only by the presence in the name of the name of the municipality of location (with the exception of such institutions with names in English when the name of the municipality appears as the first word of the name), and

---

[8] It is a permissible alternative, when it is certain that the successive names denote the same body, to assemble all the entries under the latest name with references from the other names.

* Suitable provision would be made to avoid repetition of the name of the jurisdiction or municipality in the name.

other such institutions that are commonly identified primarily by the name of the municipality even though
having legal names that are otherwise distinctive;

9.424 Local institutions of a type that are typically or frequently supported by public funds (whether or not so
supported in a particular case) whose names are quite
common and unparticularized (e.g., Public Library,
Carnegie Library, City Hospital, Musee des beaux arts)
or particularized only by the presence in the name of the
name of the municipality or location.

9.5 The name of a corporate body used in the uniform heading should be
the one by which the body is most frequently identified in its publications, except that

[Change 9.41-9.46 to 9.51-9.56]
[Change 9.5-9.62 to 9.6-9.72]

SOURCES CONSULTED

The Archives of the American Library Association (University of Illinois
Archives): RG 30/2/62, Reference Services Division, Subject File; RG
31/2/6, Resources and Technical Services Division, Executive Secretary Subject File, boxes 4, 12, 19; RG 31/11/2, Cataloging and Classification Section, Committee File, box 1; RG 31/47/5, Catalog Code Revision Committee File, boxes 1-2.

Seymour Lubetzky Papers (University of California at Los Angeles Special Collections) collection 1554, boxes 305.

Jens Nyholm Papers (Northwestern University Archives): RG 9/1/1, box 5.

Transcripts and summaries by Kathryn Luther Henderson of documents in
the John Cronin Papers (Library of Congress Cataloging Instruction
Office).

University of Illinois Archives: RG 35/1/2, Library, Dean's Office, General Correspondence, 1895-1961, box 83.

REFERENCE NOTES

1. Andrew D. Osborn, "The Crisis in Cataloging," *The Library Quarterly,* 2 (October 1941): 393-411; Kathryn Luther Henderson, " 'Treated
with a Degree of Uniformity and Common Sense': Descriptive Cataloging
in the United States, 1876-1975," *Library Trends,* 25 (July 1976):
236-237; Martha M. Yee, "Attempts to Deal with the 'Crisis in Catalog-

ing' at the Library of Congress in the 1940s," *The Library Quarterly,* 57 (January 1987): 1-2.

2. Association of Research Libraries (hereafter ARL), *Minutes of the 56th Meeting* (Chicago: ARL, 1961), 9-10; Paul Dunkin, *Cataloging U.S.A.* (Chicago: ALA, 1969), 12-13.

3. Henderson, 236.

4. Library of Congress, Special Committee on the Future of the Library's General Catalogs, "Recommendations of the Special Committee." Memorandum to the Librarian of Congress, 5 January 1951, 2 (cited in Michael Anthony Carpenter, "Corporate Authorship" [PhD dissertation, University of California, Berkeley, 1979], 70); American Library Association, Board on Cataloging Policy and Research (hereafter BCPR), "Meeting of April 20, 1951," ALA Archives, RG 31/11/2, box 1; Seymour Lubetzky, *Cataloging Rules and Principles* (Washington: Processing Dept., LC, 1953).

5. John Cronin, "Progress on Code Revision: Satisfactory or Unsatisfactory? Review of the Present Status and Recommendations for Immediate Action," ltr to Librarian of Congress, 6 March 1964, Cronin Code Rev. 1964, Misc. docs. Cataloging Instruction Office, Library of Congress (ms. notes by Kathryn Luther Henderson); Maurice F. Tauber, "Introductory Remarks," *Journal of Cataloging and Classification,* 9 (September 1953): 123-125.

6. Lewis C. Coffin, ltr to Dorothy Charles, 23 Oct. 1953, accompanied by "Proposals to the DDC Code Revision Planning Committee," prepared by Richard Angell; Lubetzky, ltr to Charles, 27 Oct. 1953, both in ALA Archives, RG 31/11/2, box 1; *Journal of Cataloging and Classification,* 12 (April 1956): 103-107.

7. *Library of Congress Information Bulletin,* 14 (17 January 1955): 9; Wyllis E. Wright, ltr to Benjamin A. Custer, 1 March 1955; Custer, ltr to L. Quincy Mumford, 21 March 1955; Mumford, ltr to Custer, 4 April 1955, all in ALA Archives, RG 31/47/5, box 1.

8. Seymour Lubetzky, ltr to Andrew D. Osborn, 31 May 1957, ALA Archives, RG 31/47/5, box 1; Paul Dunkin, "Cutter Redivivus," *Libri,* 11 (1961): 189, footnote 3.

9. Lubetzky, Ibid.; the IFLA report appeared in *Libri,* 6 (1956): 271-298.

10. Arnold Trotier, ltr to Lubetzky, 6 May 1958; John M. Dawson, ltr to Lubetzky, 11 April 1958; Paul Kebabian, ltr to Lubetzky, 28 April 1958; M. Ruth MacDonald, ltr to Lubetzky, 19 May 1958, all in ALA Archives, RG 31/47/5, box 2; F. Bernice Field, ltr to Lubetzky, 9 May 1958, ALA Archives, RG 31/47/5, box 2.

11. American Library Association, Catalog Code Revision Steering Committee (hereafter CCRC), "Minutes of Meeting at the Library of Congress, June 16, 1958," ALA Archives, RG 31/47/5, box 2; Institute on Cataloging Code Revision, Stanford University, *Summary of Proceedings* (n.p., n.d.), 5.

12. Ibid., 26-31; Laura Colvin, "Entry of All Institutions under Name rather than Place," in Institute on Cataloging Code Revision, Stanford University, *Working Papers* (Stanford, CA: n.p., 1958), V1-V35.

13. CCRC, "Minutes of Meeting in Chicago, January 28, 1960," ALA Archives, RG 31/47/5, box 2; Paul B. Kebabian, ltr to Katharine Ball, 29 February 1960, ALA Archives; RG 31/2/6, box 12, University of Illinois Archives; ALA, Cataloging Policy and Research Committee (hereafter CPRC), "Minutes, April 22, 1960," ALA Archives, RG 31/2/6, box 12.

14. Watkins, ltr to Harris, 2 February 1960; Harris, ltr to Wright, 8 February 1960, both in ALA Archives, RG 30/2/12, box 2.

15. Arnold H. Trotier, "Corporate Names," in Institute on Catalog Code Revision, McGill University, *Working Papers* (Chicago: n.p., 1960), VI1-VI13.

16. Institute on Catalog Code Revision, McGill University, *Summary of Proceedings* (Chicago: ALA, 1960), 35-38.

17. David R. Watkins, "A Reference Librarian Looks at the Proposed Catalog Code," in Institute on Catalog Code Revision, McGill University, *Working Papers* (Chicago: n.p., 1960), IX1-IX6; Maurice F. Tauber and Robert E. Kingery "Problems of Changing from the Old Rules to the New," in Institute on Catalog Code Revision, McGill University, *Working Papers* (Chicago: n.p., 1960), XI1-XI21.

18. Institute on Catalog Code Revision, McGill University, *Summary of Proceedings* (Chicago: ALA, 1960), 66; "Catalog Code Revision: Help Wanted," *Journal of Cataloging and Classification*, 10 (October 1954): 228-231; Olivia Faulkner and C. Sumner Spalding, "Experiment in the Application of the Revised Rules," in Institute on Catalog Code Revision, McGill University, *Working Papers* (Chicago: n.p., 1960), X1-X36; Institute on Catalog Code Revision, McGill University, *Summary of Proceedings* (Chicago: ALA, 1960), 78; CPRC, "Committee Minutes of Meeting, June 21-22, 1960, at ALA/CLA Montreal Conference," ALA Archives, RG 31/2/6, box 12.

19. ARL, *Minutes of the 56th Meeting* (Chicago: ARL, 1961), 12; Institute on Catalog Code Revision, McGill University, *Summary of Proceedings,* 77.

20. *Library of Congress Information Bulletin,* 19 (1 August 1960): 453-454; American Library Association, Cataloging and Classification

Section, Executive Committee (hereafter CCS EC), "Minutes, September 24-25, 1960," ALA Archives, RG 31/2/6, box 12.

21. CPRC, "Minutes of Meetings, October 27-28, 1960"; John W. Cronin, memo to members of CPRC, 27 December 1960, both in ALA Archives, RG 31/2/6, box 12.

22. Tauber and Kingery, "Administrative Implications of the New Cataloging Code," 46-60; Wright, "Report on Comparison of Results of Use of CCR Draft Code of Catalog Rules versus Present ALA Rules," 62-65; Spalding, "Proposal for Making Changes in the Catalogs to Adjust Them to the Changes in Cataloging Rules Indicated in the Draft of March 1960," 66-76, all in ARL, *Minutes of the 56th Meeting.*

23. Tauber and Kingery, Ibid., 54-56; Cronin, memo to members of CPRC, 27 December 1960, ALA Archives, RG 31/2/6, box 12.

24. Wright, Ibid., 64.

25. Spalding, Ibid.; "Major Choices to be Made on Adoption of New Cataloging Code," n.d., ALA Archives, RG 31/47/5, box 2; same title, 13 January 1961, ALA Archives, RG 30/2/62, box 2.

26. Lubetzky, *Cataloging Rules and Principles,* 56-57; ARL, *Minutes of the 56th Meeting,* 25.

27. ARL, Ibid.

28. Ibid., 34-35; Institute on Catalog Code Revision, McGill University, *Summary of Proceedings,* 78-79.

29. McCarthy, S. A., memo to members of ARL, 30 December 1960, Library, Dean's Office, General Correspondence, 1895-1961, RG 35/1/2, box 83, University of Illinois Archives; Margaret Ayrault, ltr. to Cronin, 25 April 1961, ALA Archives, RG 31/2/6, box 4; CCRC, "Meeting of January 29-30, 1961," ALA Archives, RG 31/47/5, box 2; Moon, Eric, "Who Cares about the Code?" *Library Journal,* 86 (1 May 1961): 1744.

30. Carpenter, Ibid., 147; Johannes L. Dewton, "The Grand Illusion," *Library Journal,* 86 (1 May 1961): 1719-1729; David R. Watkins, "A Reference Librarian's View of the Draft Cataloging Code," *Library Journal,* 86 (1 May 1961): 1730-1733; Watkins, ltr to members of the RSD code revision committee, 17 January 1962, ALA Archives, RG 30/2/62, box 2.

31. CCRC Steering Committee, "Minutes of Meetings on May 27-28, 1961, at Columbia University," ALA Archives, RG 31/47/5, box 2, University of Illinois Archives; Seymour Lubetzky, "Smoke over Revision," *Library Journal,* 86 (1 September 1961): 2740-2744; Paul Dunkin, "Howlers–Here and Now," *Library Journal,* 86 (1 September 1961): 2744-2749; C. Sumner Spalding, "Illusion? Delusion? Collusion?" *Library Journal,* 86 (1 September 1961): 2749-2751; Johannes Dewton,

"Holes in the Fish Net," *Library Journal,* 86 (1 September 1961): 2752-2755; Seymour Lubetzky, "P.S. to Dewton's Reply," *Library Journal,* 86 (1 September 1961): 2755, 2771.

32. The word has a long history, being first attested in 1684. *The Oxford English Dictionary* defines it as "The action of superimposing, or state of being superimposed; superposition," and gives as the most recently cited use (1907), "The superimposition of the utilitarian . . . civilisation of the West on the Indian civilisations." OED, s.v. "superimposition;" CCRC Steering Committee, Ibid.

33. The four papers were: Raudolf Engelbarts, "New York Headings," June 1961; Roger P. Bristol. "Survey of State-Supported Colleges and Universities According to ALA and *CCR* Rules," 1961; Audrey Smith, "Comparison of entries of Works of Corporate Body with Changed Name under ALA and *CCR* Rules," June 1961; and "Sample Entries Made According to *ALA Cataloging Rules* and Draft *Code of Cataloging Rules,*" ALA Archives, RG 31/2/6, box 4; Jeannette Hitchcock mentions also a Brown University study on patron reaction to the draft rules–"not statistical but qualitative"–but it never got into print (ltr to Marian Sanner, 20 March 1961; Sanner, ltr to Margaret Ayrault, 2 October 1961, both in ALA Archives, RG 31/2/6, box 12); Marian Sanner, "Studies and Surveys in Progress," *Library Resources and Technical Services,* 5 (fall 1961): 3430-3444.

34. C. Sumner Spalding, "The Quantitative Effects of Changes Cataloging Rules on the Existing Catalog," *Library Resources and Technical Services,* 5 (summer 1961): 198-206; Margaret Beckman, "Experiment in the Use of the Revised Code of Cataloging Rules," *Library Resources and Technical Services,* 5 (summer 1961): 216-220 (Beckman had volunteered her library during the McGill Institute. [Institute on Catalog Code Revision, McGill University, *Summary of Proceedings,* 59-60]); Paul S. Dunkin, "Guesstimates Unlimited: The Draft Code in Imagined Operation," *Library Resources and Technical Services,* 5 (summer 1961): 179-185; Susan M. Haskins, "Is Harvard Bound by the Past?" *Library Resources and Technical Services,* 5 (summer 1961): 189-198.

35. Audrey Smith, "Substantive Changes in the Draft Code, June 1960-July 1961," *Library Resources and Technical Services,* 5 (fall 1961): 342; Ruth C. Eisenhart, "Report on ALA Catalog Code Revision Committee Activities," *ATLA Newsletter,* 9 (19 August 1961): 14; in his report in the *Library of Congress Information Bulletin,* Spalding observed, "The alternatives having been exhausted after a full day of discussion, the present rules were decisively confirmed in their substance" (20[10 July 1961]: 398-399).

36. ARL, *Minutes of the 57 Meeting* (Cleveland: ARL, 1961), 18-19.

37. Benjamin A. Custer, "Seymour Lubetzky," *Journal of Cataloging and Classification,* 12 (January 1956): 3-7.

38. CPRC "Report of Meetings, July 10, 12, and 14, 1961," ALA Archives, RG 31/2/6, box 19; Ayrault, ltr to Cronin 25 Arpil 1961, and ltr to Paul Kebabian, 26 July 1961.

39. Kebabian, ltr to Ayrault, 1 August 1961; Sanner, ltr to Ayrault, 11 September 1961; Hitchcock, ltr to Ayrault, 17 September 1961, all in ALA Archives, RG 31/2/6, box 12.

40. American Library Association, Reference Services Division, Ad Hoc Committee on Catalog Code Revision, "Report . . . ," n.d.; Verner W. Clapp, ltr to Watkins, 19 July 1961, both in ALA Archives, RG 30/2/12, box 2; Watkins, ltr to Julia Ruth Armstrong, (28 July 1961), ALA Archives, RG 30/2/12, box 2.

41. Wright expanded the normal distribution of revised copies of the draft code to include 200 copies for ARL libraries (Wright, ltr to Paul Dunkin, 28 September 1961), ALA Archives, RG 30/2/12, box 2; Nyholm, memo to Fred Wagman and Harald Ostvold, 19 October 1961, ALA Archives, RG 31/2/6, box 12.

42. Ostvold, ltr to Wagman, 24 October 1961, ALA Archives, RG 31/2/6.

43. CPRC, Minutes of Meeting, November 8-9, 1961, 7-8, ALA Archives, RG 31/2/6, box 12.

44. Ibid., 7-8.

45. Ibid., 8.

46. Ibid., 7, 11, 14; CCS EC, Minutes, Midwinter meeting 1962, 2, ALA Archives, RG 31/2/6, box 19.

47. Ibid., 15.

48. Frederick H. Wagman, ltr to Jens Nyholm, 24 January 1962, Jens Nyholm Papers, RG 9/1/1, box 5, Northwestern University Archives.

49. ARL, *Minutes of the 58 and 59th Meetings* (Chicago: ARL, 1962), 72-74; Wagman apologized for not clearing the report first with the other committee members (Wagman, ltr to Nyholm, 24 January 1962, Jens Nyholm Papers, RG 9/1/1, box 5, Northwestern University Archives); Watkins, memo to members of the RSD committee, ALA Archives, RG 30/2/62, box 2; Cronin, memo to Librarian of Congress, 13 April 1962, Seymour Lubetzky Papers, UCLA Special Collection #1554, box 3.

50. CCRC, "Meeting of January 27-28, 1962," ALA Archives, RG 31/47/5, box 2.

51. Ibid.; Ruth C. Eisenhart, "Report on ALA Catalog Code Revision Committee Activities" *Newsletter (American Theological Library Association)* 9 (17 February 1962): 26-29; Lubetzky was originally to have

continued as editor to the end *(Library of Congress Information Bulletin)* 19 [1 August 1960]: 453-454); Lubetzky, ltr to Cronin, 12 January 1962, ALA Archives, RG 30/2/12, box 2.

52. Watkins, memo to members of the RSD committee, 17 January 1962; Watkins, Draft letter to Wright, 24 January 1962; Robert D. Stevens, ltr to Watkins, 19 January 1962; American Library Association, Reference Services Division, Advisory Committee on the Catalog Code Revision, Report, 28 January 1962; Howell "didn't want it to appear that RSD was dynamiting the code." (Julia Ruth Armstrong, ltr to Watkins, 23 February 1962); The RSD committee at one point hoped to be able to draft a compromise rule on corporate names that would be acceptable to both ARL and ALA (Isabel Howell, ltr to Ronald V. Glens, 29 March 1962), all in ALA Archives, RG 30/2/62, box 2, University of Illinois Archives.

53. CCS EC, Minutes, Midwinter meeting 1962, ALA Archives, RG 31/2/6, box 19.

54. L. Quincy Mumford, ltr to Paul Dunkin, 7 February 1962, ALA Archives, RG 31/47/5, box 2; the letter was drafted by Cronin.

55. CPRC, Minutes of Meeting, 29-30 March 1962, 3-4, ALA Archives, RG 31/2/6, box 12; Wagman took part in the meeting as well, which was held at the University of Michigan; Andrew D. Osborn, "From Cutter and Dewy to Mortimer Taube and Beyond: A Complete Century of Change in Cataloguing and Classification," *Cataloging & Classification Quarterly,* 12, nos. 3/4 (1991): 42.

56. Ibid., 4, 12.

57. Ibid., 10-11.

58. The meeting was subject to ongoing postponement. Mumford (ltr to Paul Dunkin, 7 February 1962) mentions holding the meeting "within the next month"; Cronin at the policy committee meeting spoke of a meeting "by April 15th" (CPRC, Minutes of Meeting, 29-30 March 1962, 304, ALA Archives, RG 31/2/6, box 12); "Meeting on Catalog Code Revision, May 25, 1962," stamped received in the LC processing department 13 June 1962, 2, ALA Archives, RG 31/47/5, box 2.

59. Ibid., 3.

60. Ibid., 304.

61. CCRC, "Meeting of June 16-17, 1962"; Mumford, ltr to Dunkin, 6 June 1962, both in ALA Archives, RG 31/4795, box 2.

62. ARL, *Minutes of the 60th Meeting* (Miami Beach: ARL, 1962), 15, 27-29.

63. CCRC, "Meetings of June 16-17, 1962," ALA Archives, RG 31/47/5, box 2; Ruth C. Eisenhart, "Report on ALA Catalog Code Revi-

sion Committee Activities," *Newsletter (American Theological Library Association)* 10 (18 August 1962): 11-14.

64. CPRC, "Minutes of Meeting, November 15-16, 1962," ALA Archives, RG 31/2/6, box 12; *Library Journal* 88 (1 January 1963): 46.

65. CCRC, "Meetings of July 12-13, 1963," ALA Archives, RG 31/47/5, box 2.

66. CCRC, "Meetings of January 25-26, 1964," ALA Archives, RG 31/47/5, box 2.

67. *Cataloging Service,* 109 (May 1974): 3-8.

68. The German code, *Regeln für die Alphabetische Katalogisierung,* acknowledging the great differences that separated it from its predecessor, the Prussian Instructions, was developed specifically for machine catalogs (Rudolf Lais, "Cataloging and Bibliographic Description in the Federal Republic of Germany. 1, Alphabetic Cataloguing," *International Cataloguing,* 12 (July/September 1983): 27-28.

69. Cronin, "Progress on Code Revision: Satisfactory or Unsatisfactory? Review of the Present Status and Recommendations for Immediate Action," ltr to Librarian of Congress, 6 March 1964, Cronin Code Rev. 1964, Misc. docs. Cataloging Instruction Office, Library of Congress. "It seems to me that certain members of the Code Revision Committee apparently feel that they can force the acceptance of the Spalding draft (as they tried to do with the Lubetzky draft) whether the Library of Congress approves it or not. It is not difficult to perceive a large element of face-saving in this attitude. These members of the Committee have become so identified with this aborted effort that they are now attempting to put over the impression that they have produced a serviceable code. I heartily disagree . . . "

70. Frederick H. Wagman, "The Administrator and the Research Library Catalog," *Journal of Cataloging and Classification,* 11 (October 1955): 195-196.

Chapter 8

Descriptive Cataloging

Mary Ellen Soper

INTRODUCTION

In her review of descriptive cataloging in the United States over
the period 1876-1975, Kathryn Luther Henderson notes that "descriptive cataloging is concerned to a large extent with the choice
and form of bibliographical data elements necessary to provide
access to the items in the collection, and to describe and identify the
items for purposes of selection or rejection by the user."[1] This
chapter continues that review by focusing on the development of
the *Anglo-American Cataloging Rules* from AACR1 (1967) to
AACR2 (1978) AACR2R (1988).

THE ANGLO-AMERICAN CATALOGING
(CATALOGUING) RULES

Revisions began almost as soon as the first edition of the *Anglo-
American Cataloging Rules* (AACR1) was published in 1967.[2] Library of Congress' decision, called superimposition, to apply
AACR1 only for headings new to its catalog, while continuing to
use headings previously established according to earlier rules, was
not an official revision, but affected how most libraries would apply
the new code. The availability of cataloging copy from the Library
of Congress (LC) was too powerful a force to be ignored. LC's
decisions, though meant only for its own employees, were published in the quarterly *Cataloging Service Bulletin,* and were ob-

served by many libraries throughout this country because they wanted their own cataloging to agree with that of LC so that the resulting records could be interfiled in their catalogs.

Superimposition had the effect of splintering the application of AACR1; sometimes its rules for headings would be applied, sometimes not. Predicting when to use the new code for new material and when to use forms dictated by earlier rules was a guessing game solvable either by examination of previous LC cataloging or waiting for LC to distribute the records. Superimposition may have been a feasible decision for LC, but since it affected libraries nationwide, in the long run it turned out to be unworkable. Eventually LC recognized this, and decided to abjure such applications when the next complete revision of AACR occurred.

AACR1 was published in two versions: the North American and British texts. There were various rules that the Americans and British could not agree upon, necessitating the two versions. Eventually these discrepancies would have to be received if there was to be any international sharing of bibliographic records. Soon after the North American text was published, the rules peculiar to this continent began to be canceled, and the two versions grew closer together.

AACR1 contained an almost complete revision of the rules for entries and headings, because these rules were based on the Paris Principles, the result of the decisions reached at the International Conference on Cataloguing Principles, 1961. There was international agreement on these principles, and many countries revised their cataloging codes to agree with them. But the rules for description of bibliographic materials were basically just updating previous rules derived from principles developed in the 1940s. New formats had been added, but since the description rules had been developed by LC, many smaller libraries were discontented with the rules. They found them inadequate for new formats, such as many of the newer nonbook materials, and they also objected to what they considered to be excessive detail required by the rules for more traditional materials.

Another factor that caused discontent with rules for description of materials in general arose because LC began to accept the descriptive cataloging from other countries' national bibliographies for its own use, and distributed this copy for other libraries' use. LC would adjust any headings that conflicted with AACRl and its policy of superimposition, but the physical descriptions were unchanged. It soon became apparent that other countries described bibliographic materials differently than did American libraries and such records could cause confusion in their catalogs. But the benefit of sharing bibliographic records among countries was recognized by many, so it was accepted that there was a need to revise the rules for description, based on agreement reached on the international level, similar to the agreement that produced the Paris Principles.

In 1969 the International Meeting of Cataloguing Experts was held in Copenhagen. This meeting resulted in agreement on principles of description that covered the data to be included in bibliographic descriptions for all formats, the order of these data, and the type of prescribed punctuation to be used to introduce the various data elements, as well as to be used within the elements. The International Standard Bibliographic Descriptions (ISBD) were the concrete results of these agreements. An immediate effect of development of the first ISBD for monographs was the complete revision in 1974 of AACRl's Chapter 6, rules for description of monographs, including Chapter 9, rules for photographs and other reproductions.[3] Two more revised chapters quickly followed: Chapter 12 for audiovisual media and special instructional materials was completely revised, while Chapter 14, sound recordings, was only a partial revision.[4]

With the publication of the partial revision of Chapter 14, AACRl was officially in four parts. There were also numerous rule interpretations from LC that affected its application by other libraries. The need for complete revision of the code was apparent to everyone. Work had already begun in the American Library Association (ALA) on developing new rules for the description of what was then called machine-readable data files. ALA also endorsed the first edition of the Canadian Library Association rules for nonbook materials as an interim guide for the cataloging of these materials in this country. An ALA committee was also studying audiovisual codes produced by other agencies in an effort to create a national standard for the organization of nonbook materials.

During this period the MARC (Machine Readable Cataloging) formats for all kinds of bibliographic materials were being developed at LC and quickly accepted by other libraries. Bibliographic records began to be distributed in the MARC format, and these became the basis for the development of the bibliographic utilities: OCLC (originally the Ohio College Library Center; now the Online Computer Library Center), WLN (originally the Washington Library Network; now the Western Library Network), RLIN (Research Libraries Information Network), and UTLAS (originally the University of Toronto Library Automation System). As libraries joined these various utilities in order to use automated records produced by themselves and other libraries, the need for standardization of cataloging records became increasingly important. Libraries were realizing that local practices were too expensive to continue, and that the acceptance of national standards could result in more economies through sharing. The needs of the local user were overridden by the need to reduce the cost of cataloging; whether the local user suffered as a result is still being debated. What is apparent is that the development of automated records not only in this country but also overseas, and their wide distribution, added impetus to the growing push to revise the cataloging code. ALA started planning for the second edition of AACR.

AACR2

In 1973 the Catalog Code Revision Committee, ALA, was established. In 1974 it was shifted from the Cataloging and Classification Section (CCS) to the parent Resources and Technical Services Division (RTSD) and given authority for code revision until the second edition was published. Also in 1974 the Joint Steering Committee for Revision of AACR (JSC) was formed. Initially it included representatives from ALA, the British Library, the National Library of Canada, the Library of Congress, and the Library Association. The Australians become members late. The objectives of JSC were to reconcile in a single text the North American and British versions of AACR1, to incorporate into a single text all the changes since 1967, as well as the proposed changes in process in the various countries, and to promote international interests in AACR1.

The new edition was to maintain conformity with the Paris Principles and the ISBD principles for bibliographic description of all formats. It also was to take into account the developments in automation which had been ignored in the first edition. The revision of the rules for nonbook materials were to be based on four sources: the revisions of Chapters 12 and 14, and the sets of rules developed by the Canadian Library Association, the Library Association, and the Association for Educational Communications and Technology.[5]

ISBDs for various formats had been issued by the International Federation of Library Associations (IFLA; now the International Federation of Library Associations and Institutions), or were in preparation. As work increased on the revision of AACR1 it became apparent that the ISBDs were beginning to diverge from each other. In order to correct this tendency it was decided to backtrack somewhat and prepare a general ISBD (ISBD (G)), which would set the framework for all the specific format ISBDs so they would be compatible with each other. The resulting ISBD(G) became the basis for the first chapter in the description part of the second edition (AACR2).

By 1977 it had been decided that AACR2 would put description rules before the entry and heading rules, emphasize general rules for basic choice of entry, add a rule defining when titles changed, drastically reduce the use of corporate body main entry (but the principle of main entry remained), eliminate special rules for entry of serials, delete from subheadings, omit deviations from the Paris Principles, reduce the number of alternate rules, and specify romanization of nonroman scripts either according to tables produced at LC or according to usages in published works. It was realized that the changes in the heading rules would be difficult to implement in library catalogs, but that the other changes in description and entry should have minor impact. There was interest in also taking into account the needs of other countries.

In 1978 AACR2 was published.[6] LC had decided to abandon superimposition and implement the new edition completely. The bibliographic utilities were working on ways to incorporate the changed headings resulting from the new rules into their databases. Libraries feared the amount of changes the new rules would bring, and felt they could not afford the new edition. Calls for delay in the implementation of AACR2 grew. Even parts of ALA had asked that AACR2 be delayed.

In an effort to counteract the negative reactions to AACR2, ALA and LC sponsored a series of conferences and workshops on the new code. ALA also trained trainers to go back to their states and instruct local librarians in the new code. There was much more emphasis on educating future users in the intricacies and changes the new edition brought than had been apparent with AACR1. All the furor over the new code did have a result: implementation by LC was delayed until January 2, 1981. This would give libraries the opportunity to prepare for the new code and cushion the shock of its changes.

Various studies were done to estimate the percent of headings that would be affected by AACR2. Estimates ranged from 15-50 percent, with most coming in on the low side. As tempers cooled and common sense took over, recommendations grew for libraries to adopt the new code completely and integrate records prepared according to its rules with records based on earlier rules. An integrated catalog was judged to be best for users, who were known to tend to look in only one place for records in a catalog. But many libraries decided that the advent of AACR2 was a good chance to start a new catalog in another format, based on machine-readable records. Microform or online catalogs figured in the planning of various libraries. The existing print catalog, usually in card format, was to be converted to machine-readable form eventually, as funds permitted. This resulted in two catalogs, one small but growing, based on AACR2, and usually in fiche or online, and the other, initially a much larger manual catalog, based on earlier codes.

ALA, in addition to its emphasis on training users in the new code, also began publishing manuals which were designed to explain and illustrate various parts of the code. LC also began publishing manuals for special formats.[7] In addition LC began to issue rule interpretations for AACR2 in its *Cataloging Service Bulletin.* Over the years since 1978 the rule interpretations for AACR2 and its successor have multiplied, and now have been cumulated in at least three versions for LC's interpretations, and one for interpretations from the national libraries of the larger English-speaking countries. The bibliographic utilities and many libraries regard LC's rule interpretations as part of the code to be followed as they follow the rules themselves. There were also many articles written about AACR2, some negative, but most positive or at least optimistic about the changes it would bring.

The rules for description, Part I, were thoroughly revised from AACR1, but since the ISBDs had been well publicized and had already caused parts of AACR1 to be revised, most changes resulted in few questions. A problem, however, rapidly developed with Chapter 9, machine-readable data files. Just about the time AACR2 was published, microcomputers became popular and inexpensive enough to become common in libraries. Chapter 9 had been developed to describe databases mounted on large mainframe computers and accessible through terminals. It was not structured to cover the commercially produced software and data files created for microcomputers. It would require revision to accommodate the newer formats.

In the chapter for entry (Chapter 21) the most startling change was the elimination of corporate body authorship. Now the rule spoke of emanation from corporate bodies, and established five (eventually six) categories of material which could have corporate bodies as main entry. The result of this rule was that there were many fewer main entries under corporate bodies, though they would increasingly become added entries. The lack of a rule for entry of serials, coupled with the de-emphasis of corporate main entry, resulted in most serials being entered under their titles, regardless of how indistinctive these titles were. Eventually the problem of serial entry led to development of rule interpretations that created uniform titles for many serials. This development was a change in the previous use of uniform titles, which had been used to collocate versions of individual works published with varying titles. Now uniform titles were also to be used to uniquely identify serials. Many other entry rule changes had been presaged by previous rule interpretations or changes.

The heading rules for personal, geographic, and corporate names and uniform titles included many changes, though quite a few of these had been part of AACR1, but not completely put into effect because of superimposition. If AACR1 had been fully implemented, then the shock of AACR2 would have been much less. The need for libraries to change the forms of personal and corporate names to conform with the code caused many to become interested in authority control. Controlling the forms of names, and providing references from the unused to the authorized forms, was not a new topic, but one that had frequently been ignored in card catalogs. Now that the form of catalogs was being affected by automation the interest in authority control grew rapidly. What was tolerable in card catalogs became intolerable in online catalogs, which were much more unforgiving if users entered an incorrect form of a name as a search key.

In 1980 ALA established the Committee on Cataloging: Description and Access (CC:DA), as part of CCS. It was apparent that there would be a continuing need for code revision, and CC:DA was established to serve as the center for revision efforts in ALA, and to be the ALA voice on the JSC. Nonvoting official representatives on CC:DA were selected by other RTSD sections, ALA divisions and round tables, and national library organizations outside of ALA. Suggested changes to AACR2 were to be discussed by CC:DA, and then, if approved, passed on to the JSC.

Among the topics CC:DA first discussed was the problem of the description of microforms. A basic principle in AACR2 was that the item in hand was to be described. This meant that the physical description of a microform would be derived from the microform, not its original print form. But libraries were accustomed in the past to describe the original form from which the microform copy was made in the body of the record, then in a note present the physical description of the microform. Eventually CC:DA decided not to recommend revision of the rules, but LC's rule interpretations restored the original treatment of micro- and macroform reproductions of previously existing works, so the issue was settled by continuing the description as it had always been. Only original microforms were to be handled completely according to the provisions of AACR2.

Another major topic in the early years of CC:DA was the revision of Chapter 9, machine-readable data files, so it could accommodate microcomputer software. AACR2's rules for the description of rare materials were also judged inadequate; eventually LC's *Bibliographic Description of Rare Books,* 1981, was issued to be used instead of AACR2 rules 2.12 through 2.18.

When AACR2 was finally implemented by LC in January, 1981, libraries around the country found that they could cope with the changes; one study estimated that it would increase cataloging costs less than 10 percent. The bibliographic utilities' ability to change their massive databases to conform to AACR2's heading rules no doubt was a major factor in the acceptance of the new code by libraries. Many libraries started new catalogs, but many others found they could get by with integrating the new headings with the old in their existing catalogs, though the advent of AACR2 evidently did stimulate the switch to online catalogs.

In 1981 a concise edition of AACR2, by Michael Gorman, was published by ALA. It was designed to help new students grasp the essence and basic principles of the full edition. It was also aimed at smaller libraries so they could produce bibliographic records without having to use the full text.

In 1982 CC:DA sent 35 recommendations to JSC. Later that year the first set of official revisions was published. Two more sets were to follow during the next few years.[8] By the end of 1982, Gordon Stevenson, who wrote the annual review of 1982 activities in LRTS, concluded that AACR2 had been gradually, but also largely, accepted since its publication and implementation. AACR2 was also seen as a major instrument in international standardization, which was to become increasingly important as countries began to exchange bibliographic data.

The problem of description of microcomputer files was alleviated with the publication in 1984 of guidelines for applying chapter 9 to microcomputer software.[9] In 1987 a draft revision of Chapter 9 was issued.[10] This revision not only incorporated the treatment of microcomputer software but also changed the title from machine-readable data files to computer files, which was a designation more acceptable to most people. CC:DA continued to discuss suggestions for other changes and additions. It became increasingly evident as the official and draft revisions multiplied that a new, consolidated version was needed. It was also evident that suggested changes would probably never end. Code revision had become a continuing activity, and involved great amounts of the time of members of CC:DA, not only during the two annual meetings of ALA, but also between meetings. The rule interpretations from LC also multiplied rapidly. Keeping current with the code became an arduous task during these years.

In 1986, Nurieh Musavi published the results of a survey returned by 57 heads of cataloging or technical services departments and 47 experienced catalogers in ARL (Association of Research Libraries) libraries, and 39 cataloging teachers in accredited library schools.[11] The survey asked for opinions of AACR2. Results indicated a strong, positive, overall support for the new code among both groups, though the educators were generally more positive than the catalogers. Neither group supported an AACR3 any time in the near future, though they saw the need for changes in certain rules and chapters. There was strong opposition to the development of a cataloging code radically different from an AACR2-type code.

In 1985 CC:DA began to clear recommendations for the forthcoming consolidated edition. It was involved with suggested revisions of the rules for cartographic materials, entries for performers of musical works, and suggestions on how to reduce the number of serial title changes that would require the creation of new bibliographic records. Another topic of increasing interest concerned the problem of multiple versions of works. The U.S. Newspaper Project, created to record all the newspapers published in the U.S., had to reach a decision on how to describe the many versions a particular newspaper could appear in over its lifetime. The Project decided to use a master record for each title that would include all physical manifestations of the title in one description rather than prepare separate records for each physical entity. It was proposed that this solution be extended to microform reproductions. In 1988 CC:DA created a Task Force on Multiple Versions to consider definitions and potential solutions to this problem.

The 1986 annual review of cataloging activities, published in 1987, summarized the impact of AACR2 on libraries: little or no additional staff was available to cope with implementation; increasing attention was being paid to authority control and the increased time and cost of cataloging; changes were occurring in the organization of cataloging in libraries and in the work flow of technical services departments; AACR2 seemed to have a greater effect on copy cataloging than on original cataloging; many libraries were concentrating on cleaning up their manual catalogs, relying on future online catalogs to provide the mechanics for dealing with automated records; the implementation of AACR2 provided increased impetus toward more automation; and there was little response by the general public or public service librarians to the effects of AACR2. It was concluded that the consequences of AACR2 were generally negative due to difficulties of integrating old and new headings, higher cataloging costs, lower productivity during implementation, frustrated staffs, and a more complex catalog. On the other hand, benefits included greater emphasis on authority control forced reexamination of the cataloging process, and reeducation of the library staff. Personal names accounted for most changes, followed by corporate names, series, geographic names, and uniform titles.[12]

AACR2R

In 1988 the consolidated version of AACR2 was published, though by then it was just called the 1988 revision (AACR2R).[13] It contained all the revisions made between 1978 and 1986. Despite significant changes the new version was not called a new edition, as many definitions of "edition" would ordinarily require. It was considered politically inadvisable to call it AACR3, as there were still bad feelings in the profession from the time AACR2 was published and implemented. But not everyone agreed that the fact that there was really another edition should be hidden. Sheila Intner recognized that library directors who had major investments in existing catalogs might be expected to reject a new edition, but she pointed out that cataloging rules cannot work if they fail to reflect the realities of production and distribution, and fail to meet the needs of catalog users.[14]

LC revised its rule interpretations to bring them into accord with AACR2R, though there were few major changes. It appears that LC is trying to simplify its rule interpretations and make them more stable. This should help catalogers in other libraries cope more easily with necessary changes, as in the past LC has flip-flopped on the interpretation of some rules to such an extent that it has been difficult to keep up. The editors of AACR2 had originally hoped that the code was flexible enough to allow catalogers to use their judgment in the application of the rules in order to meet the needs of their own users. In reality the advent of bibliographic utilities and the sharing of records has put increasing stress on standardization of application of the rules, which has increased the importance of LC's rule interpretations for most libraries.

In 1990 the CC:DA Task Force on Multiple Versions finished investigating the scope and definitions of materials to be considered for the multiple version approach, and began to work on a set of guidelines. It focused attention on reproductions, including microforms, reprints, and facsimiles, not on simultaneously published versions. A "hierarchical technique," or two-tiered approach was being considered. The first level would consist of the full catalog record for the original, while the second level would describe the reproduction. The subrecord would be linked to the full level bibliographic record. Access points for the reproduction would be provided. Provision of an economical and sensible display of serials issued in several formats would be made. The Task Force also examined possible revisions of AACR2R rules 0.24 and 1.11 to allow use of the hierarchical technique.

CONCLUSIONS

The cataloging codes in this country have been constantly criticized over the years, as well as praised. Much of the criticism has been very constructive, though often it was not followed, due to various factors of a political or practical nature. No doubt this criticism will continue. Technology will continue to change, and new developments will occur. Types of publications will be affected; eventually we may even see the disappearance of most information in concrete form, and instead will have to deal with it in electronic form. Basic concepts, familiar to us from cataloging practices developed in the past, such as authorship and main entry, may disappear, to be replaced by new concepts. Or perhaps they will be strengthened in the future. The only thing certain is that code revision will continue, rules will change, new rules will be added, and complaints about the cataloging code will endure. We may even finally see an official third edition of AACR. It is doubtful cataloging codes will disappear entirely, as the agitation over them, and all the work that goes into maintaining them and keeping them up-to-date is just too much fun to discontinue. More importantly, codes have a necessary and vital role in the creation of bibliographic control in our libraries, and in the growing internationalization of such control.

REFERENCE NOTES

1. Kathryn Luther Henderson. " 'Treated with a Degree of Uniformity and Common Sense:' Descriptive Cataloging in the United States, 1876-1975," *Library Trends* 25 (July 1976): 260.

2. *Anglo-American Cataloging Rules, North American Text*, prepared by the American Library Association, the Library of Congress, the Library Association, and the Canadian Library Association (Chicago: American Library Association, 1967).

3. *Anglo-American Cataloging Rules, North American Text. Chapter 6: "Separately Published Monographs,": Incorporating Chapter 9: "Photographs and Other Reproductions," and Revised to Accord With the International Standard Bibliographic Description (Monographs)* (Chicago: American Library Association, 1974).

4. *Anglo-American Cataloging Rules, North American Text. Chapter 12 Revised, Audiovisual Media and special Instructional Materials* (Chicago: American Library Association, 1975); *Anglo-American Cataloging Rules, North American Text. Chapter 14 Revised, Sound Recordings* (Chicago: American Library Association, 1976).

5. Jean Riddle Weihs, Shirley Lewis, and Janet Macdonald, *Nonbook Materials: The Organization of Integrated Collections* 1st ed (Ottawa: Canadian Library Association, 1973). (A 2d ed. was published in 1979; the 3rd ed. was published in 1989.) Library Association, Media Cataloguing Rules Committee, *Nonbook Materials Cataloguing Rules: Integrated Code of Practice and Draft Revision of the Anglo-American Cataloguing Rules, British Text, Part III* (London: National Council for Educational Technology with the Library Association, 1973). (Known as the LANCET rules.) Alma M. Tillin and William J. Quinley, *Standards for Cataloging Nonprint Materials: An Interpretation and Practical Application,* 4th ed. (Washington: Association for Educational Communications and Technology, 1976).

6. *Anglo-American Cataloguing Rules. Second edition,* Prepared by the American Library Association, the British Library, the Canadian Committee on Cataloguing, the Library Association, the Library of Congress; edited by Michael Gorman and Paul W. Winkler (Chicago: American Library Association, 1978).

7. There have been many manuals produced since AACR2 was published. Following is a sample of these:

Margaret F. Maxwell, *Handbook for AACR2: Explaining and Illustrating the Anglo-American Cataloguing Rules,* 1988 revision. (Chicago: American Library Association, 1989). (The earlier edition was for the 1978 AACR2.)

Donald C. Adcock, *Guidelines for Cataloging Microcomputer Software.* (Chicago: American Association of School Librarians, 1987). (Guidelines prepared to assist school library media specialists apply Chapter 9.)

Elizabeth W. Betz, *Graphic Materials: Rules for Describing Original Items and Historical Collections* (Washington: Library of Congress, 1982). (Augments rules found in Chapter 8, by providing additional interpretations needed for cataloging original and historical graphic materials. Chapter 8 still to be applied to modern and commercially available graphic materials.)

Cartographic Materials: A Manual of Interpretation for AACR. Prepared by the Anglo-American Cataloguing Committee for Cartographic Materials; Hugo L. Stibbe, general editor; Vivien Cartmell and Velma Parker, editors (Chicago: American Library Association, 1982). *Cataloging Government Documents: A Manual of Interpretation for AACR2.* Documents Cataloging Manual Committee, Government Documents Round Table, American Library Association; Bernadine Abbott Hoduski, editor. (Chicago: American Library Association, 1984).

Sue A. Dodd, *Cataloging Machine-readable Data Files: An Interpretive Manual* (Chicago: American Library Association, 1982).

Sue A. Dodd, and Ann Sandberg-Fox, *Cataloging Microcomputer Files: A Manual of Interpretation for AACR2* (Chicago: American Library Association, 1985).

Adele Hallam, *Cataloging Rules for the Description of Looseleaf Publications: With Special Emphasis on Legal Materials* (Washington: Library of Congress, 1986). (Guidelines to supplement AACR2).

Steven L. Hensen, *Archives, Personal Papers, and Manuscripts: A Cataloging Manual for Archival Repositories, Historical Societies, and Manuscript Libraries.* 2d ed. (Chicago: Society of American Archivists, 1989). (To replace Chapter 4 for most modern manuscript and archival descriptions. This has come to be regarded as the standard for most archives; and LC, the Research Libraries Group and OCLC consider cataloging prepared according to these rules to be fully compatible with AACR2.)

Deanne Holzberlein, *Cataloging Sound Recordings: A Manual with Examples* (New York: The Haworth Press, 1988) (Monographic supplement to *Cataloging & Classification Quarterly;* no. 2.)

Library of Congress, Office for Descriptive Cataloging Policy, *Bibliographic Description of Rare Books: Rules Formulated Under AACR2 and ISBD (A) for the Descriptive Cataloging of Rare Books and Other Special Printed Materials.* (Washington: Library of Congress, 1981). (LC will use these rules for any books published before 1801 instead of AACR2 rules 2.12-2.18.)

Nancy B. Olson, *Cataloging of Audiovisual Materials: A Manual Based on AACR2,* 2d ed., edited by Edward Swanson and Sheila S. Intner. (Mankato: Minnesota Scholarly Press, 1985). (Excludes music and cartographic materials, but covers non-musical sound recordings.)

Photographic Cataloging Manual, American Museum of Natural History, Dept. of Library Services; project director, Nina J. Root; principal authors, Diana Shih and Miriam Tam (New York: The Museum, 1984). (For collections of photographs with non-art subject matter.)

Richard P. Smiraglia, *Cataloging Music: A Manual for Use with AACR2* 2d ed. (Lake Crystal, MN: Soldier Creek Press, 1986).

Wendy White-Hensen, *Archival Moving Image Materials: A Cataloging Manual* (Washington: Library of Congress, Motion Picture, Broadcasting and Recorded Sound Division, 1984). (Comprehensive instructions for cataloging materials in film and TV archives, within framework of Chapter 7.)

8. *Anglo-American Cataloguing Rules, second edition. Revisions,* Joint Steering Committee for Revision of AACR (Chicago: American Library Association, 1982); *Anglo-American Cataloguing Rules, second edition. Revisions,* 1983 (Chicago: American Library Association, 1984); *Anglo-American Cataloguing Rules, second edition. Revisions, 1985* (Chicago: American Library Association, 1986).

9. American Library Association, Committee on Cataloging: Description and Access, *Guidelines for Using AACR2 Chapter 9 for Cataloging Microcomputer Software.* (Chicago: American Library Association, 1984).

10. *Anglo-American Cataloguing Rules, second edition. Chapter 9. Computer Files, Draft Revision,* edited for the Joint 3 Steering Committee for Revision of AACR by Michael Gorman (Chicago: American Library Association, 1987).

11. Nurieh Musavi. "An Evaluation of AACR2," *Library Resources & Technical Services* 30 (April/June, 1986): 137-148.

12. Janet Swan Hill, "The Cataloging Half of Cataloging and Classification, 1986," *Library Resources & Technical Services* 31 (October/December 1987): 321-332.

13. *Anglo-American Cataloguing Rules, second edition. 1988 Revision.* Prepared under the direction of the Joint Steering Committee for Revision of AACR, a committee of: the American Library Association, the Australian Committee on Cataloguing, the British Library, the Canadian Committee on Cataloguing, the Library Association, the Library of Congress; edited by Michael Gorman and Paul W. Winkler (Chicago: American Library Association, 1988).

14. Sheila Intner. "The Case for AACR3," *Technicalities* 8 (April 1988): 6-8.

Chapter 9

The Transformation of Serials Cataloging 1965-1990

Lori L. Osmus

THE SERIALS CATALOGER'S WORLD IN 1965

In 1965, a cataloger's desk was likely to include a typewriter, catalog card stock, the red book, *A.L.A. Cataloging Rules for Author and Title Entries,* and the green book, *Rules for Descriptive Cataloging in the Library of Congress,* both published in 1949. There was plenty of cataloging to be done, because funds available for acquisitions, particularly in academic libraries, had increased 14-fold in the previous ten years.[1] At the same time, there was a shortage of professional catalogers, and library administrators were seeking ways to reduce cataloging backlogs and lower the cost of cataloging, such as through shared cataloging.

However, serials catalogers were left out of shared cataloging ventures in the 1960s,[2] and were often on their own in applying the cataloging rules, that were written primarily for books. Library of Congress (LC) rule interpretations were not made public as regularly and in as much detail as they are now, and few applied to serials. Even the post-1956 *National Union Catalog* included only serials represented by LC printed cards, not those of other libraries.[3] Not only could LC supply only a fraction of serials cataloging, it was very slow in appearing due to LC's policy of waiting to catalog a serial until all the issues of the first volume had been received and bound. With little guidance or need for standardization, each library could follow its own practices for cataloging serials, resulting in a wide variety in description as well as in choice and form of entry. It was no wonder that one author felt serials cataloging will probably be the last bastion of rugged individualism."[4]

One reason serials cataloging was rugged was latest entry cataloging, used in the United States for most of the twentieth century, which required a serials cataloger to provide the whole history of the serial in the cataloging. This often required extensive searching through printed bibliographies, so familiarity with bibliographic tools was regarded as an important part of a serial librarian's knowledge. When all necessary information was in hand, the cataloger typically typed the cards for the main entry, to be duplicated as unit cards for each added entry in the catalog, and sets of cards were made for other library locations. Holdings may have been given only on the main entry card, or the library user may have been referred to a separate catalog of serial records, which also had to be maintained.

It was a challenge to keep serials cataloging records up-to-date in this environment. Since the body of the serials cataloging record was based on the latest issue of the serial, it could be out-of-date as soon as the next issue arrived. When a serial's main entry or title changed, latest entry practices dictated changing the main entry and descriptive paragraph to describe the latest issue, shifting all of the older information to the notes area. This usually meant pulling and retyping all the cards for the serial in the catalog. However, by 1965, librarians had hoped that computers could soon be used to reduce the drudgery involved in cataloging, although they were also apprehensive about the other changes computers might bring.

LOOKING TO THE FUTURE FROM 1965

In 1964, Margaret C. Brown, Chief of the Processing Division of the Free Library of Philadelphia, was asked to appraise the next 20 years in librarianship and in particular, cataloging. She correctly predicted the elimination of much human labor due to automation, the need for greater cooperation among libraries, reduction in the need to duplicate bibliographic control of the same titles, and the resulting importance of standardization to allow records to be compatible.[5] Paul S. Dunkin, also writing at that time, mentioned that machines may realize Jewett's dream of a central store of cataloging data.[6] Brown described a dream that is today approaching reality on a small scale: "It has been suggested that the day after the day after tomorrow a reader may, by placing himself at the right end of a coaxial cable select, retrieve, and have printed any material in a designated library."[7]

During the early development of computers, few libraries understood them, and they were regarded as magical and mysterious as well as a source of anxiety.[8] Barbara Markuson points out that initially,

> There was a bad period of oversell–the computer was described as a 'brain,' people would be replaced by these machines, and almost all problems would be solvable. . . . The difficulties inherent in automation of bibliographic control systems were grossly oversimplified.[9]

Some of the earliest efforts in library automation were directed at serials control, and through problems and failures, programmers and librarians developed a better grasp of the complexities involved in library automation and the limitations of existing technology. Despite the difficulties, "there was widespread belief that most libraries of any significance would, in the future, be responsible for developing and managing their own local computer operations."[10]

THE WINDS OF CHANGE, 1965 TO 1970

While libraries began working on their own local automation projects, developments also began on a national level. The five-year period that began with the much-heralded publication of a useful printed tool for serials, the third edition of the *Union List of Serials,* would end on the brink of being able to produce a national database of machine-readable information giving description and location of serials. The latter was the goal of a project called the National Serials Data Program (NSDP). It entered Phase 1, preliminary design, in 1967, as a joint venture of the National Agricultural Library (NAL), the National Library of Medicine (NLM), and the Library of Congress, with the Joint Committee on the Union List of Serials acting in an advisory capacity.[11]

Similar plans were being developed on an international level. Collaboration between Unesco and the International Council of Scientific Unions to develop UNISIST, a scientific information system, resulted in the 1970 recommendation for the establishment of the International Serials Data System (ISDS), an international registry of serial publications. Some means were needed to uniquely identify serials, and work to develop this, in the form of an International Standard Serial Number (ISSN), began in 1970 based on the pending American National Standard Number for Serial Publications.[12]

Meanwhile, the LC Information Systems Office began working on the Machine Readable Cataloging (MARC) Project, and by 1968 had developed the MARC format for monographs. In August 1969, LC published a working document of the MARC serials format. This allowed NSDP to begin Phase II, a pilot project to build a national database of serials information.[13]

The suitability of the *Anglo-American Cataloging Rules* (AACR), published in 1967, for computer-based cataloging purposes was questioned, but most libraries were more concerned about the heading changes it required. LC solved the heading change problem for the time being with its policy of superimposition. Other new rules in AACR caused problems for serials catalogers. Although there was now only one rule, rule 6, for entry of serials, it was difficult to apply because it required catalogers to analyze whether a serial was really one of the types listed for title entry and what titles were considered generic and therefore exceptions to the rule. AACR rule 6D recommended successive entry cataloging for serial title changes, but a footnote indicated LC would continue latest entry cataloging. This was not LC's desire, but was required of them by the Catalog Code Revision Committee under pressure from the research library community, who felt it important to have access to records giving the entire history of a serial. Since the only serials cataloging available in the *National Union Catalog* was LC's, and this was the model for national practice, this decision perpetuated latest entry cataloging in all libraries.[14]

In September 1968, LC announced some changes to make its serials cataloging practices more efficient. Good news for libraries was that LC would begin cataloging many English-language periodical-type serials from the first issue, which would result in serials cataloging for many new serials appearing much faster than before. However, there was a down side–LC would discontinue reprinting cards to reflect changes in serials except as LC was able to recatalog titles that had ceased publication.[15] Even with these changes, by the end of 1970 the requirement that LC continue latest entry cataloging had the result that "its serials cataloging operation had become backlogged so seriously with titles awaiting recataloging to the latest title or body that there was little time to handle serials that had never been cataloged at all."[16]

THE ACCELERATION OF AUTOMATION, 1971 TO 1975

By the early 1970s, it was becoming clear that automation based on local developments was proceeding too slowly to solve pressing problems facing all libraries, and in fact initially resulted in additional work. The economic stringency that progressed during the decade forced libraries to move from individual automation projects to more cooperative ventures. With cooperation came a greater need for standardization.

When Frederick Kilgour wrote of his "Concept of an On-Line Computerized Library Catalog"[17] in 1970 it was called "the latest vision of the Holy Grail."[18] However, when the Ohio College Library Center (OCLC) began operation on August 26, 1971,[19] many of Kilgour's visions soon came to pass. By 1975, OCLC's database contained 1.5 million bibliographic records,[20] and its membership included 12 networks of libraries outside of Ohio.[21] Other networks that would eventually rival OCLC were also being formed, such as BALLOTS in 1971 and the Research Libraries Group (RLG) in 1974.

In this atmosphere, efforts to create national and international databases of serial records increased. The draft international standard of the ISSN was approved in October 1972,[22] and responsibility for creating ISSNs was assigned to the International Serials Data System (ISDS), which was to consist of national and regional centers reporting to an international center. In the United States, NSDP was embarking on its third phase toward building a serials database, and also agreed to become the ISDS center for the United States. By the end of 1973, the NSDP database included 5,200 records.[23] Also, 1973 was the first year that MARC serial records were distributed. OCLC began supporting the MARC serials format in July 1974, but it was three more years before it could print cards for serial records.

The creation of a national serials database was not happening quickly enough for a group of librarians who formed the Ad Hoc Discussion Group on Serials Data Bases at the June 1973 American Library Association Annual Conference. They proposed a cooperative effort, to be known as the CONversion of SERials Project (CONSER), to convert approximately 200,000 to 300,000 serial records to machine-readable form in a two- to three-year period. NSDP and the Canadian ISDS center, ISDS/Canada, would also be CONSER participants, assigning ISSNs to the records input, or creating base records on which the others could build. The founders of CONSER were also concerned about the confusion and lack of communication in the creation of serial records, and needed to reconcile a number of contradictory standards before the Project was able to begin in 1975, with OCLC as its vehicle.[24]

Differences between the International Standard Bibliographic Descriptions (ISBDs) for monographs and serials were one source of conflict. The ISBD, first developed by the International Federation of Library Associations for monographs in 1971, is concerned with description, and lists required data elements to describe an item, assigns them an order, and prescribes punctuation. When an ISBD for serials (ISBD(S)) was drafted in 1974, it conflicted with the ISBD for monographs (ISBD(M)) by promoting the creation of a distinctive title when the title was generic, rather than using the title proper as it appeared on the issues.[25] This distinctive title was similar to a unique title called the key title created by ISDS in conjunction with assigning ISSNs. Library of Congress began using the draft ISBD(S), and announced its practices for creating distinctive titles.[26] Some of these differences were resolved when members of the ISBD(S) revision meeting in October 1975 agreed to adopt the title proper concept of ISBD(M).[27] In October 1975, work also began on a general ISBD (ISBD(G)), to assure that all future ISBDs would be compatible.

AACR Chapter 6, Separately Published Monographs, was revised and published as a supplement to AACR in 1974 to incorporate ISBD(M). It was also used by serials catalogers for place of publication and publisher, except for prescribed punctuation. This was mentioned in *Cataloging Service* bulletin 112, which also detailed a number of rule interpretations for serials, designed to reconcile current serials cataloging practices and ISDS requirements, as well as addressing problems arising when serial records are converted to machine-readable form.[28]

There were also conflicts between the cataloging rules and ISDS guidelines in determining entry of serials and what constitutes a title change, requiring a new ISSN. When work on revising AACR began in 1974 to incorporate the ISBDs and other changes, controversy erupted over entry of serials, and the library literature was filled with heated debate. In July 1975, the American Library Association's voice in code revision, the Cataloging Code Revision Committee (CCRC), decided to ask the Joint Steering Committee for the Revision of AACR(JSC) to draft a rule that would require title main entry for all serial publications.[29]

Title changes of serials were expensive and time-consuming, but also became a source of humor when David C. Taylor championed the frustrations of many serials librarians with the publication of the serial *Title Varies* beginning in 1973. In July 1974, he presented the first "Worst Serial Title Change of the Year Award" at the ALA Annual conference in New York.[30]

LC was able to triple its serials cataloging productivity when in 1971 it enlarged its serials cataloging staff[31] and also announced that it would abandon latest entry cataloging, as of May 31, 1971.[32] The existence of both latest entry and successive entry records in many library catalogs was another problem faced by the CONSER participants. Although the result would be some duplication of records, CONSER decided to allow both forms of cataloging because of the extensive recataloging that would otherwise be necessary, and uncertainty about how the revision of AACR would affect entry of serials.[33] In November 1975, the CONSER Project officially began, when OCLC loaded the base file, consisting of approximately 80,000 records contained in the *Minnesota Union List of Serials* and the composite records from the Library of Congress

MARC serials files.[34] Machine-readable records for serials were about to become more available than ever before.

No library yet had an online catalog serving all the functions of a card catalog because the technology was still too expensive. Libraries were experimenting with other forms of catalogs, such as computer-produced book-format catalogs, and computer output microfilm. Microforms were becoming more commonplace for serial publications as well, due to their low cost and space-saving attributes, although many catalogers were still uncertain how to deal with them.

THE MOMENTUM CONTINUES, 1976 TO 1980

When the United States celebrated its bicentennial, many of the major players in the next 15 years of serials cataloging were already present: CONSER, ISDS, NSDP, ISSN, ISBD(S), and of course MARC(S). The end of 1980 would also see the retirement of an old friend, AACR, with its revision taking over on "Day One" of 1981. It was a half-decade of getting ready for AACR2 as well as becoming aware of the benefits of CONSER. It was not all peaceful cooperation, either, as more networks flourished and competition between them intensified.

As the input period for AACR2 ended in early 1976, the CCRC reconsidered its 1975 request for title entry of all serials and decided instead to endorse the concept of limited corporate authorship for all materials. While not being completely compatible with ISDS, at least this allowed the majority of serials to be entered under title, while avoiding a special rule for entry of serials.[35] The RTSD Serials Section Ad Hoc AACR Revision Study Committee provided a forum for the discussion of serials cataloging developments. When all was said and done on AACR2 revision for serials, the Ad Hoc AACR Revision Study Committee was made a standing Serials Section committee, renamed the committee to Study Serials Cataloging in 1978.[36]

In June 1976, LC reached full operational status in CONSER, inputting and authenticating records online, and these records were then distributed on the MARC serials tapes.[37] CONSER benefited LC by eliminating the need for LC to do original cataloging for approximately 25 percent of the new serials it received.[38] To better use and create serial records of universal benefit, LC announced in the winter of 1977 that its description of a serial would no longer be limited to the volumes actually owned by LC, but would be based on all known information.[39] LC was supposed to accept full responsibility for CONSER when the file-building phase ended in 1977, but when budget restrictions prevented it from doing so, OCLC agreed to take over management of CONSER from the Council on Library Resources.

CONSER met its goal of creating a database of around 200,000 records by the end of 1977, with 15 participants,[40] but there was no end in sight of records to be input. To avoid duplicate records, in 1978 CONSER participants agreed to begin inputting only successive entry records for title changes back to 1967, and as many others as feasible.[41] LC was having difficulty keeping up with CONSER authentication and modifications to records, and plans to decentralize this effort were under discussion in 1980. The next phase of CONSER hoped to add locations and holdings to records, and to accomplish this, a standard format for holdings data was needed. The American National Standards Institute (ANSI) Committee Z39.40 worked on this for several years and published its standard for summary holdings statements in 1980.

The activities of NSDP continued with greater efforts to encourage publishers to use ISSNs. NSDP seized a golden opportunity in 1977 when the United States Postal Service wanted to devise a control number to identify serial publications to be regulated for second-class and controlled circulation mailing. Due to negotiations by NSDP, the ISSN was chosen for this purpose, and became a requirement as of January 1979.[42]

Fear of AACR2 grew as its publication date approached. By the time it was published, December 7, 1978, library representatives meeting at LC had already voted to delay its adoption by one year, to January 1, 1981. LC began making decisions on optional and alternative rules, and also made exceptions due to pressure from the American library community. Late in 1980, at the request of other research libraries, LC, NLM, and NAL agreed to postpone application of the AACR2 rules for microform reproductions,[43] and AACR conventions for these were still being followed ten years later. The rules also resulted in non-distinctive titles for many serials by limiting corporate body entry, so LC came to the rescue in mid-1979 with guidelines for constructing a "unique serial identifier" for these serials. Unfortunately, this unique serial identifier, later to be known as a uniform title for serials, was incompatible with ISDS key titles in some cases.

Libraries studied how to cope with the changes coming with AACR2. The greatest amount of change was going to result from LC's policy of desuperimposition, changing headings to the new forms they should have had under AACR, rather than from AACR2 itself. Many libraries planned to close their catalogs rather than deal with the increase in recataloging. Serials catalogers worried about what to do with serial records that would span the closing date of the catalog, and whether check-in records for serials needed to be changed to match the revised catalog entries.

Bibliographic networks looked for ways to flip names in authority records and map old headings into new ones, and the networks themselves also experienced change. Acknowledging that its clientele had grown far beyond Ohio academic libraries, OCLC changed its governance structure in December 1977 and also changed its name to simply OCLC, Inc. The Washington Library Network began operation, and BALLOTS developed a new file design that would allow each library to see its own records as well as those of other libraries. In 1978, the Research Libraries Group (RLG) chose BALLOTS for its technical processing needs, and announced plans for the Research Libraries Information Network (RLIN).[44] Enticed by sophisticated search capabilities and the ability to see their own records, a number of large research libraries soon joined RLIN, and questions arose over how those who were CONSER participants could continue to contribute records without access to OCLC. By 1980, competition between OCLC and RLIN was intense.

ADJUSTMENT TO AACR2 AND MORE NEW TECHNOLOGY, 1981 to 1985

Catalogers bravely faced the 1980s with AACR2 in hand as Day One of its use dawned on January 2, 1981. Many of the old cataloging standbys had fallen into obsolescence during the past 15 years, replaced by more complete and up-to-date machine-readable counterparts. The post-1956 *National Union Catalog* stopped including records for serials. *New Serial Titles* began to be produced from the CONSER tapes, but stopped showing holding libraries, which then became available only on OCLC.[45] There was also some thought that perhaps catalogers themselves were on the way out.

Online catalogs began to seem more attainable as the development of microcomputers gave libraries a choice over fully integrated mainframe systems. Automated systems required machine-readable records, so conversion projects increased, with serials cataloging benefiting from the ongoing work of the CONSER Project. However, it would be some time before most CONSER records would be in AACR2 form. Libraries still needed to decide whether to recatalog their serials to successive entry, and how to link new titles to old titles on records not in AACR2 form.

Voluminous LC rule interpretations began to spell out serials cataloging rules, standards, and practices in more detail than ever before. Among these, the most important for serials were those limiting what to consider a title change, and changing the order of preference for qualifiers in uniform titles. Three sets of amendments to AACR2 were issued, until in 1984, JSC decided to publish a consolidated edition of AACR2 by the end of the 1980s.[46]

Policy changes were made in CONSER to reduce the workload of the national centers. Participants were allowed to amend and update some records in 1979, but in 1984 this was expanded to allow CONSER members to modify LC-authenticated records and authenticate their own records.[47] In late 1983, the CONSER Abstracting and Indexing Project began, and added data indicating where serials were abstracted and indexed to 50,000 records by the end of 1985.[48] Another new element in CONSER was the United States Newspaper Project (USNP), which began in 1982 with six libraries.[49] Newspapers had long been neglected in serials cataloging, and the goal of USNP was to remedy this by cataloging all the available newspapers in the United States and selectively preserving on microfilm those in danger of disintegration. Users of CONSER records who assign subject headings to their serials were disturbed by an unfortunate incident in July 1985 which caused all member-assigned LC subject headings to be dropped from CON-

SER records.[50] A consulting team studied CONSER in 1985 and made recommendations for its future. By the end of 1985, the CONSER database contained 530,794 records, of which 335,134 were authenticated.[51]

As libraries coped with AACR2 heading changes and began developing online catalogs, authority control seemed in need of the same cooperation as existed for serials cataloging through CONSER. LC had been creating machine-readable name authority records since April 1, 1978.[52] The Name Authority Cooperative Project (NACO) was developed to allow other libraries to contribute name authority records to LC's database. In 1980 the CONSER Advisory Committee announced that new participants in CONSER must also participate in NACO,[53] but NACO participation is not limited to CONSER members.

NACO benefited from another project which came to fruition in 1985, the Linked Systems Project (LSP). "The purpose of LSP is to link the automated systems of the national library and the three major networks on a mutually rewarding basis."[54] The first use of LSP was to exchange authority records between NACO participants, who have access through LSP to the LC Name Authority File. LSP has many other possibilities in bringing together the various networks to allow them to function as one national network.

Competition continued between the networks, but was less sharp as each network encountered problems. OCLC, which changed its name to Online Computer Library Center in 1981,[55] contended with its membership over various issues in 1983.[56] In 1985, OCLC announced the Oxford Project, to completely redesign its products and services, as well as its telecommunications network. RLIN suffered from serious system problems during 1982, culminating in total collapse of the serials file in April 1982, but eventually recovered.[57]

The networks needed to decide what to do when LC began cataloging many serials at a partial level in 1981[58] due to budget cuts.[59] This evolved into minimal level cataloging (MLC) for other materials by 1983,[60] and other libraries began to realize that requiring full bibliographic control for all materials would limit what they could catalog. Efforts began to reconcile various national minimal level cataloging standards.

Long efforts to develop standards for holdings achieved success when in 1985 the National Information Standards Organization (formerly ANSI) approved standard Z39.44 which covered both summary and detailed serials holdings statements. LC and eight southeastern United States research libraries began work on a MARC communications format for serials holdings in 1982, and it was also approved by 1985.

FINE TUNING AND NEW FORMATS, 1986 TO 1990

During the last years of the 1980s, the cataloging rules grew ever more friendly to the needs of serials catalogers as well as more compatible with ISBD(S) and ISDS guidelines. Serials catalogers had opportunities to become better informed due to a series of Serials Cataloging Regional Institutes, held during 1986 and 1987, utilizing experts in the field. Cataloging practices for newspapers and microforms received considerable attention due to the United States Newspaper Project and work by the Association of Research Libraries (ARL) on *Guidelines for Bibliographic Records for Preservation Microform Masters (Serials)*. As alternative formats, such as CD-ROMs and online databases, became more widespread, it became clear that integration of the MARC formats was necessary to allow an item which had characteristics of more than one format to be adequately described in cataloging. When the revised AACR2 was issued in 1988, it was welcomed as a part of a gradual finetuning process rather than as a harbinger of drastic change. Cataloging was becoming more sensible and flexible, and moving away from its traditional orientation to books and card catalogs.

USNP started as a Project but became a Program by 1984. Since USNP was to involve cataloging newspapers and then microfilming some of them, it seemed redundant to follow the existing standards that would have required creating separate records for the microfilm. Therefore, USNP developed the "master record concept," in which holdings of all formats of a title were attached to one bibliographic record, and the different formats were distinguished by codes in the local data records of the holdings. In December 1989, LC and the Council on Library Resources sponsored the Multiple Versions Forum, which reached consensus in favor of a method similar to the master record concept. Called the "two-tier hierarchical approach," it involves describing the version-specific data of a serial in the MARC holdings record attached to the bibliographic record of the serial as a whole.[61] This was supported by ARL as it developed its standards for the bibliographic control of preservation microfilms. Adoption of this method depends on how soon networks are able to implement the MARC holdings format and any changes to it necessary to use this method.

The LC rule interpretations on criteria for changes in title proper were incorporated in the 1988 revision of AACR2. The British Library proposed that AACR2 include a general statement on uniform titles for serials, and this was sent to JSC for consideration in 1990. Although efforts were abandoned to make the ISDS key title and ISBD(S) title proper identical, ISDS guidelines were reformulated to allow for inclusion of the ISBD(S) title proper if it differs from the key title.[62] New editions of the ISBDs were published in August 1987, and ISBD(S) was altered to allow linking entry notes to give the key title and ISSN, in 1990, an LC rule interpretation brought U.S. practice into greater conformity with ISBD(S) and eliminated much bracketing in serials cataloging. LCRI 12.0B1 accomplished this by allowing the use of the whole publication as the prescribed source of information for all areas of the description with the exception of the title/statement of responsibility and edition.[63]

Serials catalogers have further guidance on the creation of machine-readable serial records thanks to the *CONSER Editing Guide,* published in 1986 in looseleaf form, with occasional updates. Updating of CONSER's mission statement and organization resulted from the study by consultants in 1985, and in 1987 CONSER was renamed the Cooperative Online Serials Program. This acknowledges that it is no longer a project, but an ongoing effort by 22 participants creating 65,000 new records a year.[64]

Due to the longstanding problem of how to allow RLG non-OCLC members to actively contribute records to the CONSER database, the Linked Systems Project (LSP) is being investigated for transfer of CONSER records. In late 1986, the NACO Project taking place through LSP was extended and renamed the National Cooperative Cataloging Project,[65] and in 1989, National Coordinated Cataloging Operations.[66] In 1987, eight libraries keyed bibliographic records directly into LC's system.[67] LC's Serials Record Division joined LSP on May 11, 1988, and began creating authority records and cataloging serials directly on OCLC. "With the adoption of LSP, [LC's) serial cataloging sections are among the few units in the Library working in a totally online cataloging mode."[68] At the end of 1990, 37 institutions had contributed 78,723 new name authorities and 812 new series authorities through LSP.[69] The next step will be for libraries to key data directly into their utilities for transmittal to LC. This sharing of cataloging and authority work is making cataloging more uniform and LC cataloging less distinguishable from that of participating libraries. Ultimately, LSP may allow access to records in all the major networks from one terminal and result in the need for less original cataloging.

Early in the 1980s it was thought that original cataloging would soon be performed entirely by machine, making catalogers obsolete. As research into the applications of artificial intelligence increased, it became apparent that expert systems could be designed to aid catalogers, but were unlikely to be sophisticated enough to replace catalogers in the near future. Automation has made cataloging more complex, with more standards, codes, and interpretations to understand and apply than ever before. By the mid-1980s employers were keenly aware of a shortage of catalogers, and that the predictions that there would be no need for professional catalogers had proven false.

There is always more than enough work for serials catalogers, not only due to the explosion of new serials published each year, but due to the need to recatalog old ones as they change. Cancellation projects are often mounted to cut old subscriptions in order to pay for new ones, so serials catalogers are faced with massive recataloging to close holdings, as well as an influx of new serials. In addition, the implementation of the MARC holdings format in some libraries has added a new dimension to the information to be converted and maintained on serial records.

LC revealed that its 1989 backlog included 2,543,000 serials,[70] and revised its priorities and hired new staff in order to work toward a goal of reducing the backlog 30 percent by the end of fiscal 1993.[71] More minimal level cataloging will also be done. LC also experimented with "whole book cataloging," having one person catalog one title completely, and included some serials cataloging in the experiment.

There is always more to do to serial records because serials are always changing. In 1990, Mary Ellen Soper found that 18 percent of the serial records she examined were not up to date,[72] and Annalisa Van Avery reported that 50 percent of OCLC serial copy required adjustments to meet current standards.[73] Users of online catalogs are becoming more sophisticated and want more than just bibliographic descriptions of serials; they want to find citations to articles, or even the full text of the articles themselves. Electronic journals, leased databases, and fiscal restraints may eventually shift the library's role from an owner of materials to a provider of access, and serials catalogers will be faced with describing ever more nebulous materials.

THE SERIALS CATALOGER'S WORLD IN 1990

In 1990, many serials catalogers still have desks, but some may instead have a workstation equipped with a computer to access the library's local online catalog or a national bibliographic utility. Serials catalogers need to be able to interpret records prepared according to a long history of rules, and would probably have on hand at least a blue book, AACR, published in 1967; a tan book, AACR2, published in 1978; and a green book, AACR2 revised, published in 1988. In addition, to create MARC serial records, the serials cataloger would need a copy of the MARC serials format as applied by the bibliographic utility in use, and would be aided by having access to the *CONSER Editing Guide* and a cumulation of the LC rule interpretations, plus the latest *Cataloging Service Bulletin*. If a cataloger has a typewriter, it is probably used to type cataloging worksheets for input into the utility by other staff, although worksheets can be handwritten as well. A new cataloger would probably be annoyed if faced with typing a card. Much of the work of catalogers today consists of editing copy from a utility, or from the local online catalog for recataloging.

When recataloging, strong feelings of responsibility to follow current national standards cause catalogers to agonize over past practices and how much effort to devote to bring old records up to par. Should a cataloger feel guilty if a latest entry record is not split up into successive entry records? Is it wasted effort to catalog print and microform editions on separate bibliographic records according to current standards, when a change in practice is likely in the next few years?

With access to hundreds of thousands of serial records online at a terminal, a serials cataloger in 1990 is less inclined to seek cataloging information in printed bibliographies. If it is found in a source such as the *National Union Catalog: Pre-1956 Imprints,* the forms of entry and description are likely to be so out-of-date as to be useless. The current rules eliminate the need to perform extensive research into the history of a serial by allowing cataloging from the issues in hand, with a "Description based on": note in the cataloging. The ease of finding copy and changing serial records would seem like a dream come true to a serials cataloger of 1965. However, the complexity introduced by automation tempers this euphoria.

LOOKING TO THE FUTURE FROM 1990

As serials catalogers today approach a crossroads in providing access to information that will be difficult to catalog using traditional methods, they feel as uneasy as their counterparts of 1965 who were worried about the possible impact of computers on their work. New methods of cataloging serials may need to be developed along with the new formats, and demands for online catalog access to serials at the article level as well as the title level will stretch cataloging resources. In addition, the goal of universal bibliographic control has not yet been attained, even though a hit rate of 90 percent or more in the bibliographic utilities satisfies most needs. Some method also needs to be developed to keep serials cataloging records even more up-to-date than they are, although the quality of serials cataloging has improved a great deal due to the efforts of the CONSER participants. In the next 25 years, the goal of serials catalogers will remain the same, to organize serials information in ways that will enable library users to efficiently find what they seek. By whatever name serials catalogers may be known in the future, the work they do to achieve this goal will still be a necessary and important component of librarianship.

REFERENCE NOTES

1. Richard M. Dougherty, "Manpower Utilization in Technical Services," *Library Resources & Technical Services,* 12, no. 1 (Winter 1968): 77.

2. Kathryn Luther Henderson, "Serial Cataloging Revisited–A Long Search for a Little Theory and a Lot of Cooperation," in *Serial Publications in Large Libraries,* ed. Walter C. Allen (Urbana, Il: University of Illinois, Graduate School of Library Science, 1970), 79.

3. Ibid.

4. Robert D. Desmond, "1968: A Summary Treatment of the Year in Serials," *Library Resources & Technical Services,* 13, no. 3 (Summer 1969): 389.

5. Margaret C. Brown, "A Look at the Future Through Bifocals," *Library Resources & Technical Services,* 9, no. 3 (Summer 1965): 267.

6. Paul S. Dunkin, "1965: Year of the Big Book," *Library Resources & Technical Services,* 10, no. 2 (Spring 1966): 175.

7. Brown, "A Look at the Future Through Bifocals," 266.

8. Ibid., 262.

9. Barbara Evans Markuson, "Bibliographic Systems, 1945-1976," *Library Trends* 25, no. 1 (July 1976): 314.

10. Ibid., 323.

11. William H. Huff, "Serial Observations–1967," *Library Resources & Technical Services,* 12, no. 2 (Spring 1968): 195.

12. Joseph W. Price, "International Cooperation in Serials: Problems and Prospects," *Drexel Library Quarterly,* 11, no. 3 (July 1975): 33.

13. Richard 0. Pautzsch, "The Year's Work in Cataloging–1969," *Library Resources & Technical Services,* 14, no. 2 (Spring 1970): 183.

14. Henderson, "Serial Cataloging Revisited," 80.

15. "Cataloging of Serials in the Library of Congress," *Cataloging Service,* 83 (September 1968): 3.

16. Dorothy J. Glasby, "Historical Background and Review of Serials Cataloging Rules," *Library Resources & Technical Services,* 34, no. 1 (January 1990): 85.

17. Frederick G. Kilgour, "Concept of an On-Line Computerized Library Catalog," *Journal of Library Automation,* 3, no. 1 (March 1970): 1-11.

18. Phyllis A. Richmond, "The Year's Work in Cataloging and Classification," *Library Resources & Technical Services,* 15, no. 2 (Spring 1971): 154.

19. Nancy Campbell, "People, Programs, and Events: 1971 to 1991," *OCLC Newsletter,* 191 (May/June 1991): 22.

20. Carol F. Ishimoto, "Cataloging and Classification," *ALA Yearbook* (1976): 129.

21. Campbell, "People, Programs, and Events," 22.

22. Price, "International Cooperation in Serials," 33.

23. Hans H. Weber, "Serials '73–Review and Trends," *Library Resources & Technical Services,* 18, no. 2 (Spring 1974): 146-147.

24. Jim E. Cole and Olivia M. A. Madison, "A Decade of Serials Cataloging," *The Serials Librarian,* 10, no. 1/2 (Fall 1985-Winter 1985-1986): 109-114.

25. Marlene Sue Heroux, "Automated Serials Cataloging," *The Serials Librarian,* 9, no. 3 (Spring 1985): 74-75.

26. "Serials with Generic Titles," *Cataloging Service,* 110 (Summer 1974): 3.

27. Mary Sauer, "Automated Serials Control: Cataloging Considerations," *Journal of Library Automation,* 9, no. 1 (March 1976): 8-11.

28. "Serials-Rule Interpretations," *Cataloging Service* 112 (Winter 1975): 10-13.

29. Paul Fasana, "Serials Data Control: Current Problems and Prospects," *Journal of Library Automation,* 9, no. 1 (March 1979): 31.

30. H. W. Hall, "Serials '74: A Review," *Library Resources & Technical Services,* 19, no. 3 (Summer 1975): 200-201.

31. Daisy Ashford, "Serials in Review: 1972," *Library Resources & Technical Services,* 17, no. 3 (Spring 1973): 168.

32. "Cataloging of Serials," *Cataloging Service,* 99 (April 1971): 1.

33. Richard Anable, "CONSER: Bibliographic Considerations," *Library Resources & Technical Services,* 19, no. 4 (Fall 1975): 347-348.

34. John R. James, "Serials '75–Review and Trends," *Library Resources & Technical Services,* 20, no. 3 (Summer 1975): 261.

35. John R. James, "Serials in 1976," *Library Resources & Technical Services,* 21, no. 3 (Summer 1977): 221.

36. William H. Huff, "Serials," *ALA Yearbook,* (1979): 262.

37. William H. Huff, "Serials," *ALA Yearbook,* (1977): 300.

38. Dorothy J. Glasby, "Serials in 1979," *Library Resources & Technical Services,* 24, no. 3 (Summer 1980): 278.

39. "Serial Entries," *Cataloging Service,* 120 (Winter 1977): 8.

40. William H. Huff, "Serials," *ALA Yearbook,* (1978): 287.

41. Dorothy J. Glasby, "Serials in 1978," *Library Resources & Technical Services,* 23, no. 3 (Summer 1979): 210.

42. Glasby, "Serials in 1979," 277.

43. "Chapter 11," *Cataloging Service Bulletin,* 11 (Winter 1981): 15-16.

44. Marilyn H. Jones, "Year's Work in Cataloging and Classification: 1978," *Library Resources & Technical Services,* 23, no. 3 (Summer 1979): 262-263.

45. Marcia Tuttle, "Serials," *ALA Yearbook* (1982): 259.

46. Michael Gorman and Arnold Wajenberg, "Cataloging and Classification," *ALA Yearbook* (1985): 88.

47. Marcia Tuttle, "Serials," *ALA Yearbook* (1985): 260.

48. Germaine C. Linkins, "Technical Services in 1984 and 1985: Serials," *Library Resources & Technical Services* 30, no. 3 (July/September 1986): 244-245.

49. Benita M. Weber, "The Year's Work in Serials: 1982," *Library Resources & Technical Services,* 27, no. 3 (July/September 1983): 252-253.

50. Linkins, "Technical Services in 1984 and 1985: Serials," 244.

51. Marcia Tuttle, "Serials," *ALA Yearbook,* (1986): 294.

52. Jones, "Year's Work in Cataloging and Classification: 1978," 266.

53. William H. Huff, "Serials," *ALA Yearbook* (1981): 270.

54. Michael Gorman and Arnold Wajenberg, "Cataloging and Classification," *ALA Yearbook* (1986): 104.

55. Constance Rinehart, "Descriptive Cataloging in 1981," *Library Resources & Technical Services,* 26 (1982): 257.

56. Joe A. Hewitt, "Technical Services in 1983," *Library Resources & Technical Services,* 28, no. 3 (July/September 1984): 206-207.

57. Crystal Graham, "Serials Cataloging on RLIN: A User's Viewpoint," *Serials Review,* 9, no. 3 (Fall 1983): 91.

58. Weber, "The Year's Work in Serials: 1982," 248.

59. Tuttle, "Serials," (1982), 257.

60. Hewitt, "Technical Services in 1983," 213-214.

61. *Multiple Versions Forum Report* (Washington: Network Development and MARC Standards Office, Library of Congress, 1990), 7-9.

62. James W. Williams, "Serials Cataloging in 1987," *The Serials Librarian,* 15, no. 1/2 (1988): 66.

63. "12.0B1," *Cataloging Service Bulletin,* 47 (Winter 1990): 41.

64. Williams, "Serials Cataloging in 1987," 70.

65. Michael Gorman and Arnold Wajenberg, "Cataloging and Classification," *ALA Yearbook* (1987): 102.

66. Janet Swan Hill, "Cataloging and Classification," *ALA Yearbook* (1990): 91.

67. Ibid.

68. "Serial Record Division Celebrates First Anniversary as LSP Participant," *Library of Congress Information Bulletin,* 48, no. 43 (October 23, 1989): 377.

69. "NACO Training at LC," *Library of Congress Information Bulletin,* 50, no. 5 (March 11, 1991): 91.

70. "LC's Arrearage," in "AL Asides," *American Libraries,* 21, no. 10 (October 1990): 841.

71. "Library Develops Plan to Cut Arrearages," *Library of Congress Information Bulletin,* 49, no. 10 (May 7, 1990): 170, 174.

72. Mary Ellen Soper, "What You See May Not Be What You Get: Errors in Online Bibliographic Records for Serials," *The Reference Librarian,* 27/28 (1990): 201.

73. Annalisa R. Van Avery, "Recat vs. Recon of Serials: A Problem for Shared Cataloging," *Cataloging & Classification Quarterly,* 10, no. 4 (1990): 59.

Chapter 10

Minimal Level Cataloging: Past, Present, and Future

Andrea L. Stamm

One of the chronic dilemmas facing libraries today is the problem of maintaining adequate bibliographic control of their collections in the face of inadequate or shrinking staffing. The currently popular and viable solution to this dilemma is to perform minimal level cataloging (MLC) on a specific portion of the cataloging backlog and/or currently received acquisitions. MLC, or less-than-full cataloging (full cataloging being determined by the cataloging rules of the period and to a great degree by the Library of Congress standard), is not a new concept, however, and has been in existence over the decades under various names such as "brief cataloging," "simplified cataloging," or "limited cataloging."[1] It is difficult to define MLC, as elements of it changed over time and depended on constantly evolving standards. What all concepts had in common was a less-than-full bibliographic record, created in order to speed up processing. This then increased cataloging production and made otherwise unavailable material immediately available to the user. MLC also became a significant cost-cutting measure.

HISTORICAL PERSPECTIVE

In the days before bibliographic networks and their resulting supply of cataloging copy, libraries had to do more original cataloging, since they had no source for copy other than the Library of

Congress and the *National Union Catalog.* When catalogers could
not keep pace with current acquisitions, they were forced to backlog
materials without copy until such time as copy became available, or
a cataloger could process the item originally.

In response to a growing arrearage as well as in an effort to
establish "a more satisfactory balance of the relative interest and
value of the various materials, the service demands of the Library,
and the capacity of the cataloging staff,"[2] the Library of Congress
(LC) announced its standards for "limited" cataloging in 1947. A
modified explanation of limited cataloging appeared in 1951 in
Cataloging Service[3] when the program was officially begun. From
1951 to 1962, limited cataloging restricted the descriptive data,
most particularly the collation and notes, as well as added entries. In
announcing the discontinuance of limited cataloging in September
1963, LC specifically mentioned these limitations as unsatisfactory
as well as the need for a single set of cataloging rules for all publications.[4]

NEED FOR A NATIONAL STANDARD

In the 1970s, the addition of various automation-related developments greatly complicated the cataloging process. Content-desig-
nated MARC bibliographic and authority records, online authority
files, and bibliographic utilities all had a significant impact on the
operations and workflow of catalog departments across the United
States. Cataloging tools such as LC's *Rule Interpretations* made
cataloging more consistent, but also more complex. It became clear
that even with the use of cataloging copy from bibliographic networks, catalogers would not be able to perform full level cataloging
on all materials received. As discussion proceeded for the second
edition of the *Anglo-American Cataloging Rules,* levels of bibliographic description were formulated, including rule 1.0D1, a "first
level," now commonly called "Level One," which is a "less than
full" level of cataloging.[5] Level One applies only to bibliographic
description; it is not intended to discuss access points. Concurrently
in 1978, the *National Level Bibliographic Record–Books* (NLBR)
was being drafted for LC, and it contained its own standards for a
"national level" MLC machine-readable record. "The minimal

level record is designed to provide the information needed to identify an item, i.e., the complete descriptive block, from title to series, in accordance with ISBD (and AACR2), plus ISBN and class number (or other shelf number) and, for author access where appropriate, a main entry. These data elements include but are not limited to those specified for Level One cataloging in AACR2. The minimal level is intended for use with ephemeral or marginal materials or materials which the cataloging organization feels do not warrant the high cost of full cataloging but nevertheless should be maintained under a degree of bibliographic control."[6]

LIBRARY OF CONGRESS' IMPLEMENTATION OF MLC

In November 1979, LC announced the adoption of MLC, with an AACR2 "Level Two" bibliographic description, for monographs of the lowest cataloging priority, i.e., Priority 7 (changed to Priority 5 in 1981). These items were either worth retaining but not worth the expense of full cataloging, or backlogged items that would not otherwise receive full level cataloging.[7] LC/MLC was intended to extend bibliographic coverage to more materials. In the initial phase (1980-1984), records could be searched by author/title, title, and LC card number search keys, and contained a main entry when appropriate, title, edition, publication and distribution data, physical description, series, and some notes. MLC did not provide for subject access, classification beyond a single LC class letter at the end of the 050 field, or authority work. The public was cautioned that LC/MLC was not performed by professional catalogers, and therefore these records might not conform to AACR2 or LC's *Rule Interpretations.* Headings might not be under authority control. LC began distributing LC/MLC serial records in January 1983, and monographs including microforms in the Fall of 1983 in the Minimal Level Cataloging Service.[8]

Hampered by the inability to apply full content designation or to make added entries in the in-process Automated Process Information File (APIF), in the second phase of LC/MLC (1984-September 1986), LC expanded the record and moved the LC/MLC file from the APIF file to the Books master file.[9] This "enhanced MLC," or "MLC Plus," also included additional fixed fields, one added entry when main entry is under title, and a series traced differently. MLC Plus was considered to be a better product since it contained more data elements and because its location in the Books file permitted full and correct content designation, thereby becoming a more accurate record.[10] Authority work was performed, if needed, to break a conflict.

In the third phase (September 1986-September 1990), other data elements were added, including uniform titles and certain notes. Provisions for added entries (7xxs) were liberalized: one 7xx was permitted when the record was under a main entry and two 7xxs were permitted when the piece was under title main entry. Provisions for authority work were also considerably broadened. In January 1989, LC changed its distribution of MLC books from a separate service to the "Books All" service. Maps, visual materials, and music are also mentioned as already being distributed in the MARC subscription tapes.[11]

Since September 1990, LC has added a new feature to its MLC records: the MARC field 653 provides access through subject terms in an uncontrolled vocabulary. For foreign-language material, subject terms are translated into English. For English-language MLC materials, 653s are added when the title does not reflect the subject content.[12] This development acknowledges the importance of subject access and addresses the primary failure of keyword and Boolean operators in subject searching–their dependency on the vocabulary used in the text. Foreign-language materials, in particular, benefit from translation into English, presuming most people in the United States would first search for a subject using the official language of the country. Even for English language materials, keyword/Boolean obviously cannot retrieve what is not present in the text. The "common" or translated term, added by LC in the uncontrolled subject field, is a step in the right direction, but it still does not provide in one place access to all materials having the same subject. Is the user well served by this compromise?

In December 1990, LC announced a revision of its cataloging priorities and levels of cataloging for monographs, serials, and microforms.[13] In this first major revision of priorities since 1981, all Priority 4 materials receive MLC because of their perceived low research value. Materials appropriate for Priority 4 include (providing they have not been given a higher priority for other reasons) children's books, college-level textbooks, official publications of foreign countries, privately printed works, and state and local government publications. Anthologies, applied arts and crafts, secondary-level textbooks, popular instructional and devotional publications, popularization in all subjects, sports and recreation, and unrevised reprints rarely receive a higher priority.[14] In addition, materials that have been in LC's arrearages for three or more years are also given MLC treatment.

BIBLIOGRAPHIC NETWORKS'
IMPLEMENTATION OF MLC

During this gradual evolution of LC/MLC, the bibliographic networks were busy formulating their own standards for MLC. After much debate in the Research Libraries Group and analysis by members of its Technical Systems and Bibliographic Control Program (BIBTECH), an "RLG Base Level Standard–Books" was approved in July 1983 for inclusion into its bibliographic utility, the Research Libraries Information Network (RLIN).[15] It closely paralleled the NLBR Minimal Record, but differed in some key areas. For example, the RLG mandatory if applicable inclusion of other title information went beyond NLBR Minimal Record requirements, while the romanized title was not included in the RLG Base Level, but was mandatory if applicable in the NLBR Minimal Record standard. By October 1984, the two standards matched almost exactly. Although the cost of entering an RLG Base Level record into RLIN is the same as inputting a full level record, RLIN gives four searching credits for each original full level record input, and no credits for inputting a Base Level record into the database.

The Ohio College Library Center (OCLC) concurrently developed its own version of MLC standards called "Level K," which corresponds to AACR2 Level One description.[16] It also differs slightly from the NLBR Minimal Record standard. For example, first place of publication and series statements are optional in Level K. OCLC does not penalize its members for inputting Level K records: they receive a full credit for inputting them.

REVIEW OF THE LITERATURE

Even though the concept of less-than-full cataloging has been around for more than four decades, and despite its controversial and evolving nature, there is surprisingly little formally published information appearing in the literature.

Discussion of "limited" cataloging occurred in the late 1940s and early 1950s in several of LC's *Cataloging Service* bulletins.[17] In the 1950s, three journal articles appeared, and are still worth reading. Jolley described and supported LC's "limited" cataloging efforts.[18] Wright described the minimum amount of information needed in "short cataloging," and suggested that instead of supplying subject analysis, we needed far more subject bibliographies. He also suggested that catalogers should use judgment, applying varying degrees of cataloging fullness in different parts of the same library.[19] Winchell approached full versus "limited" cataloging from the reference librarian's point of view. She argued that added entries may determine the usefulness of the catalog, and stated that "it goes almost without saying that careful selection of added entries is of first importance."[20]

The next significant article on the topic appeared in 1979. Forman promoted the concept of using a short record circulation system. He maintained that such a system, in conjunction with a state or regional full bibliographic database made available to all, would satisfy the majority of users.[21]

A 1982 study of British libraries by Seal, Bryant, and Hall included discussions on a "short entry catalogue" and its effects on processing costs and library users. They concluded that for monographic materials, a short entry lacking added entries, series, and subject headings met the needs of 97 percent of users.[22]

In 1984, Douglas and Leung reported on surveys sent to ten institutions and bibliographic networks as well as to the heads of cataloging of the 115 Association of Research Libraries.[23] Using the intentionally undefined term of "brief" records, they found some surprising results. The perceived value of a "brief" record seems to have greatly increased between a 1979 OCLC survey in which 74.5 percent of its members were opposed to the concept of a brief record, and the 1984 survey in which only 9 percent (or 7 of the 74 libraries responding) reported that they were not already involved in a "brief" project and could think of no conceivable reason to start one. Nineteen of the 50 (38 percent) engaged in current "brief" projects reported that these records might eventually be updated either on an in-house system, through retrospective conversion, or by being updated by an LC record. However, once the record was entered into a bibliographic utility, it would likely not be updated.

Also in 1984, Gorman reported on another survey of the 25 institutions represented in ALA's Technical Services Directors of Large Research Libraries (commonly known as "Big Heads").[24] In this group, eight of the 25 institutions (32 percent) responded that they were using the NLBR Minimal Record in their cataloging, while 14 (56 percent) were using a non-NLBR Minimal Record standard for at least some of their materials. Nearly all of the libraries made some or all of their MLC records available to other libraries through RLIN, OCLC, other utilities, or publication of its catalog. Materials receiving MLC treatment were designated by type, language, subject, or other "local conditions."

A third survey on MLC was conducted in 1989 by the Association of Research Libraries' Office of Management Studies. In the draft results received by "Big Heads," of the 79 libraries responding, 54 used some form of MLC at that time, eight were planning to use MLC within three to five years, one tried it and discontinued it, and 16 were not using it at all.[25]

In 1986, the *Journal of Academic Librarianship* published "Minimal-Level Cataloging: A Look at the Issues–A Symposium" composed of six papers offering a well-balanced overview of the topic.[26] Included were a cogent survey of MLC issues such as its philosophy, use of staff, and network involvement by Horny, an anti-MLC viewpoint by Ross and West, alternative solutions by Rhee, links between local and national cataloging systems by Crowe, and two pro-MLC viewpoints from Michigan's Marko and von Wahlde and Kent State's Somers and Kamens.

Markiw's "the Use of Minimal-Level Cataloging in Bibliographic Control" discussed the implementation of MLC at the University of Kentucky Libraries.[27] Two surprising ideas surfaced here. First, Kentucky considers some MLC temporary (high priority books waiting for full cataloging copy) and some MLC permanent (juvenile books and a playscript collection). Second, a personal name subject heading is added for certain art materials, although no other subject headings are supplied.

Three relevant articles were presented at the 1990 International Federation of Library Association's conference in Stockholm. In "Cataloging Simplification: Trends and Prospects," Horny discussed American MLC practices as well as LC's draft proposal for simplifying the International Standard Bibliographic Description for Monographs or ISBD(M).[28] Langballe discussed Norwegian and other Scandinavian efforts to simplify the ISBD and MARC format, basing change on the principle that information is given only once.[29] Berg reported on a Norwegian pilot project of brief cataloging.[30]

At the 1990 American Library Association Annual Conference, Horny spoke about the process of determining MLC standards for videorecordings in her paper "What You See Is What You Get (So What Do You Do?)."[31]

Although not the primary topic of discussion, MLC is at least touched upon in several other published articles. Neville and Snee's "Aging of Uncataloged Monographs" mentioned that studies of online searching indicate that subject searching accounts for more than 50 percent of all online searches. Browsers looking for "unknown" but potentially useful items may not be well served when using MLC records lacking subject access.[32]

Mandel's "Trade-offs: Quantifying Quality in Library Technical Services" used MLC in a hypothetical cost-effectiveness analysis.[33] Graham's "Quality in Cataloging: Making Distinctions" discussed what elements of the catalog record are essential (versus merely useful), and made a case for an emphasis on "lean" records.[34] Harris's "Historic Cataloging Costs, Issues, and Trends" included a cataloging-cost survey with "less than AACR2 or brief" cataloging as a method of cutting costs.[35] Lowell's "Local Systems and Bibliographic Utilities in 1992: A Large Research Library Perspective" surveyed ALA's "Big Heads" and discovered that in 1989, 2,253,000 "less-than-full" records appeared on their local systems while only 547,000 were on the bibliographic networks. Predictions of MLC material on local systems in 1992 suggest that

3,418,000 MLC records will be present, but only 1,040,000 will be loaded into the utilities. Over 2,000,000 MLC records would thus not be available nationally.[36]

Other sources of information on MLC have been numerous recent articles in LC's *Cataloging Service Bulletin* and its *Information Bulletin,* occasional discussions in bibliographic network newsletters such as RLG's *Operations Update* and OCLC's *Newsletter,* as well as more current forms of publishing such as electronic publishing on NOTIS-L.

There is also a vast amount of "unpublished" documentation available on the topic of MLC. Minutes of ALA's "Big Heads" over the last decade are full of such lively discussions. RLG's BIBTECH meetings likewise frequently discussed MLC. An unpublished report by the University of Chicago on OCLC member use copy also discussed MLC, and concluded that MLC does not meet the needs of the seven libraries surveyed.[37]

MLC AT NORTHWESTERN

One institution's experiences with MLC can provide concrete examples of the kinds of decisions libraries must make. In past years, Northwestern University Library (NUL) used less-than-full cataloging for certain designated categories of materials such as pamphlets, works considered to be ephemeral, and certain items obtained in large gifts. Such cataloging decreased over time, especially since 1971, with the implementation of our automated processing system Northwestern Online Total Integrated System (NOTIS) and the availability of cataloging copy. Even though all of the arrearages of the general collections were brought under bibliographic control in the form of brief online bibliographic records, accessible under author, title, and series, the books themselves remained in a backlog area. As MLC was being discussed on the national level in the 1970s, NUL realized that an automated processing system would not do away with a growing arrearage. Existing cataloging staff could not keep up with the increasing acquisitions as well as existing arrearages. The implementation of some form of MLC could be a solution to the problem.

After the publication of the NLBR Minimal Record, RLG's Base

Level, and AACR2's Level One standards, NUL considered the various options, and implemented a slightly enhanced NLBR Minimal Record in 1982. NUL/MLC includes, in addition to the NLBR Minimal Standard, the first place of publication, one added entry, if there is a title main entry, title added entries for variant or "catch" titles (in order to partially take the place of full subject analysis), and one Library of Congress subject heading. All headings (except, occasionally, a series) are under authority control. NUL/MLC records are permanent records, not meant to be upgraded anytime in the future.

SUBJECT ACCESS IN NUL/MLC

The inclusion of subject headings in MLC is extremely uncommon. Northwestern carefully considered the advantages and disadvantages of including an LCSH heading. Both public services and technical services staff agreed that patrons would be best served by adding a subject heading, thus assisting patrons who search for a "non-known" item. This is borne out by several recent articles such as Neville and Snee.[38] In 1985, Holley said "User behaviour in the online catalogue as seen through transaction log analysis shows a much higher level of subject searching than many would have expected. Even in most research libraries, the majority of users are coming to the online catalogue with a subject search in mind."[39]

The costliness of providing a subject heading was also considered. As original catalogers were already needed for NUL/MLC to establish names and series, they could also fairly easily add a single LCSH heading. Paraprofessionals performing copy cataloging do not establish names, series, or subjects, and therefore are not the appropriate level to perform NUL/MLC. Since 1971, Northwestern has tried to keep its online catalog "clean," so when the concept of supplying a non-LCSH subject heading was briefly discussed, it was immediately dismissed, for it would only "pollute" the catalog. In order to make this subject analysis cost-effective, the catalogers were given the option of assigning the single most appropriate LCSH subject heading, if easily determined, or assigning a slightly more "general" subject heading than would be performed on full level cataloging, if the "general" subject heading would save the time and expense of establishing a new subject heading or geographic place needed for full level cataloging.

SELECTION OF MATERIALS RECEIVING NUL/MLC

Special collections pamphlets, local dissertations, art exhibition catalogs, some collections of nearly homogeneous materials, such as books in a specified series or by a designated author, some ephemeral materials, some microforms, and some Africana materials are currently receiving MLC Cataloging at NUL. They are selected because full level cataloging often requires complicated corporate body authority work (e.g., art exhibition catalogs and Africana materials), or because full level description and subject analysis may be difficult and time-consuming (e.g., pamphlets and microforms).

Materials are selected to receive NUL/MLC in one of two ways: by type of material or title-by-title basis. For example, science materials in certain series designated by the science bibliographer receive such NUL/MLC treatment. This treatment is adequate because the user accesses this material by series, author, title, or subject. In another case, most art exhibition catalogs receive NUL/ MLC. This decision is based on an algorithm developed by the art bibliographer, and takes into account the length of the book, the amount of text in it, if it is a museum catalog, and whether or not it is of local interest. This is actually not a complicated formula, and takes the cataloger little time to decide on the appropriate level of cataloging.

Selection for NUL/MLC treatment more often occurs on a title-by-title basis. In the case of the Africana materials, after it has been determined that there is no cataloging copy in the bibliographic utility, a bibliographer quickly scans the remaining materials and designates those that should receive MLC. The time spent making this decision is minimal, thus keeping the procedure cost-effective. The bibliographer is influenced by such factors as: low research value of materials, projected low use of materials, and the timeliness of ephemeral materials (political party pamphlets, for example). The ultimate decision, however, rests with the cataloger, not the bibliographer, because the cataloger alone has the knowledge of cataloging rules to decide what is adequate access in cataloging.

NUL/MLC TIME STUDIES

The NUL Catalog Department performed several time studies of NUL/MLC over the years. Results from a 1983 study of the general backlog showed that the time savings averaged 48 percent over full level cataloging. For science materials, the time saving was 50 percent. In a 1982 time study, Special Collections political pamphlets averaged a one-third time savings. In 1990, a study of Africana materials revealed a time savings of 32 percent. All studies demonstrate significant time savings, the varying numbers dependent on the relative difficulty of the materials themselves.

Based on the time studies mentioned above, as well as discussions with Northwestern original catalogers, we can draw some conclusions on the specific elements that save time in NUL/MLC. The elimination of multiple added entries, particularly corporate bodies, saves the most time. A significant amount of time is saved in subject analysis since only one subject heading is assigned, and that heading may be less specific than it would have been at the full level. Some time savings occurs in the descriptive portion of the record, where decisions are made easily about multiple publishers, printers, and the need for notes. Probably the least time savings occurs in classification, where a complete Dewey classification number is always provided, although it is permissible in NUL/MLC to assign a broad classification number using a shorter notation.

EVALUATION OF NUL/MLC

NUL/MLC is not appropriate to all materials. First, NUL/MLC should only be performed if it saves time, and therefore permits the cataloging of another title that would otherwise not receive cataloging. Works of *belles lettres* by a single author rarely save time, since subjects are not assigned anyway, and they usually lack corporate headings and uniform titles.

Second, NUL/MLC should not be performed if it seriously inhibits access to the material. NUL/MLC allows only a main entry or a single added entry, rarely both (some cataloger's judgment is permitted, of course!). In AACR2, certain types of materials routinely require added entries.[40] For example, in works of mixed responsibility (rule 21.8) at least two persons or bodies perform different kinds of activities. When a work is a collaboration between an artist and writer (rule 21.24), the choice of a single access point is inadequate. Likewise, works that are modifications of other works (rule 21.9) and works of shared responsibility (rule 21.6) also require at least two access points. It is clear that for all the complicated cases listed in AACR2's chapter 21, MLC is inadequate.

Another type of material heavily collected at NUL is conference proceedings. These materials usually require more than one access point, even if they are cataloged under conference main entry, which is often merely a repetition of the title. Patrons sometimes ask for such publications by their editor, or by their corporate sponsor (organizer of the conference) since often the exact title of the publication or even its name is not consistent within the publication itself. NUL/MLC is clearly inadequate in this instance.

The last category of material that does not receive adequate access in NUL/MLC is material for which there is no easy-to-determine single subject heading. Exceptions are regularly made to the policy of a single heading, as long as it does not take the cataloger much time to determine the additional subject heading and its proper formulation. Many of the Library's books are small studies, often mimeographed papers, studying the relationship among three separate and unrelated subjects. It is impossible to find one or even two subject headings to adequately cover this material. By the time the subject analysis of the three topics is completed, it becomes clear that full level cataloging should be performed on this material.

Despite the disadvantages of NUL/MLC, Northwestern is, overall, pleased with it, and continues to utilize it for appropriate materials. Cataloging production is of course the major advantage: thousands of titles that might not otherwise have been cataloged have been given adequate access in the Library's catalog. Nor has the Library received any complaints about having MLC records mixed in with full level records in the catalog. NUL/MLC also enables a greater variety of materials to be rescued from the backlog, put on the shelves with other items on the same subject, and made instantly available for patron browsing.

FUTURE DIRECTIONS OF MLC

In the ideal world, we would all rather see full level records in our national and local databases than less-than-full records. However, since MLC access is better than no access at all, it is clear that MLC, in some form, will endure in the future. In a recent "Big Heads" meeting, Murray-Rust expressed the public services point of view. "Public Services librarians are also interested in productivity. Public Services encourage Technical Services to find ways to push more material through in a shorter amount of time."[41]

While the bibliographic utilities will continue to accept MLC records, member libraries will continue to upgrade them to full level records when cataloging for their own institutions. This trend, first cited by Douglas and Leung in 1984[42] was reconfirmed by the University of Chicago in 1990.[43] OCLC, in particular, encourages its members with at least a Full Mode authorization to make such upgrades by giving them a $2.00 credit for each upgrade.[44]

Institutions will increase their MLC cataloging efforts in the future. Lowell surveyed the 25 largest research libraries in the United States, and they predicted adding an estimated 1,165,000 less-than-full records to their local databases between 1989 and 1992.[45] In order to help control their arrearages, the Library of Congress will continue to catalog many thousands of items annually using MLC. In 1990, Rather reported that LC had increased their MLC cataloging by 50 percent.[46]

With the advent of the uncontrolled subject terms in their MLC records, LC has recognized the importance of subject access in MLC records. A prediction for the more distant future is that subject access, in some form, will come to be part of the national standard for MLC treatment. Perhaps LC will reconsider the wisdom of uncontrolled subject headings, or add another level of subject access similar to Northwestern's, which uses LCSH.

The recent trend toward cataloging simplification by the Library of Congress has centered on the ISBD(M).[47] Horny states that

"Further pressures are now making it necessary to carefully study the importance of data which has been routinely supplied. These pressures are likely to produce close scrutiny of all cataloging standards with the intent of reaching general agreement about a level of cataloging which will be officially recognized as more than minimum and widely acceptable without need for enhancement.[48] In this era of cooperative cataloging, this is, indeed, the direction for which we should strive.

REFERENCE NOTES

1. Heartsill Young, ed., *The ALA Glossary of Library and Information Science* (Chicago: American Library Association, 1983), 31.

2. "Gradation of Cataloging in the Library of Congress," Library of Congress, Processing Department, *Cataloging Service* 13 (December 1947): 1.

3. "Limited Cataloging," Library of Congress, Processing Department, *Cataloging Service* 23 (May 1951): 1-4.

4. "Discontinuance of Limited Cataloging," Library of Congress, Processing Department, *Cataloging Service* 61 (September 1963): 1.

5. *Anglo-American Cataloguing Rules,* 2d ed., 1988 revision. (Ottawa and Chicago: Canadian Library Association, American Library Association, 1988), 15. (hereafter cited as *AACR2*).

6. "Draft Introductory Statement concerning 'National Level Bibliographic Record–Books'." Prepared by Processing Services, Library of Congress, *LC Information Bulletin* 37 (November 10, 1978): 692-696.

7. "Library of Congress to Create Minimal Level Cataloging Records," *LC Information Bulletin* 38 (November 2, 1979): 457-460.

8. Library of Congress, Processing Services, Cataloging Distribution Service, "Announcement," October 1983 and "Notice to MARC Serials Subscribers," January 17, 1983.

9. "Minimal Level Cataloging-Monographs," Library of Congress *Cataloging Service Bulletin* 36 (Spring 1987): 41.

10. Letter from Lucia Rather to Karen Horny, dated May 23, 1985.

11. Library of Congress, Processing Services, Cataloging Distribution Service, "Notice to US MARC Subscribers," December 1988.

12. "Guidelines for Applying Field 653 to MLC Records." Library of Congress *Cataloging Service Bulletin* 50 (Fall 1990): 48-51.

13. "LC Revises Cataloging Priorities and Levels of Cataloging," *LC Information Bulletin* 49 (December 17, 1990): 441.

14. Ibid., 442.

15. "RLG Base Level Standard–Books," Research Libraries Group *Memo,* July 31, 1983.

16. Ohio College Library Center, "Level I and Level K Input Standards," *Technical Bulletin* 30 (December 9, 1977), 2p.

17. Check Nancy B. Olson's *Cataloging Service Bulletin Index* under "Minimal Level Cataloging." No. 1-52, Summer 1978-Spring 1991. (Lake Crystal, MN: Soldier Creek Press, 1991).

18. L. Jolley, "A Note on 'Limited' and 'Simplified' Cataloguing in the Library of Congress," *Journal of Documentation* 8, no. 2 (1952): 99-105.

19. Wyllis E. Wright, "Full, Medium and Short," *Journal of Cataloging and Classification* 1, no. 4 (1955): 196-199.

20. Constance M. Winchell, "The Catalog: Full, Medium, or Limited," *Journal of Cataloging and Classification* 1, no. 4 (1955): 199-206 (quotation from p. 203).

21. Michael Gorman, "Short Can Be Beautiful," *American Libraries* 10, no. 10 (1979): 607-608.

22. Alan Seal, Philip Bryant, and Carolyn Hall, *Full and Short Entry Catalogues: Library Needs and Uses* (Claverton Down: Bath University Library, 1982), 2.

23. Nancy E. Douglas and Shirley Leung, "Use of the Full MARC Record: Myth and Reality," in *Academic Libraries: Myths and Realities,* eds. Suzanne C. Dodson and Gary L. Menges (Chicago: Association of College and Research Libraries, 1984), 177-182 (hereafter cited as *Academic Libraries*).

24. Michael Gorman, "Report on the Technical Services Directors of Large Research Libraries Survey of Minimal-Level Cataloging," *Information Technology and Libraries* 3 (December 1984):382-384.

25. "Draft Brief Analysis of the Association of Research Libraries QUICK-SPEC Survey on the Use of Minimal Level Cataloging and Cataloging Priorities Conducted on Behalf of the Library of Congress," in *Draft Recommendations of the Committee on Cataloging Priorities and Levels of Cataloging (Library of Congress)* distributed to ALA's Technical Services Directors of Large Research Libraries by Henriette D. Avram, June 22, 1989, Attachment 6, June 15, 1989.

26. Karen L. Horny, "Minimal-Level Cataloging: A Look at the Issues–A Symposium," *Journal of Academic Librarianship* 11, no. 6 (January 1986): 332-334; Ryburn M. Ross and Linda West, "MLC: A Contrary Viewpoint," 334-336; Sue Rhee, "Minimal-Level Cataloging: Is It the Best Local Solution to a National Problem?" 336-337; William J. Crowe, "Local Needs, Shared Responsibilities," 337-338; Lynn Marko and Barbara von Wahlde, "BRC (Brief Record Cataloging) at Michigan," 339-340; Jeanne Somers and Harry Kamens, "A More Detailed Study of One Library's Experience," 341-342.

27. Michael Markiw, "The Use of Minimal-Level Cataloging in Bibliographic Control," *Georgia Librarian* 25 (Fall 1988): 65-67.

28. Karen Horny, "Cataloguing Simplification: Trends and Prospects," *International Cataloguing and Bibliographic Control* 20, no. 3 (April/June 1991): 25-28.

29. Anne M. Hasund Langballe, "Brief Cataloguing in Card and Online Catalogues," *International Cataloguing and Bibliographic Control* 20, no. 3 (April/June 1991): 28-31.

30. Øivind Berg, "Current Problems with the MARC/ISBD-Formats in Relation to Online Public Access of Bibliographic Information" (Paper delivered at the 56th IFLA General Conference, Stockholm, Sweden, 18-24 August, 1990, booklet 4).

31. Karen L. Horny, "What You See Is What You Get (So What Do You Do?): An Administrator Looks at Minimal Level Cataloging" (Paper delivered at the American Library Association Annual Conference, June 23, 1990, Chicago).

32. Ellen P. Neville and Antonia M. Snee, "Aging of Uncataloged Monographs," in *Academic Libraries,* 273-276.

33. Carol A. Mandel, "Trade-offs: Quantifying Quality in Library Technical Services," *Journal of Academic Librarianship* 14, no. 4 (September 1988): 214-220.

34. Peter S. Graham, "Quality in Cataloging: Making Distinctions," *Journal of Academic Librarianship* 16, no. 4 (September 1990): 213-218.

35. George Harris, "Historic Cataloging Costs, Issues, and Trends," *Library Quarterly* 59, no. 1 (January 1989): 1-21.

36. Gerald R. Lowell, "Local Utilities and Bibliographic Utilities in 1992: A Large Research Library Perspective," *Journal of Academic Librarianship* 16, no. 3 (July 1990): 140-144.

37. "University of Chicago Library Report on Member Copy Use Survey, January-March 1990, Version 2." (Unpublished paper distributed to ALA's Technical Services Directors of Large Research Libraries), 13.

38. Neville and Snee, "Aging of Uncataloged Monographs," 275.

39. Robert P. Holley, "Subject Cataloguing in the USA," *International Cataloguing* 14 (October 1985): 43-45.

40. *AACR2,* Chapter 21.

41. [American Library Association] Technical Services Directors of Large Research Libraries "Minutes, January 11, 1991 Meeting, Chicago," 3.

42. Douglas and Leung, "Use of the Full MARC Record," 181.

43. "University of Chicago Library Report on Member Copy Use Survey," 13.

44. Illinois Office of the Secretary of State, *Information Bulletin* 232 (July 1, 1991): 5.

45. Lowell, "Local Utilities," 143.

46. [American Library Association] Technical Services Directors of Large Research Libraries "Minutes of the June 22, 1990 Meeting, Chicago," p. 3.

47. "Proposal to Present Guidelines for the Application of ISBD(M) for Contemporary Material" (Washington, DC: Library of Congress, August 1989).

48. Horny, "Cataloguing Simplification," 28.

PART V:
SUBJECT ACCESS

Chapter 11

Subject Cataloging

Tschera Harkness Connell

The catalog is used to present the resources of a library or a group of libraries to its users. The user approaches the catalog with an information need articulated in the form of a query. A search formulation of that query is matched against the bibliographic records (document representations) in the catalog. If the need is stated clearly, if the need is translated and searched in the catalog so that both the need and the constraints of catalog design are taken into consideration, if the information contained in the collection of documents is well represented in the bibliographic records, and if the bibliographic records match the search formulation, then the user is probably successful.

It is easy to see that there are many points along the way that influence whether the user finds the information needed. The quality and quantity of the collection of documents represented in the catalog are the first considerations. The accuracy of input into the system is also important. In terms of document representation, how well do the bibliographic records reflect the documents they represent? What standards were used for the construction of the bibliographic records? Are the standards adequate? How current is the vocabulary used in the catalog? How consistently is the vocabulary applied? How effective is the structure of the catalog in guiding the user to other items related to but different from the user's original request?

The responsibilities of catalogers center around the issues represented by these questions. Subject catalogers concentrate on providing access to what the document is "about." The process involves:

(1) analyzing individual documents to determine what concepts are expressed; (2) representing the identified concepts by the language of the system (classification and/or subject headings); (3) making entries for the identified concepts; and (4) linking related concepts so that groups of similar documents can be retrieved.

BACKGROUND AND HISTORY

Arranging Entries in the Printed Catalog

Probably the oldest form of catalog is the classified catalog where the entries are arranged systematically according to their subject relationships. In this form of catalog, the subjects are frequently expressed by the use of symbols, numbers, or other notation. Therefore, the use of a classified catalog requires consulting an alphabetical subject index to the classification scheme. In contrast, for an alphabetical subject catalog no separate index is needed. Verbal subject entries are arranged in alphabetical order without regard to subject relationships or hierarchies. Subject relationships, if expressed, are in the form of linking references. An extension of the concept of an alphabetical subject catalog is the dictionary catalog where all entries (author, title, series, as well as subject) are arranged in a single alphabet.

The ease of using a catalog directly without the necessity of first consulting an index contributed to making the alphabetical arrangement a popular form of catalog in the United States during the latter part of the nineteenth century. The decision made in 1898 by the Library of Congress to adopt the dictionary arrangement, and the subsequent decision to publish its cataloging in the form of catalog cards, eventually made the dictionary catalog the predominant form of catalog in the United States. Since that time, classification has been used in the United States primarily as a shelving device and subject cataloging has emphasized subject headings as a means of access. The remainder of this chapter focuses on the tradition of verbal subject access to library materials in the United States.

Goals for Subject Cataloging

The rules for subject headings in a dictionary catalog are largely the result of the work of Charles A. Cutter. Cutter's "objects" for the subject catalog and his "means" to achieve them, published in his *Rules for a Printed Dictionary Catalogue* (1876-1904), are the foundation for American subject cataloging theory and practice. Since that time others have expanded and adapted Cutter's principles, but no new rules for subject cataloging have been published in the United States.

Cutter's goals for subject cataloging were: (1) to enable the user of the catalog to find a particular document of which the subject is known; (2) to find other documents on the same subject or related subjects; and (3) to assist the user in selecting from the entries retrieved, the document(s) most suited to his or her information need. To fulfill these goals, Cutter stressed that the subject cataloger must always consider the convenience and point of view of the user.[1]

Cutter suggests that the best way to achieve the first goal is to enter a document under its specific subject, choosing a subject heading that is neither broader nor narrower than the subject content of the work. In practice, this principle of specificity is coupled with the principle of direct entry. A book about coyotes, for example, will be entered under the subject heading, "Coyotes," not under the heading "Animals–Vertebrates–Mammals–Carnivores–Dogs–Coyotes."

Specificity is a difficult concept to apply. Part of the problem is definition. The concept changes in context. Specificity as just described refers to the principle of assigning a term that is coextensive with the subject of the document. In practice, specificity is dependent upon the level allowed by the indexing language. This means that a cataloger assigns the most specific term that covers the material of the book *and* that is allowed by the list of uniform headings (controlled vocabulary) used in the catalog. If the subject of the book is more specific than any of the controlled vocabulary terms, then a more general term is assigned. The user must know to look under the specific heading and then, if nothing is found, to use a more general term.

Specificity is also influenced by the depth of indexing. It can mean the most specific term that is coextensive with the whole book, a particular percentage of the book, a single chapter, section, or part of the book In this sense, the concept of specificity is determined largely by administrative policy.

In order to enable the user to find out what the library has on a given subject (Cutter's second goal), it is necessary to enter documents on the same subject under the same subject heading. This can be done one of two ways. If a subject can be expressed in more than one way, entries for each work on the subject can be entered under each way of expressing the subject. Alternatively, Cutter advocated a principle of unity which requires entries for each work on a subject to be entered under one uniform, distinct heading chosen to represent the subject. In order to choose a single uniform subject heading to represent a topic, decisions must be made between synonyms, differences in spelling, and language. Preference is given to common usage if common usage is known. Common usage may differ among different groups of users. For example, in most libraries in the United States, common usage would mean choosing the English rather than a foreign language term. However, the users of a Hispanic neighborhood library might find "SIDA" more helpful than "AIDS." When choices are made between synonyms, variant spellings, language, or any potential terms, cross-references are used to lead the user from a term not chosen to a term that represents the wanted material. In addition, using a uniform heading to represent a specific subject requires providing "see also" references to alert the user to subject headings that represent related material. A user interested in the topic AIDS may also be interested in information about the drug AZT which has been used in the treatment of AIDS. Therefore, the user who has found the heading AIDS should be made aware of potentially useful material under the heading for AZT. Providing a network of references and assigning a uniform heading for each subject are the means by which catalogers have traditionally tried to overcome the scattering of subjects that occurs in an alphabetical arrangement.

Cutter's third objective, to assist the user in the choice of a book, has received little attention in the library literature. According to Cutter, one way to achieve this goal is to highlight distinguishing literary or topical characteristics of each document by including descriptive notes on the entry. Implementing Cutter's ideas and/or finding additional ways to achieve this goal may be the critical element in making large online catalogs effective.

Subject Headings Lists

Keeping a record of headings used in a catalog is necessary in order to maintain a system of uniform headings. Early lists were prepared locally by each library. In 1895, the American Library Association produced the first widely accepted universal list (*List of Subject Headings for Use in Dictionary Catalogs*). This list was intended for medium-sized libraries and was based upon headings used in several prominent libraries of the time. As Library of Congress cataloging became widely available through the printed card program, librarians naturally became interested in having a list of headings used by the Library of Congress. The Library of Congress first published its list in 1909 under the title *Subject Headings Used in the Dictionary Catalogues of the Library of Congress*. The title was changed in 1975 to *Library of Congress Subject Heading* (LCSH). Although there are other sources for headings, especially for specialized libraries, the primary source for subject headings in the United States is LCSH.

LCSH

The Library of Congress subject headings are made available in many forms. The best known form is the printed three–volume hardcover version known as the "red books" because of the color of the bindings. Because this is the form most often available to library patrons, this will be the form referred to by the term LCSH in the remainder of this section.

The Library of Congress subject heading system is based on literary warrant which means that headings are based on the materials cataloged at the Library of Congress. In libraries that specialize in subject areas not well represented in LCSH, catalogers may need to supplement the list from other sources. However, even for libraries that have similar collecting interests as the Library of Congress, LCSH is not a stand alone tool. LCSH is an incomplete listing of the subject headings used in the Library of Congress catalogs. Most personal and place names are excluded. As well, subdivisions which are used to restrict a heading to a more specific meaning are not listed with all the possible subject headings with which they may be used. For the cataloger, this means that the terms in a subject heading string must be synthesized from more than one source. For the user, this means the need to know (or find out) that there are potentially helpful terms that are not listed in LCSH.

Each new edition of LCSH is a partial accumulation of headings and references in current use. Obsolete headings are dropped, old terminology is replaced, and new headings are added. Excluded are histories of the development of individual subject headings. This means that unless libraries have changed or replaced outdated headings, the user may miss relevant material. One recurring criticism of LCSH has been the inability of the Library of Congress subject heading system to keep current. However, many libraries have great difficulty keeping up with the changes that are made. Even though librarians may have access to auxiliary tools or to online versions of Library of Congress subject headings which give information about old and new terms, users have to depend on the catalog and/or the red books. Many obsolete subject terms are still in catalogs of American libraries.

For the cataloger, choosing terms and/or synthesizing terms and subdivisions from a list is difficult. It is not always obvious which of several headings is most appropriate. Even by looking at other records that have the heading, it is not always obvious what policies determined the assignment of that particular heading. Since the time of Cutter no code of principles has been adopted by the library community to aid in the process of subject cataloging. In the absence of a code, librarians have turned to guides for using the Library of Congress system.

Until recently, the basic guide to the Library of Congress system has been David Judson Haykin's 1951 discussion of the system and of Library of Congress subject cataloging practice.[2] In 1984 the Library of Congress published its *Subject Cataloging Manual: Subject Headings* (SCM:SH). Now in its fourth edition (1991) the manual provides guidelines and procedures for assigning Library of

Congress subject headings. The introduction to the third edition notes that the guide is valuable for both input and retrieval:

> Practicing subject catalogers wishing to assign subject headings in the spirit of LC's own policies and practices should find it indispensable. . . . Reference librarians may wish to consult it in order to understand how subject headings are assigned and thereby develop successful strategies for finding material in a subject catalog.[3]

Because of the central role that the Library of Congress plays in national and international cooperative efforts, the policies of the Library of Congress have become the operating standard for most of the libraries in the United States.

TODAY AND TOMORROW

Divergent Purposes

Cutter's first two objects are frequently endorsed, but are difficult to implement. Much of the difficulty is that the "finding" function and the "collocating" function of the catalog are fundamentally in conflict. To help a user "find a particular document" requires access points that emphasize the item's uniqueness. These access points must help the user separate that item from other items that may be similar. Collocating items in a catalog means grouping them by their similarities.

Theoretically, the use of uniform headings in conjunction with a well-developed system of references can balance the fragmentation effect of alphabetically arranged specific and direct entries. This theoretical catalog assumes that catalogers apply headings consistently, remove old headings, and update entries regularly. Practically, few libraries have had the resources to implement and maintain such a system.

Ironically, the trend toward using bibliographic utilities as the principal source of cataloging has exacerbated the problem. Cooperative cataloging efforts provide basic descriptions of much of the published literature in library collections. However, many of the structural elements of the catalog are not the kinds of data that can be obtained in prepackaged form. Building a structure of a catalog is dependent upon the local collection and on local users. If the structure is not provided by the library, then the burden of making connections among headings is shifted to the user. Some libraries provide copies of LCSH near the catalogs for patrons to use. However, in addition to being an incomplete listing of headings used in the Library of Congress system, LCSH lists many headings not used by the local library because the local library has no material on the particular topic. These two seemingly conflicting situations–incompleteness on the one hand and the listing of headings not used on the other–are not likely to be understood by the majority of library patrons.

For the user, even if the network of references is extensive, logical, and well-maintained, the process of following a series of references will not result in finding all materials in the library on a particular subject. Catalog records usually represent the document as a whole. Parts of documents and periodical articles are not cataloged. One result of whole document cataloging is that a user performing a comprehensive search must also consult more general headings in order to locate material of which only a part is specifically related to the topic. This is difficult because "see also" references are made from a general heading to a more specific one but seldom from the specific to the general.

The near impossibility of performing the "finding" and the "collocating" functions equally well is frequently noted in library literature. There is no consensus on which of these (or any other) functions should be emphasized. David Judson Haykin wrote that "the primary purpose of the subject catalog is to show which books on a specific subject the library possesses. Its use as a source of general subject bibliography . . . is of secondary importance."[4] Haykin's view, however, is not universal. Reference departments would still like to find all the documents about the same subject by consulting the same subject heading. Even better would be a system that would enable the user to find "all the best of them."[5] Catalogs, as presently designed, do not attempt to supply critical evaluations of documents. The library community lacks consensus on the purpose of the subject catalog. Although disagreement over goals is a longstanding problem, the problem has intensified with the presence of the online catalog.

Online Catalogs

Today's catalogs, online or manual, contain records that reflect not only current cataloging standards but also traditions or prior technologies and earlier times. Library collections (and therefore library catalogs) represent the output of recorded knowledge throughout the ages. This means that even if there were no inaccuracies and inconsistencies in indexing over the years, shifts in how subject disciplines are perceived would create variations in the subject vocabulary used in catalogs. This fact, in addition to problems of practice and language previously discussed, contributes to the complexity of the catalog as a tool for information access.

The potential of the computer is often heralded as the solution to subject access problems. No longer is there a need for reliance on linear alphabetical access. Computers can be programmed to mix and match data elements in ways not possible in manual systems. Online catalogs can be designed to allow users to search for material using key words in the title, Library of Congress subject headings, and classification. Providing access through words (verbal access) and/or symbols (classification) is no longer a mechanical issue. Technologically, it is possible to do both.

However, online catalogs are just the newest innovation in a long line of innovations in library catalogs and catalog technology. Historically, new technologies solve some problems but then create new ones. For example, time and more especially space constraints of paper catalogs have made it difficult for catalogers to provide as many access points as they might have desired for a particular item. It is only now with the computer that we have the technology to implement the concept of multiple access points to any great degree. Increasing the number of headings assigned to individual items, however, also increases the number of records for which the headings are used. The large size of many online catalogs means that users often retrieve sets of records that are too large to be of any practical use.

Retrieving large numbers of items is not a problem that is new with the computer. However, traditional means of dealing with the problem are not effective in the online catalog. In a card catalog environment the user could refine a search with a glance at the subdivision groups filed behind the subject heading. The "place" of subdivisions in the alphabetical catalog facilitated browsing. "Place" in the online catalog has little meaning and browsing is more difficult to achieve. In the online catalog the use of subdivisions makes retrieval more difficult because the user must match exactly a long subject heading string. Even if the system provides the user with a complete list of headings and subdivisions used in the catalog, the process of using the list and retrieving the records often requires two steps. In the traditional catalog the user could find the approximate place of a subject and then browse through the entries. Searching by approximation and browsing are much more difficult to achieve in an online catalog. The trend toward assigning more headings to documents must be accompanied by a refinement of Library of Congress subject headings to allow users to discriminate among items.

Another example of an old problem solved but a new one created is that computers allow us to expand the conceptual approaches to the catalog by combining different fields, or parts of fields, in a single search. Combining parts of fields in a single search, however, can create a problem of "false drops" (records that match the mechanical search formulation but that are irrelevant to the conceptual request). For example, a user who is looking for material on the psychological aspects of creativity is probably not interested in the title *Dying: A Psychological Study with Special Reference to Individual Creativity and Defensive Organization* which could be retrieved by a system that searches main headings and subdivisions independently.

New Expectations

With any new technology comes a change in practices and expectations. It is common for online catalogs to represent the holdings of more than one library or information center. From a catalog the user can find out if an item exists, *and* if it is available. In some cases the item can be paged right from the terminal. These are becoming expected features by users of online catalogs.

Additional expectations for catalogs are likely to develop. For example, the widespread use of computers to access periodical indexes and other bibliographic databases (such as DIALOG) may shift the expectations for these databases to the online catalog. However, the present Library of Congress subject heading system is not designed to accommodate the assignment of headings to portions of documents or periodical articles. The additional load on the system will create similar problems as the assignment of more headings to whole documents. In large general databases, users will need more assistance in discriminating among items retrieved.

Some will argue that we need to combine other bibliographic retrieval systems and online catalogs, especially as it becomes more common to access both from a single computer terminal. However, common access means that the boundaries between the systems are less visible to the user but it does not mean that the boundaries are not there. Differences related to content and scope are not easy, and perhaps not desirable, to change. "Access" to a gourmet restaurant, a grocery store, and a McDonalds from a single shopping center does not make those options for obtaining food the same. Furthermore, it is unlikely that combining those food sources into a "single system" would be satisfactory. Hildreth points out that because multiple retrieval systems and multiple search techniques are available through a single terminal, the librarian has a new responsibility: "to understand the differences and to interpret these differences in a meaningful way for users."[6]

Again, the issue is one of goals. What is it that subject cataloging should achieve? What services do we as a profession want the subject catalog to provide? For example, is helping the user find the critically acclaimed "best" documents on a particular topic a viable goal? If the answer is yes, then how might it be accomplished? Would it be possible to link bibliographic records to published reviews?

Once goals are defined, then subject cataloging traditions can be evaluated in terms of the desired goals. What are the relationships between searching techniques and traditional input standards? Which input traditions assist the user in searching? Which searching techniques work and in what circumstances? For example, when is it useful to use classification rather than verbal access? When is it useful to use controlled vocabulary rather than natural language? When is it best to use both? Can context-sensitive on-screen "helps" guide the user to the techniques most likely to work in his or her current search situation?

Which subject cataloging traditions need more explanation? Under what circumstances would references explaining the conditions of use for a particular heading be helpful? Would it be helpful to include a date that a new heading is first used in the system so that the user might be prompted to use a different heading for material published before that date? Which elements on the bibliographic record are most useful for retrieval? Which for discrimination among items? Do we need more information on the bibliographic record? Do we need less?

The answers to these questions could provide standards for subject cataloging and guidelines for the development of user interfaces. Well designed user interfaces are needed to allow users to exploit the catalog without necessarily learning all the intricacies of subject cataloging or of system design.

In early American library history cataloging was the concern of the profession as a whole. How to provide access to library collections occupied the conference agendas of library directors and catalogers. With the emergence of online catalogs an interest in improving subject access has again become an active concern of the entire library community. Hopefully, with many minds working on problems of subject access, the profession will be able to define what it wants to accomplish and then find effective ways for achieving the goals.

REFERENCE NOTES

1. Charles A. Cutter, *Rules for a Dictionary Catalog,* 4th ed., rewritten (Washington, DC: Government Printing Office, 1904).

2. David Judson Haykin, *Subject Headings: A Practical Guide* (Washington, DC: Library of Congress, 1951).

3. Library of Congress. Office for Subject Cataloging Policy. *Subject Cataloging Manual: Subject Headings,* 3rd. ed. (Washington DC: Cataloging Distribution Service, Library of Congress, 1990), xiii.

4. Haykin, *Subject Heading,* 1.

5. Constance McCarthy, "The Reliability Factor in Subject Access," *College & Research Libraries* 47 (1986): 53.

6. Charles R. Hildreth, *Intelligent Interfaces and Retrieval Methods for Subject Searching in Bibliographic Retrieval Systems* (Washington, DC: Cataloging Distribution Service, Library of Congress, 1989), 11.

Chapter 12

The Dewey Decimal Classification: 1965-1990

John P. Comaromi

The last quarter century of the life of the Dewey Decimal Classification (DDC) began with the publication of Edition 17 in 1965 and ended with the publication of Edition 20 in 1989. The two editions are the most dissimilar philosophically in the history of the Classification (Edition 15 [1951] had no philosophical underpinning and can hardly be called an edition of the DDC). This chapter attempts to explain the bases for the dissimilarity.

EDITIONS 1 THROUGH 16

First, a few paragraphs on the history of the DDC up to 1965 are needed to provide the reader the lay of the land upon which the events would take place. Editions 2 through 14 (1885-1942) were stable with respect to the meaning attached to a DDC number. This was called "integrity of numbers." The editor for Edition 14 was fired upon its publication. When his assistant (who had worked with the apostles of Melvil Dewey) was passed over, he quit. There was now no one on the scene who knew the DDC editorially. Thus was apostolic succession riven, and the stage set for the debacle whose destructive effects are still felt in the Dewey world–indeed, in librarianship.

Edition 15–both Schedules and Index–was prepared by amateurs. Integrity of numbers was forgotten in the avalanche of change (and reduction) that took place in what was to have been the Standard Edition of the DDC. The furor over and rejection of Edition 15 were so widespread that the DDC's owner (Forest Press, a division of the Lake Placid Education Foundation) was forced to redo the Index and issue a revised 15th edition. (At the Library of Congress where DDC numbers were provided for LC cards by the Decimal Classification Section it was decided that both Edition 15 and Edition 14 numbers would be supplied for items in those topics where the editions differed.) The cost of the revised edition and the mismanagement of finances during the 1940s brought Forest Press to the unhappy situation of having insufficient funds to pay for the development, printing, and publication of Edition 16.

To the rescue came the Library of Congress, who agreed to appoint an editor (to be paid by Forest Press) and to see to it that future editions would be developed. The first person appointed to oversee editorial operations was David Haykin. Because he advocated keeping pace with knowledge (which would destroy integrity of numbers), he was forced from the editorship by the two advisory committees responsible for protecting the interests of DDC users during the development of Edition 16. Ben Custer replaced him in 1956. Performing a splendid juggling act to maintain the old and provide the new, Custer produced Edition 16 in 1958–for which efforts he deservedly earned the Melvil Dewey Medal. As a firm bond to Edition 14 had been made in the casting of Edition 16, librarians (a conservative lot by nature and duty) were pleased with the present and confident of the future. This brings us now to the preparation and publication of Edition 17.

EDITION 17

An excess of success curses future efforts by lulling those who enjoy such success into believing errors in efforts to be made are as unlikely as they are unwelcome. Custer decided (no doubt by the prompting of his assistant editors, or at least with their collusion) that intellectual rigor needed to be imposed upon the rickety intellectual structure of the DDC. He decided further that the Index was not to be used for arriving at a DDC number expeditiously or, too often, at all. No, DDC users would have to dig in either the Index or the Schedules or both to arrive at a proper number. Upon hearing of Custer's new Index (in which one would have to look under Dancing *to begin to find* a number for the Waltz), Carlyle Frarey, an Editorial Policy Committee (EPC) member (the Committee advised Forest Press on the reasonability of the efforts of the DDC editors), remarked that it would now be easier to enforce the dictum never to classify from the Index. When users came to use the new Index, they were not amused; some were furious. In a review the head cataloger of a large public library wrote:

> To me, the Index, in which the editors obviously take a great deal of pride, is one of the most infuriating weaknesses of Dewey 17. It seems to be designed not only to prevent the slothful from attempting to use it to class a book directly but effectively to discourage anyone from using it at all.[1]

Another reviewer went further:

> This index is time-wasting, and a caricature of Dewey's formidable achievement. Of the 15th edition, John Metcalfe said that "Dewey now needs to be saved more from his editors than his enemies." The same statement is true of the 17th edition.[2]

The editorial office was furious with Olding's conclusion, all the more because it was true. The negative reception to the Index was so great that (as it did for Edition 15) Forest Press issued free an expensive revised Index based upon the style of the highly successful Edition 16 Index.

Was anything else amiss with Edition 17? Unfortunately, yes.

(1) The new Introduction was decidedly murky (and would continue to be so through Edition 19).
(2) The basis of organization that permeated the Classification–organize by discipline or field of study–was good in itself when not carried to extremes or applied wrongheadedly, as it was here and continues to be until this very day. For instance, in Edition 20 the writing style of business letters was relocated from business correspondence (651.75) to literary composition (808.066651). This perversion began in Edition 17, and is now almost complete.
(3) The first divisional phoenix (complete recasting of an XX0 class) ever produced was for 150 Psychology; it had not been

done well–less than a decade later many librarians called for an extensive revision of the division. This was the first in an unbroken string of misbegotten recastings of major fields of study, recastings that discouraged technical services staff and disserved the public through the confusion wrought.

(4) Rigorous structure required the use of multiple zeros for standard and other subdivisions; this made for long numbers, which set American librarians (no matter how enamored they are of size) to grumbling and thoughts of defection.

Can anything good be said of Edition 17? Actually, not much. The one new device that made the lot of classifiers considerably easier was the provision of an auxiliary table for geographical places. In the past if one wanted to append place to a topic, one had to go to the history numbers for places, extract the meaningful digits from the history number, and append them to the base number of the main topic. For instance, if one had a travel book on Canada, resort had to be made to the history number for Canada (971) from which the meaningful digits for Canada (71) had to be extracted and then appended to the base number for geography (91), thus providing 917.1 for a travel book on Canada. This was called "divide like." Edition 17 provided for synthesis an auxiliary table whose numbers could be appended to whatever base number. It was clever, useful, and appreciated, and a harbinger of auxiliary tables to come.

To sum up the nature of Edition 17: theoreticians loved it; many who had to use it were not so affectionate–some were disgusted and a few were repulsed.

EDITION 18

In 1968 Deo Colburn, who had run the financial affairs for the Lake Placid Club and Forest Press for many years, was replaced by Richard Sealock. Here began the professionalization of Forest Press that in varying emphases has continued to this day.

Edition 18 appeared in 1971. In the flush era when formal education and libraries were considered to be more closely linked than they are now seen to be, the DDC sold well. Almost half of its sales went to foreign buyers. Still, all was not well with the Classification.

(1) The Index returned for the most part to the style that had failed in Edition 17. This time, however, little criticism of the Index was made public. In fact, since the furor of Edition 17, relatively little substantial criticism of the DDC has been aired. Whether librarians have concluded that their words go unheeded or whether once-vocal librarians have decided to vote with their feet and march to the Library of Congress Classification cannot be determined for certain; the silence is certainly unnerving to the DDC producers, however. (Conversion to LCC began seriously after the publication of Edition 15. It may have abated since then, but it has never died away. In 1951 more than half of all college libraries and a sprinkling of universities used the DDC. By 1974 half of all college libraries and a few universities used the DDC. By 1985 one-fourth of all college libraries and still fewer universities used the DDC. As for public libraries, whose allegiance to the DDC was almost universal at mid-century, now several large systems and their satellites use the LCC–Baltimore, Buffalo, Chicago, Cleveland, and Minneapolis among them. During the same four decades foreign use of the DDC increased, and officially recognized translations or adaptations were made into Arabic, French, Italian, and Spanish.) One EPC member did a study comparing Edition 17's second Index to Edition 18's Index. It showed that it took Edition 18 Index users 25 percent longer to succeed half as well as users of Edition 17's second index. The results did not deter either the Editor from providing, the EPC from recommending, or Forest Press from publishing an equally feckless Index for Edition 19. A survey of OCLC libraries in Wisconsin elicited the comment that Edition 19's Index was "the most expensive useless volume" known to him. (He may have said "the most useless expensive volume"; either way is apt.) This is about the best of the succinct critiques of the Edition 17-19 indexes.

(2) The two phoenixes for Edition 18 (340 Law and 510 Mathematics) were botched for different reasons: the first for an absence of nerve, the second for an abundance of ignorance. When the citation order was to be mandated for law, Custer

asked British and American librarians which of two citation
orders they preferred:

(a)   34 + topic + jurisdiction
      That is, 34   law
                5.6   criminal law/evidence
             0973   United States
      = 345.60973.

(b)   34 + jurisdiction + topic
      That is, 34   law
                7.3   United States
              056   criminal law/evidence
      = 347.3056.

The first gathered law by topic, and would not need a jurisdiction indicated for the favored country, state, province, county,
or city. The second gathered all of the law of a jurisdiction to
one place–a good practice, perhaps, in libraries that gather the
law of many jurisdictions. The vote was split down the middle
(one wonders why British opinion weighed as heavily as U.S.
opinion, but not for long), so Custer cut the baby in half,
thereby frustrating both women claiming the child. That is:

    34 + branch of law + jurisdiction + topic
     34   law
       5   criminal law
         .73   United States
           0   place holder
              6   evidence.
    = 345.7306.

Of course, no one was happy with this Byzantine solution.
(The British eventually used Option B from Edition 19 that
permitted their preferred citation order. The U.S. preferred
citation order has never been given as an option at all, even

though the oversight and cavalier treatment of U.S. opinion was called to the attention of the Editorial Policy Committee.) The first draft of the phoenix for 510 Mathematics was met by gentle, and not so gentle, ridicule at the hands of American mathematicians. A modified draft–one not much better than the first–was not reviewed by the same mathematicians, nor by anyone else, but it was published in Edition 18 nevertheless. It was promptly savaged by Australian mathematicians. Its structural problems have not been addressed to this day, however. A few howlers, such as indexing Turing machines to economics and engineering numbers and providing a number for Solid trigonometry, have been removed in Edition 20.

On the plus side, the continued development of the auxiliary tables (1-standard subdivisions; 2-places and individual persons; 3-literature and works about it; 4-language; 5-racial, ethnic, and national groups; 6-languages; and 7-persons as groups) made life a little easier for classifiers. Edition 18 was easier to use than Edition 17. Theorists and reviewers generally admired it; those who had to use it had considerably less approbation.

In 1974 an extensive survey was made of the use of the DDC in the United States and Canada.[3] Four innovations were to grow from the survey: (1) a new introduction; (2) a new index; (3) a manual; and (4) DDC workshops. But these lay in the future and depended upon the arrival of an editor more heedful of the complaints and solicitous of the needs of the DDC's public. Custer was of the sink-or-swim school of classification. He believed that the DDC structure itself provided all the buoyancy an intelligent, assiduous classifier needed. He objected to the production of a manual for users, an index that indicated directly a broad range of frequently sought topics à la Melvil Dewey. Some librarians and many theoreticians (especially British) agreed with his moral stance. The present Editor did not agree then nor does he now with such a stance; the idea that less help produces more learning is counter to the experience of our race.

In 1977 Richard Sealock, who had firmed up and formalized relations between Forest Press (the owner of the DDC) and the Library of Congress (whose Decimal Classification Division produced the contents of the DDC) and had in Edition 18 fashioned one of the most elegant of DDC editions, was replaced by John Humphry (the New York State Librarian). During Humphry's tenure (1977-1985) he encouraged, developed, and cemented many international relationships that have helped to propel the DDC to its preeminence on the classification scene. He oversaw the Italian and Arabic translations (the entire remaining stock of the latter is–or was–stored in Kuwait City), and developed a worldwide network of agents to distribute the DDC.

EDITION 19

Edition 19 appeared in 1979. Its Index has already been commented on. The phoenix for 324 Political process was the first not to have to suffer adverse criticism. The phoenix for 301-307 Sociology raised a storm of protest from those inimical to the unequal treatment of the sexes that the schedule presented and from those inimical to skeleton phoenixes for muscular bodies of literature. The vociferous criticism prompted an expanded 301-307 that was published in 1982. It was covered in pink and eventually embraced with a rare affection.

The 1980s and a new Editor (John Comaromi) arrived at the same time. He promptly saw to it that two of the desiderata exposed by the 1974 Survey were met:

(1) The *Manual on the Use of the Dewey Decimal Classification: Edition 19* was published in 1982.[4]
(2) During the early 1980s, Comaromi gave over 50 all-day workshops to more than a thousand catalogers in all corners of the U.S. and in Toronto, Ottawa, and Vancouver, Canada.

The 1980s saw a revolution and a diminution in DDC affairs. The revolution came via the development of the online Editorial Support System (with Inforonics, Inc.) that would enable the editors to produce the print tapes for Edition 20. (Edition 19 had been produced by computerized photocomposition, but everything had been keyed in by an outside contractor, which made the database not amendable to editorial manipulation.) Karen Markey used tapes in the Council on Library Resources study to evaluate online subject retrieval. Her seminal work has produced a battery of useful articles and further studies by her.[5] It was hoped that the tapes would be made available to the public at an early date, but the absence of a MARC format for classification data (now available) and other computing considerations delayed their distribution. The diminution came in 1988 when the Lake Placid Education Foundation (Forest Press's parent organization) sold the copyrights of the DDC to OCLC (Online Computer Library Center), thus removing the salutary freedom of action that the Press had enjoyed for six decades. But, then, the absorption of a library classification by a bibliographic utility may turn out to be a liaison beneficial to both parties.

In 1985 John Humphry stepped down. His successor at the New York State Library succeeded him at the Press. (Melvil Dewey was also a New York state librarian. The Greeks may have had a word for such a hiring pattern; I cannot think of one.) Peter Paulson's appointment was proven to be as beneficial to the DDC as those of his predecessors. He maintained all the professional publishing expertise and international contacts established by Sealock and Humphry even as he publicized the DDC in the United States more fully and adeptly than heretofore, set more DDC publications in the works than heretofore, and established for the first time educational programs for DDC users in need of them.

EDITION 20

Edition 20 appeared in 1989. Its Index was better than that of Edition 19; but it still fell far short of fulfilling the frequently expressed desire to have Library of Congress subject headings keyed to DDC numbers, it still indexed thousands of schedule terms that are topics in no one's book, and it still did not index thousands of terms that librarians look for. To its credit, however, it can be said that the Index has 10 percent more numbers in 60 percent of the space. Moreover, no one gets the "cross-reference-runaround" (that is, one does not get the entry Waltz see Dance [or Dancing] that fouled the pages of the indexes to Editions 17 through 19). One now reads Waltz form for the music and Waltzes for the dance. The public must be happy with such indexing assistance. But they should be less happy with the form of entry. That is, the LCSH form of these topics are Waltz for the dance and Waltzes for the music, much more appropriate forms of entry. Edition 13's [the last edition prepared fully by the apostolic editors] entries for them are

Waltz   music composition
            piano music
Waltzing   amusements
            ethics.

(The last suggests that the editors would have been amazed at the propinquity of today's dance partners. One should note that linguistic eccentricities haunt the DDC Index to this very day, and will probably continue to do so.)

The major phoenix of Edition 20 (a minor one was done for British Columbia T2-711) was done for 780 Music. The Decimal Classification Division applies the DDC to monographs or sets that are music or on music. Recordings are not classed. Unbound scores and parts are not classed. Because of the lack of both experience in classing works of music and a body of cataloging records that contain a DDC number for each item, it was felt that the editors could not devise a phoenix for 780. No one, other than the British, was calling for one; but that call was enough to lead Forest Press to contract with several British librarians to produce a phoenix for 780. A provisional form of it was published in 1981, and supposedly tested. Criticism of it led to the form found in Edition 20. Praise for the phoenix has been spotty; criticism of it has not. Here are a few comments from American librarians that were gathered for a survey to assist in the planning of Edition 21:

> Bring back the DDC19th 780s. This number building is not necessary and it makes the numbers too long. (We go to six digits beyond the decimal so important numbers get chopped off.)

> Need provision for 1 piano 4 hands and 2 pianos 8 hands. Also the treatment of vocal music is inconsistent with that of instrumental music with regard to scores vs. treatises. Also, we do not like the use of facet indicators.

The recent changes did not solve the problem of "folk vs. popular" or "vocal vs instrumental."

Music! The new idea makes sense, but excessively long numbers are formed for common simple items [such as songs].

I detest rev. 780. It may be fine for specialized music libraries, but is a pain for general libraries. I hope that if 700-770 is revised, regular DDC number building will be followed, not the bizarre and complex number building of 780. Also hope standardized and understandable terminology will be used, not terminology for specialists only.

Regarding DDC 20, it has been disastrous for us in the 780s. Patrons can make no sense of that entire collection now. It just shows that these major revampings do not do any good unless you have the funds to recatalog the entire collection. What is meant to be clarification becomes confusion. The complaint I had concerning the movement of the opera production books to 792.5–just plain stupid and silly. Put them back in the 780s.

The revision of the 780s was too drastic. Our public services librarians and patrons do not understand the necessity of all the needless changes. And why did we allow the British to dictate our Music needs?

780s: Complete revision has given us a fascinating intellectual construct, a less chauvinistic way of dividing the universe of music . . . and a practical disaster. Already we have books on rock intershelving with the operas. I cannot believe it was truly necessary to do such violence in 782-785, so that orchestra music has been bulldozed into the space formerly occupied by secular vocal music, to name only the most reprehensible example of many. This is urban renewal using atom bombs.

Stability is of greater value in a library classification than present-day revisers evidently believe. I do not want to discard all my old music collection: there are books and scores 30 years old that are as useful as much of what I will buy this year. I do not see any likelihood of getting much of it reclassified; my library has never done that, and its technical services division is shrinking. Even to classify new purchases *consistently* in either old or new numbers is unlikely: economic pressures force administrations to look for cheaper cataloging, not better cataloging, and no one has the time to make sure the Dewey number found on OCLC is from a particular edition, much less to change it if it is not. The result I foresee is complete chaos in large parts of the 780s in about 5 years, building to a peak of confusion around 2005, with lingering effects for the rest of my life. The alleged benefits of the new classification will not truly be realized in this library (nor, I suspect), in most others for at least a quarter century.

What's done is done. I can only plead for **NO MORE COMPLETE REVISIONS!** At least keep the whole numbers the same.

To which may be added the gist of two conversations the Editor had with two head catalogers: The first worked at a large university library and moaned that the 780 phoenix would probably force the library to convert to the Library of Congress Classification; the second worked at a *large* county system in California and asked when we were going to revise the phoenix as no librarian in the branches wanted to use it.

The last two comments on the 780 phoenix dealt primarily with the policy of having phoenixes at all. The Editor neither participated in nor has seen evidence of any discussion of any policy of revision other than that supporting the destructive path of the phoenix. His present view can be seen in the first paragraph of a document he recnetly wrote:

Of making many phoenixes there seems to be no end. Our American public and I agree that they should be halted. The very idea of phoenixing seems to me to have been embraced without a sufficient regard for the disruptive results that each entails, or the expensive result where one is not accepted, or without considering other ways to have continual revision. Wherever revision is needed (admittedly in many places in the Classification), *gradualism* would have been a better policy . . . that is, revise on all fronts that need it, but do so slowly, to the end that both librarians and the public can handle with aplomb the vibrations that set their intellectual order to shaking. Do not toss an entire discipline in the air only to reassemble its parts into a new but dubious structure (which seems to have been the case in Editions 17-20).

Unfortunately, the Editor's view is not shared by the other members of the party that produce the DDC. The pleading of the DDC's public for no more phoenixes is likely to be disregarded as it has been for the past quarter century.

Can anything good be said about Edition 20? Yes.

(1) The rewritten Introduction has met with almost universal approval and high praise. One cataloging teacher admonished the Press not to touch it for Edition 21. (This was a third desideratum of the 1974 Survey.)

(2) The inclusion of the Manual and its general quality earned high marks (more than a few catalogers and the Editor himself consider the 1982 Manual to have been better–and in many places more useful still than the present Manual). Especially highly regarded are the maps, flowcharts, and the this-number-vs.-that-number notes. One respondent to the planning survey wrote: "Probably the best approach to intelligent classification in print. It should be used as a text in schools of library science."

(3) The note system has been beefed up by the inclusion of many notes from the 1982 Manual, strengthened by the see-also references, and made approachable through the editors' desire to have the DDC used consistently and well.

(4) Although not a part of Edition 20 itself, a great effort to provide instruction on the use of the new edition has been made, and will continue to be made.

DDC IN USE

Not only is the DDC developed at the Library of Congress, it is also applied more intensively and extensively than anywhere in the world. The number of *titles* receiving DDC numbers for the years 1965-1990 are listed in Table 12.1.

TABLE 12.1. Number of Titles Receiving DDC Numbers at the Library of Congress for the Years 1965-1990.

	1965	21,497
	1966	25,565
	1967	46,087
	1968	71,641
	1969	74,366
	1970	73,525
	1971	68,132
	1972	80,462
	1973	84,474
	1974	90,739
	1975	100,302
	1976	94,020
	1977	100,797
	1978	104,721
	1979	120,678
	1980	116,543
	1981	101,974
	1982	101,297
	1983	117,535
	1984	123,439
	1985	123,719
	1986	114,709
	1987	102,854
	1988	102,414
	1989	103,128
	1990	109,237
Total	26 years	2,373,855

Forest Press and the DDC editors have produced works other than the full and abridged editions of the DDC and their updating serial *DC&: Decimal Classification Additions, Notes and Decisions.* The chronological list in Table 12.2 may convey to the reader the sense of assistance that the Press is attempting to provide.

To return to the opening question of this essay: Why are Editions 17 and 20 philosophically dissimilar? (It may take a suspension of

TABLE 12.2

1967	Classification for small Spanish libraries
1968	Introduction to the Dewey Decimal Classification for British Schools (2nd ed.)
1974	French translation
1975	Survey of the Use of the Dewey Decimal Classification in the United States and Canada
1976	The Eighteen Editions of the Dewey Decimal Classification (a history)
1977	Introduction to the Dewey Decimal Classification for British Schools (3rd ed.)
1980	Spanish translation
	Proposed Revision of 780 Music
1982	301-307 Sociology: Expanded Version Based on Edition 19 Manual on the Use of the Dewey Decimal Classification: Edition 19
1983	Melvil Dewey: The Man and the Classification
1984	Arabic translation
1985	004-006 Data Processing and Computer Science and Changes in Related Disciplines: Revision of Edition 19
1986	Dewey Decimal Classification for School Libraries (British and International ed.): revision and expansion of the Introduction to the Dewey Decimal Classification for British Schools
1988	Italian translation
1989	Dewey Decimal Classification 200 Religion Class: Reprinted from Edition 20 of the DDC; with a Revised and Expanded Index, and Manual Notes from Edition 20
1990	*DC&: Additions, Notes and Decisions.* 5: no. 1- Beginning in the later issues of volume 4, *DC&* began to contain letters to the editor accompanied by responses from the Decimal Classification Division and articles on the condition and application of the Classification. These features are continued in volume 5. Joining them is a feature styled "Editors' Choice" that contains classification assistance for DDC classifiers.
1991	Educational packages

disbelief to consider them as being dissimilar.) Their editors differed as to the extent and means of providing assistance to classifiers. Individuals make a difference here as anywhere, for good or ill.

REFERENCE NOTES

1. Frances Hinton, (Review of the Dewey Decimal Classification), *Library Resources & Technical Services* 10 (Summer 1966) 396.

2. R. K. Olding, (Review of the Dewey Decimal Classification), *The Australian Library Journal* 14 (December 1965): 207.

3. John P. Comaromi, Mary Ellen Michael, and Janet Bloom, *A Survey of the Use of the Dewey Decimal Classification in the United States and Canada* (Albany, NY: Forest Press, 1975).

4. John P. Comaromi and Margaret J. Warren, *Manual on the Use of the Dewey Decimal Classification: Edition 19* (Albany, NY: Forest Press, 1982).

5. Karen Markey and A. N. Demeyer, *Dewey Decimal Classification Online Project: Evaluation of a Library Schedule and Index Integrated into the Subject Searching Capabilities of an Online Catalog: Final Report to the Council on Library Resources* (Dublin, OH: OCLC, 1986).

PART VI:
INDEXING

Chapter 13

Indexing, in Theory and Practice

Marie A. Kascus

"There is no greater literary sin than the omission of an Index, and if I had my way, even novels would be provided with charts of this kind to their multifarious contents."

E.B. Osborn, *Literature and Life*

"And in such indexes, although small pricks to their subsequent volumes, there is seen the baby figure of the giant mass of things to come at large."

William Shakespeare, *Troilus and Cressida*

"An index can suggest life's incongruities with a concision the most powerful biographer will have trouble matching. . . . As for the author's own pleasures, there are few keener than seeing the index of his book. It hardly matters how fleeting are the appearances of some of the indexed terms in the text of the book he has written. How learned the author feels just seeing those hundreds of alphabetical subjects and names, and how organized, as if someone had finally gone into his brain and– all for the gentle reader's sake–put those heaps of clutter into a gleaming row of file cabinets."

Thomas Mallon, *The Best Part of Every Book Comes Last*

INTRODUCTION

Given the length of its history, one might assume that indexing is a well-understood and established field. Ironically, this is not the case. Perceptions of indexing range on a continuum from that of a "quaint and unhurried perversity"[1] to that of "a complex decision process involving perceptual discrimination, concept formation, and problem solving."[2] For Milstead, "cataloging and indexing are conceptually the same activity."[3] For Anderson, "indexing and classification are the same fundamental operation."[4] Others would disagree. While there is no consensus as to the precise relationship of cataloging and classification to indexing, they are viewed as complementary activities. Unlike indexing, however, cataloging and classification are well established and guided by an accepted set of procedures and performance measures.

Despite a long history marked by significant progress, indexing is not well understood. However it is perceived, indexing is clearly a key element in information access and information retrieval and needs to be better understood. The indexing process is a remarkable achievement of distillation from the complete text of a document to the essential concepts that identify the document for efficient retrieval. The process is as relevant for closed systems, such as books, as it is for open systems, such as databases. Despite its failure to achieve broad recognition and its imperfections, indexing, in theory and practice, is a complex analytic process and an important tool for research and scholarship.

The purpose of this chapter is to present a kaleidoscopic overview of indexing through time beginning with a brief discussion of its origins and focusing on some of the major milestones along the way in the development process that have marked progress in the field. Given the dimensions of the task, what follows is a thumbnail sketch of some of the events and people that have impacted the field and brought it to its present level of development through a discussion of: indexing literature, indexers as professionals, professional organizations, the golden age of machine indexing and indexing evaluation, and a view toward the future and what is needed to move the field further along to the next logical stage of development.

INDEXING–EARLY HISTORY

The origin of indexing has been traced back to the existence of manuscripts in the fifth century, but according to Witty, its actual development was limited until after the introduction of printing from movable type in the fifteenth century.[5] Witty's study of indexes in fourteenth century manuscripts and fifteenth century printed books led him to characterize early indexing practice as crude in its use of catchwords from the text and imprecise in its rough alphabetic arrangement. The use of subject headings was limited prior to 1550 and was thought to be an invention of the sixteenth century. According to Witty, these indexes were not much of an intellectual challenge for their makers.

In 1987, Rabnett did a more thorough analysis of the technique of early indexes and corroborated Witty's earlier observation of their crudeness and imprecision.[6] While Witty did not view these early indexes as posing a challenge to their makers, Rabnett noted that these early indexes reflect the technique that was to be improved over time but not essentially changed in terms of selecting concepts and expressing them in the language of the indexing system at hand.[7]

Indexing evolved from indexes to individual works to multiple volume indexes to collective indexes. W. E. Poole is credited with introducing the concept of indexing multiple issues of many periodicals resulting in 1882 in the *Index to Periodical Literature,* a monumental achievement at the time and an inspiration for others to follow.[8] H.W. Wilson's efforts in starting the *Readers Guide to Periodical Literature* in 1901 marked another important milestone in indexing in that each article in the periodicals indexed was listed under author and subject and excellent cross references were provided to link related subjects.

In this early period, indexes were either taken for granted, if they were there, or ignored, if they were not, but they were not looked at analytically or critically. This followed much later.

INDEXING LITERATURE

Indexing history and tradition are well represented in what Wellisch considers the first major work on indexing written in 1879 by H. B. Wheatley entitled, *What Is an Index?*[9] This is a question that is as relevant today as it was when it was posed more than 100 years ago. The substantial literature of indexing is best reflected in the annotated bibliography meticulously compiled by Hans Wellisch entitled, *Indexing and Abstracting: An International Bibliography.* Volume I of this monumental work covers the literature of indexing from 1856-1976,[10] and Volume II covers the literature from 1977-1981.[11] The topics under which the literature is organized provide an indication of the breadth and depth of the literature and the thoroughness of its coverage in this comprehensive bibliography. Among the main topics included are: principles and theory, indexing languages, indexing systems, tests of indexing languages, citation indexes, indexing techniques, index production, indexing specific formats, indexers, indexing as a profession, indexing around the world, history of indexing, and humor in indexing. This bibliography contains over 4,000 entries in the original two volumes with entries arranged in chronological order. The organization of the references makes it possible to examine the evolution of the field in both its intellectual and practical aspects. A current awareness bibliography updating these two volumes has appeared in regular installments in the publication, *The Indexer,* beginning with Volume 15, issue 1 in 1986.[12]

Collison's *Indexes and Indexing*[13] and Knight's *Training in Indexing*[14] are good examples of textbooks on indexing practice for those who want a detailed study of the intricacies of indexing, and they filled a real void in their time for those seeking practical training. Good general textbooks on the subject of indexing are sparse, but the book by Borko and Bernier entitled *Indexing Concepts and Methods*[15] is recognized as the most comprehensive treatment of indexing with a balanced presentation of both the principles and practice of indexing. Craven's *String Indexing* is a good example of the kind of specialty books that have appeared in indexing.[16] Two recent books, Wellisch's *Indexing from A to Z*[17] and Lancaster's *Indexing and Abstracting in Theory and Practice*[18] are welcome additions from two prominent educators and should become classics in the field. Mulvany's *Indexing Books,* is a practical and thorough guide for beginners as well as professionals written by a professional indexer.[19]

The journal literature on indexing is scattered in terms of Bradford's Law with about one-third of all of the literature appearing in a small number of journals directly related to the topic, about one-third appearing in journals related but not mainly on the topic, and the remaining one-third scattered throughout a larger group of journals not related to the topic.[20] Some of the most interesting work has appeared in the overlap with information science involving indexing problems in information retrieval and has appeared in such journals as *American Documentation, Journal of the American Society for Information Science, Journal of Documentation,* and *ASLIB Proceedings.* Other good sources of indexing scholarship are *Library Quarterly, Drexel Library Quarterly,* and *Special Libraries.*

One English language title that deals exclusively with the topic is *The Indexer* published jointly by the British, American, Australian, and Canadian Societies of Indexers. *The Indexer* has a broad following with subscribers in 52 countries, so it is obviously serving a need. The journal itself is an interesting curiosity. A sample of recent issues includes articles on English-language dictionaries, the business side of indexing, the oldest index in existence, the latest in indexing software, natural language processing and automatic indexing, and why indexes fail searchers. A feature section includes reviews of praised indexes and censured indexes as well as news of general interest to indexers. The articles tend to be practical in nature rather than research oriented. While its original focus was on book indexes, *The Indexer* has broadened this focus in recent times to include the application of indexing principles in general and mechanical and technical developments in the field.

A useful source of information on current developments in the field is the *Newsletter of the American Society of Indexers* which has recently changed its title to *Key Words.* The newsletter began publication in 1970 and provides professional indexers with a forum for exchanging ideas and keeping current in the field. A regular feature of interest is "The Electronic Shoebox" which includes announcements and reviews of new software to help indexers with the mechanical aspects of indexing.

Doctoral dissertations on indexing have continued to bring research to bear on specific indexing problems and have contributed to the growing knowledge base. A recent check of *Dissertation Abstracts International* provided a count of 43 doctoral dissertations on indexing in the Library and Information Science field. About one third of these dissertations were completed in the last decade. Good examples are Artandi's *Book Indexing by Computer,*[21] Weinberg's *Word Frequency and Automatic Indexing,*[22] and Dykstra's *The Structured Encoding of Document Contents: A Logico-Linguistic Study of PRECIS as a Possible Model in the Shift from Indexing to Automatic Text Analysis.*[23]

What is most readily evident in scanning the literature of indexing is the imbalance between the abundance of practical descriptions on the intricacies of indexing, and the sparsity of empirical studies that are important to the further development of indexing as a science.

INDEXING AS A PROFESSION

As a profession, indexing is not widely recognized. In part, this relates back to how indexing has evolved through the years. G. Norman Knight indicates that prior to the formation of the Society of Indexers in 1957, he had been indexing books and periodicals for over 30 years and "he had never met and did not know the name of a single other person in this field."[24] For those immersed in it, indexing is clearly an intellectually challenging activity. For the uninitiated, indexing is perceived to be a narrow and arcane specialty. Some see indexing as so simple that anyone, including a machine, can do it. Others recognize that it is so complex, that it has yet to be reduced to an algorithm for machine processing. A sense of the complexity of indexing was nicely articulated in a recent article in *Byte*. According to the author, "the dark side of document image processing is the question of retrieval; indexing documents properly and consistently for later retrieval isn't a low-order clerical task, but a complicated exercise that requires knowledge engineering."[25]

As professionals, indexers are not widely recognized. In discussing indexers as a group, Dorothy Thomas provides a useful profile that includes three broad categories of individuals. The largest category consists of independent contractors and free-lancers, many of whom are subject experts in a particular field; the second largest group are salaried individuals including trained librarians, who specialize in indexing for hard copy or databases; and the third category are educators, who contribute the fewest indexes but who teach, conduct research, and prepare the other two categories of individuals to put theory into practice.[26] Since indexing operated largely as a cottage industry with individuals working independently, indexers remained isolated as a group and had no formal means of exchanging ideas until the formation of professional organizations for that purpose.

PROFESSIONAL INDEXING ORGANIZATIONS

Professional organizations are a comparatively recent phenomenon given the long history of indexing and indexers. These organizations provided a formal mechanism for indexers to exchange ideas on the issues that challenged them. The British Society of Indexers was founded in 1957 in Great Britain by G. Norman Knight, and its American counterpart, the American Society of Indexers, was founded more than a decade later in 1969 with inspiration from Theodore C. Hines.[27]

These professional organizations played an important role in the development and improvement of indexing practice. Prior to the establishment of these professional organizations, the availability of training and education in indexing was limited. With the establishment of these organizations came a greater awareness of indexing as a knowledge base, and courses began to appear under the auspices of these professional organizations as well as at various university library schools. In the early years, there were just a few such courses, but Thomas notes that by the twentieth anniversary of the American Society of Indexers in 1988, there were 50 academic courses available throughout the country.[28] The importance of curriculum development cannot be overstated, since it gave recognition to indexing as a knowledge base and encouraged the solidification of the knowledge base by educators who could test theories and conduct experiments to strengthen the science and improve the practice of indexing.

The American Society of Indexers uses a variety of means to reach a broad spectrum of individuals involved in indexing activities. These include training and continuing education opportunities, the encouragement of local chapters, and various publications such as standards and guidelines, information on becoming an indexer, a register of indexers, a directory of indexing courses, and a bi-monthly newsletter. ASI sponsors an annual conference in different locations throughout the country, and, in 1988, published the proceedings of that conference in a volume entitled, *Indexing: The State of Our Knowledge and the State of Our Ignorance.*[29]

The growth of the American Society of Indexers from 257 members in 1970 to over 700 members in 1988 attests to steady progress in professionalizing indexing and providing a support system for indexers.[30] While the increase in membership in ASI attests to its growing viability as an organization, it is probably fair to say that there are still more people involved in indexing activities than are reflected in the membership figures of the ASI.

The American Society of Indexers began its work entirely on a volunteer basis, and its strength has been a cadre of capable and dedicated individuals who have generously contributed their time and talent in serving the organization and the profession. In an effort to better achieve its goals, ASI has begun to formalize its organizational structure through the establishment of a national headquarters with a paid professional staff to manage the organization on a permanent basis. This has enabled ASI to take a giant leap forward in centralizing and coordinating the important work of the organization, thereby contributing significantly to advancing indexing as a profession.

These professional organizations have been instrumental in establishing awards to recognize the work of indexers. The British Society established the Wheatley Medal to honor its first recipient, Henry Wheatley, in 1962. In 1978, at the request of the American Society of Indexers, the H. W. Wilson Company created an American award comparable to the Wheatley Medal with a citation and a cash award to the indexer and a citation to the publisher of the index. The first recipient of the H. W. Wilson award was Hans H. Wellisch in 1979 for *The Conversion of Scripts: Its Nature, History, and Utilization.*[31]

INDEXING SOFTWARE

Indexing practice has progressed from indexing out of a shoebox, to indexing on a floppy disk, to indexing on a hard disk. Indexes have progressed from handwritten, to typewritten, to computer transmitted via modem directly to the publisher. Microcomputer programs such as MACREX, CINDEX, and INMAGIC to name a few, are helping indexers with the mechanical aspects of indexing and freeing them up to concentrate on the intellectual aspects. With the proliferation of new indexing software, there is a need for comparative information in deciding what software works best for the indexing task at hand. Linda Fetters prepared a guide to seven indexing programs including Bookdex, Newdex, The Index Editor, and MACREX.[32] Much change has taken place in the area of indexing programs since that initial article. The fourth edition of *A Guide to Indexing Software* is available from the American Society of Indexers.[33]

The availability of inexpensive microcomputers and the emergence of a variety of indexing software packages on the market have advanced the practice of indexing significantly in terms of facilitating the mechanical work of sorting and organizing entries. They open up a whole range of new possibilities for indexers in the future.

THE GOLDEN YEARS OF MACHINE INDEXING AND EVALUATION

Three events in the twentieth century combined to give indexing a significant boost forward in its development. The first was the exponential growth of the literature and the need for improved access to information by scholars and researchers in the scientific fields. The second was the advent of the computer which gave promise as a tool to provide better and faster access to information and ushered in the period of machine indexing. The third was the experience applied from the emerging field of information science with its emphasis on mathematical models and empirical testing. This combination of factors set the stage for an intense period of creative activity directed at analyzing indexing and retrieval systems using mathematical models and establishing performance criteria that could be used to evaluate indexing systems.[34] The information explosion in science provided the need to improve access and retrieval, the computer provided the tool to manipulate large volumes of data, and the information science field provided the impetus and the methodology to evaluate indexing and retrieval systems.

This transitional period with its intense intellectual activity can be characterized as a golden age in indexing. The work of H. P. Luhn in the early 1950s is particularly significant. Salton credits Luhn with recognizing the potential of computers for information retrieval and introducing the idea of machine indexing using the computer to do the mechanical work of matching and sorting key-words as well as the intellectual work of analyzing the content of a document.[35] Luhn's methodology involved term weighting based on the frequency and placement of words in the text and resulted in KWIC (Keyword-In-Context) indexes. Luhn actually made a dis-tinction between what he called a dissemination index, that would be generated by machine quickly and easily, and a retrieval index, that would be thoughtfully and thoroughly prepared. For Luhn, "machine products could never reach the level of perfection of which humans are capable," but he saw a need and a purpose for such indexes and took the lead in exploring the ways in which the computer could best serve the indexing process.[36]

Another early application of the computer to the task of indexing was the work of Eugene Garfield in 1959. Capitalizing on the strengths of the computer as a tool in manipulating the large volume of data resulting from the information explosion in science, Gar-field created citation indexes.[37] Garfield described a citation index as an association-of-ideas index providing an ordered list of cited articles, each of which is accompanied by a list of citing articles.[38] While Garfield did not originate the idea, he took excellent advan-tage of the computer's ability to quickly and easily manipulate large volumes of data. With the increased habit of citation during this time, citation indexes provided a tool for quantitative study and an interesting means of communicating and evaluating information.

The influence from the emerging discipline of information sci-ence is clear. Much of the stimulus for evaluating indexing systems during this period came from the information science field which heavily emphasized empirical testing and quantitative measures. The Cranfield projects, under the leadership of Cyril Cleverdon, are especially noteworthy because of the significant body of literature they generated and their implications for evaluating indexing systems. The Cranfield projects are regarded as landmark experiments in indexing evaluation. These projects ushered in a period of intense experimentation and research that raised consciousness about the complexity of the indexing process and its importance in efficient and effective retrieval. In Cranfield I, Cleverdon compared four indexing languages (Universal Decimal Classification, faceted classification, coordinate indexing uniterms, and alphabetic subject headings) using a database of 18,000 and 1,200 subject searches, and reported no significant difference among the four indexing languages with each operating at the same level of recall performance retrieving 80 percent of the known relevant documents.[39] In Cranfield II, Cleverdon continued his work testing various index language devices in isolation and in combination to measure their impact on performance.[40] The Cranfield experiments represent the first significant use of recall and precision to evaluate the performance of indexing systems. Cleverdon acknowledged the contribution of Karen Sparck Jones, whose research documented the symbiotic relationship between the exhaustivity of indexing and the specificity (precision) of the indexing language.[41]

The Cranfield projects, and the plethora of experiments inspired by them, represent an exciting and important period in the dialogue and debate on the problems and complexities inherent in establishing factors that could be universally used to evaluate indexing systems. Of the many similar experiments in evaluating indexing systems undertaken during this time, the one thing that they shared in common was the use of various mathematical models. As exciting and important as these experiments were in their implications for indexing, they were not without their critics. The experiments involved different index languages, file sizes, sources of questions, and primary performance measures causing others, such as Bourne, to conclude that these differences would make it difficult to make meaningful generalizations about the various indexing systems involved.[42]

Swanson and others criticized the test design of the Cranfield experiments as well as the incorrect interpretations of the Cranfield data. Swanson's research led him to conclude that "consistently effective fully automatic indexing and retrieval is not possible" because the intellectual problem of meaning is not reducible to a rule-based algorithm for machine processing.[43] Experiments using computers in book indexing led others, such as Borko,[44] and Kochen and Tagliacozzo,[45] to conclude that fully automated indexing was not possible.

Lancaster's criticism of Cranfield revolved around his concern that recall and relevance were not intrinsically meaningful and, therefore, could not be used to compare the performance of other systems with different documents, requests, and user requirements.[46]

Fairthorne's simple, yet insightful observation, that "to test is not to evaluate" adds a basic but important dimension to the discussion and debate precipitated by these early efforts in analyzing indexing and establishing the factors that could be generalized and applied universally to the evaluation of indexing systems.[47]

The importance of this experimental work in indexing evaluation begun in the 1950s and 1960s cannot be overstated. However, while much was accomplished during this period, more questions were raised than answers provided. What became clear is the lack of a solid theoretical base for indexing and the urgent need for one in order for further progress to take place in the field.

In the early 1970s Masse Bloomfield continued the discussion on indexing evaluation, directed at finding a "rational basis for indexing and some means to evaluate it," in a five part series on evaluation in indexing in *Special Libraries*.[48] Based on his review of the indexing evaluation literature, including the Cranfield experiments, Bloomfield determined that it was necessary to examine indexing apart from the retrieval system as a whole in order to obtain a theoretical understanding of the indexing process. Bloomfield made a careful distinction between indexing for machines, for machine searching, and indexing for printed indexes, for human searching, which he felt had become blurred in the literature and caused some to draw inappropriate conclusions about the latter.[49]

In the search for a theoretical basis for indexing, Bloomfield offers six characteristics of subject indexes. Bloomfield's characteristics are (1) breadth of vocabulary (number of different index terms in the subject index); (2) depth of indexing (number of index terms assigned to a document to describe its contents); (3) use of general or specific terms; (4) use of "see" and "see also" references; (5) indexing format; and (6) inclusion of titles or other qualifying phrases.[50] Of the six characteristics, Bloomfield stated that only three could be compared quantitatively (1,2,4), and the others (3,5,6) were capable of subjective evaluation only. He further stipulated that each characteristic would have to be evaluated separately and a weighting formula developed to arrive at a complete picture.

Artandi's indexing characteristics, while established in the context of searching, are similar to those of Bloomfield. Artandi's characteristics are "specificity and size of the index language, the network of relationships that exist between terms, the exhaustivity of the indexing, and the arrangement and physical characteristics of the file."[51]

For Lipetz, there are two concepts that define and shape the field of indexing: "the nature of indexes and the usefulness of indexes."[52] Lipetz sees the nature of indexes as the complex of decisions that have to be made as to what to include, how much to include, and how to include it with usefulness integrally related to the nature of indexes. According to Lipetz, both concepts require empirical data to establish what works most effectively and what use is made of indexes.

For Lancaster, performance evaluation for indexing is measured from the perspective of the user in terms of coverage of the literature, recall ratio (ability to yield relevant literature), precision ratio (amount of effort required to discover relevant literature), and a novelty factor (ability to uncover relevant references unknown to the user).[53] On the practical side, Lancaster emphasized the importance of vocabulary control in indexing consistency as a way of bringing the language of the indexer into coincidence with the language of the searcher.[54]

The experimental work in machine indexing and the evaluation of indexing and retrieval systems begun in the 1950s and 1960s marks the beginning stages in an ongoing movement to find a rational theoretical basis for indexing and a methodology for comparison in differentiating good indexing from bad indexing. Separating the art, from the craft, from the science is important. In this context, Lipetz sees indexing as meeting the requirements for a mainstream science with progress coming first from the field and basic theory or broad understanding developing later and often leading to further refinements of practice and to new applications.[55]

The indexing field has had a long history and has experienced a dramatic growth as a result of the impact of machine processing and computer technology. Yet, despite its long history and increased breadth and depth as a field, indexing is not well understood. The lack of a generally accepted theoretical base weakens it as a science and makes it difficult to reach any consensus on what are the essential criteria to be used in measuring performance. The theory and practice of indexing need to be brought into coincidence, so that they inform, enrich, and stimulate each other. More work needs to be done on the theoretical side to establish a generally accepted set of principles of indexing that can guide future progress in the field.

A VIEW TO THE FUTURE

New challenges for indexing and indexers are not difficult to find. Online Public Access Catalogs (OPACs) and electronic journals are two cases in point. The rapid proliferation of OPACs has raised concerns as to how best to comparatively evaluate them. For Chitty, the solution is found in indexing. In an article on "Indexing in the Online Catalog," Chitty states that "the online public access catalog (OPAC) is fundamentally an indexing application," and, as such, the OPAC can be analyzed in terms of the kind of indexes constructed and the way in which the indexes are searched.[56] The theory and practice of indexing are here applied to the evaluation of OPAC design. The electronic journal, in itself a challenge in bibliographic control, was the forum for an interesting discussion on the importance of indexing electronic journals. In the June 25, 1991 issue of the electronic publication, *Newsletter on Serials Pricing,* concern was expressed about the need to index electronic journals in order for them to be a viable publishing force in the future.[57] The dual issues of how to index and who would do the indexing brought some interesting responses from those on the electronic network. Resolving these issues poses new challenges and opportunities for today's indexers. Along with the challenges come new opportunities for indexers to share ideas and to exchange information over the

Internet on the list Index-L, the Indexer's Discussion Group (IN-DEX-L@BINGVMB).

Machines have clearly stimulated and positively influenced the development of indexing and will continue to impact the field in the future, but they remain an aid to the process and not a substitute for it. The hope and expectation for the future is that artificial intelligence and expert systems, which capture human intelligence within the computer system, could alter the present dynamic, increasing our understanding of the indexing process and significantly advancing the theory and practice of indexing. Artificial intelligence and expert systems are well poised to inspire the next golden age of indexing, but the final outcome remains uncertain.

APPENDIX

INDEX

A systematic guide to items contained in, or concepts derived from, a collection. These items or derived concepts are represented by entries in a known or stated searchable order, such as alphabetical, chronological, or numerical.

INDEXING

The process of analyzing the informational content of records of knowledge and expressing informational content in the language of the indexing system. It involves: 1) selecting indexable concepts in a document; and 2) expressing these concepts in the language of the indexing system (as index entries); and an ordered list.

INDEXING SYSTEM

The set of prescribed procedures (manual and/or machine) for organizing the contents of records of knowledge for purposes of retrieval and dissemination.

Definitions from *ANSI 1968 Basic Criteria for Indexes Z39.4[58]

*The Standard for Indexes is currently undergoing revision and the revised standard should be published soon: ANSI-NISO Z39.4-199X

REFERENCE NOTES

1. Mark Rabnett. "The First Printed Indexes: A Study of Indexing Techniques in Some Incunabula." *Cataloging and Classification Quarterly.* Vol. 2, No. 3/4 (1982): p. 101.

2. Harold Borko and Charles Bernier. *Indexing Concepts and Methods.* New York: Academic Press, 1978. p. 214.

3. Jessica Milstead. "Indexing for Subject Catalogers." *Cataloging and Classification Quarterly.* Vol. 3, No. 4 (1983): p. 37.

4. James D. Anderson. "Indexing and Classification: File Organization and Display in Information Retrieval" in *Indexing: The State of Our Knowledge and the State of Our Ignorance, ed. B. Weinberg.* New York: Learned Information, Inc., 1989. p. 71.

5. Francis J. Witty. "Early Indexing Techniques: A Study of Several Book Indexes of the Fourteenth, Fifteenth, and Early Sixteenth Centuries." *Library Quarterly.* Vol. 35, No. 3 (July 1965): p. 148.

6. Rabnett, "The First Printed Indexes," p. 87.

7. Ibid.

8. Robert L. Collison. *Indexes and Indexing.* 3d rev. ed. London: Ernest Benn Limited, 1969. p. 18.

9. Henry B. Wheatley. *What Is an Index? A Few Notes on Indexes and Indexers.* 2d ed. London: Society of Indexers, 1879.

10. Hans H. Wellisch. *Indexing and Abstracting: A Guide to International Sources.* Santa Barbara, CA: ABC-Clio Press, 1980.

11. Hans H. Wellisch. *Indexing and Abstracting 1977-1981: An International Bibliography.* Santa Barbara, CA: ABC-Clio Information Services, 1984.

12. Hans H. Wellisch. "Indexing and Abstracting: A Current-Awareness Bibliography Part 1" *Indexer.* Vol.15, No.1 (April 1986): pp. 29-35.

13. See note 8 above.

14. G. Norman Knight, ed. *Training in Indexing: A Course of the Society of Indexers.* Cambridge, MA: M.I.T. Press, 1969.

15. See note 2 above.

16. Timothy C. Craven. *String Indexing.* Orlando, FL: Academic Press, 1986.

17. Hans H. Wellisch. *Indexing from A to Z.* New York: H. W. Wilson, 1991.

18. F. W. Lancaster. *Indexing and Abstracting in Theory and Practice.* Champaign, IL: Graduate School of Library and Information Science, 1991.

19. Nancy C. Mulvany. *Indexing Books.* Chicago and London: University of Chicago Press, 1994.

20. Hans H. Wellisch. "The Literature of Indexing" in *Indexing: The State of Our Knowledge and the State of Our Ignorance, ed. B. Weinberg, Medford, NJ:* Learned Information, Inc., 1989, p. 3.

21. Susan Artandi. *Book Indexing by Computer,* PhD dissertation, Rutgers-The State University, New Brunswick, New Jersey, 1963.

22. Bella Hass Weinberg. *Word Frequency and Automatic Indexing,* PhD dissertation, Columbia University, New York, 1981.

23. Mary Dykstra. *The Structured Encoding of Document Contents: A Logico-Linguistic Study of PRECIS as a Possible Model in the Shift From Indexing to Automatic Text Analysis,* PhD dissertation, University of Sheffield, 1986.

24. Knight, *Training in Indexing,* p. 6.

25. Christopher Locke. "The Dark Side of DIP." *Byte* Vol.16, No.4 (April 1991): pp. 193-204.

26. Dorothy Thomas. "Book Indexing Principles and Standards." in *Indexing: The State of our Knowledge and the State of Our Ignorance,* ed. B. Weinberg, Medford, NJ: Learned Information, Inc., 1989. pp. 123-124.

27. Borko and Bernier, *Indexing Concepts,* p. 222.

28. Thomas, "Book Indexing Principles and Standards," p. 125.

29. Bella Hass Weinberg, ed. *Indexing: The State of Our Knowledge and the State of Our Ignorance.* Proceedings of the 20th Annual Meeting of the American Society of Indexers, New York City, 1988. Medford, New Jersey: Learned Information, Inc., 1989.

30. Thomas, "Book Indexing Principles and Standards," p. 123.

31. Thomas, "Book Indexing Principles and Standards," p. 129.

32. Linda Fetters. "A Guide to Seven Indexing Programs Plus a Review of the Professional Bibliographic Style." *Database.* Vol. 8, No. 4 (December 1985): pp. 31-38.

33. Linda Fetters. *A Guide to Indexing Software.* 4th. ed. Washington, DC: American Society of Indexers, 1992.

34. Charles P. Bourne. "Evaluation of Indexing Systems." in *Annual Review of Information Science and Technology,* ed. C. Cuadra. Washington, DC: American Documentation Institute, Vol.1 (1966): p. 171.

35. Gerard Salton. "Historical Note: The Past Thirty Years in Information Retrieval." *Journal of the American Society for Information Science.* Vol. 38, No. 5 (September 1987): p. 376.

36. H. P. Luhn. "Keyword-in-context Index for Technical Literature (KWIC Index)." *American Documentation.* Vol. 11, No. 4 (October 1960): p. 295.

37. Eugene Garfield. "Citation Indexes for Science." *Science.* Vol. 122, No. 3159 (July 15, 1955): pp. 108-111.

38. Eugene Garfield. "Science Citation Index-A New Dimension in Indexing." *Science.* Vol. 144, No. 3619 (May 8, 1964): p. 650.

39. Cyril Cleverdon. "The ASLIB Research Project on the Comparative Efficiency of Indexing Systems." *ASLIB Proceedings.* Vol. 12, No. 12 (December 1960): pp. 421-431.

40. Cyril Cleverdon. "Cranfield Tests on Index Language Devices." *ASLIB Proceedings.* Vol.19, No. 12 (December 1967): pp. 608- 620.

41. Cyril Cleverdon. "Review of the Origins and Development of Research." *ASLIB Proceedings.* Vol. 22, No. 11 (November 1970): p. 545.

42. Bourne, "Evaluation of Indexing Systems," p. 180.

43. Don R. Swanson. "Historical Note: Information Retrieval and the Future of an Illusion." *Journal of the American Society for Information Science.* Vol. 39, No .2 (March 1988): p. 95.

44. Harold Borko. "Experiments in Book Indexing By Computer." *Information Storage and Retrieval.* Vol. 6 (May 1970): pp. 5-16.

45. Manfred Kochen and Renata Tagliacozzo. "Book Indexes as Building Blocks for a Cumulative Index." *American Documentation.* Vol. 17, No. 2 (April 1967): p. 59.

46. F. W. Lancaster. *Information Retrieval Systems: Characteristics, Testing, and Evaluation.* New York: Wiley, 1968: p. 130.

47. Robert A. Fairthorne. "Some Basic Comments on Retrieval Testing." *Journal of Documentation.* Vol. 21 (December 1965): pp. 267-270.

48. Masse Bloomfield. "Evaluation of Indexing 1. Introduction." *Special Libraries.* Vol. 61, No. 8 (October 1970): p. 429.

49. Masse Bloomfield. "Evaluation of Indexing 5. Discussion and Summary." *Special Libraries.* Vol. 62, No.2 (February 1971): p. 99.

50. Bloomfield, p. 97.

51. Susan Artandi. "The Searchers-Links Between Inquirers and Indexes. *Special Libraries.* Vol. 57, No. 8 (October 1966): p. 572.

52. Ben-Ami Lipetz. "The Usefulness of Indexes." in *Indexing: The State of our Knowledge and the State of Our Ignorance,* ed. B. Weinberg, Medford, NJ: Learned Information, Inc., 1989. p. 113.

53. F. W. Lancaster. "The Evaluation of Published Indexes and Abstract Journals." *Bulletin of the Medical Library Association.* Vol. 59 (July 1971): p. 481.

54. Lancaster, "Information Retrieval Systems," p. 8.

55. Lipetz. "The Usefulness of Indexes," p. 112.

56. A. B. Chitty. "Indexing for the Online Catalog." *Information Technology and Libraries.* Vol. 6, No. 4 (December 1987): p. 297.

57. Marcia Tuttle. *Newsletter on Serials Pricing Issues.* n.s., No. 4 (June 25).

58. American National Standards Institute. *Basic Criteria for Indexes.* New York: ANSI, 1968. Z39.4-1968.

Chapter 14

Some Post-War Developments in Indexing in Great Britain

Mary Piggott

DEFINITION

The term "index" has no precise definition. From the Latin for "informer" or "pointing finger," it has been used to designate any label, list, table, or catalog that enables a thing to be identified and/or a reference to be located. It has been applied in libraries to lists that facilitate access to collections (or to catalogs of collections) through author, title, and subject designations, and in bibliographies similarly to lead to entries and groups of entries. As an adjunct to a published text an index provides help in locating subjects written about and references cited within that text. Published on its own, or more frequently together with abstracts, an index pinpoints and locates specific articles and topics that have appeared in a variety of publications.

There is no limit to the elaboration of an index except that dictated by common sense. If an index becomes too complicated to use as the means of easy identification of a subject and access to its location, it ceases to be informative and hence to be an index.

For the purpose of this article, indexing has been considered in two of its functions. The first is that of naming the general subject of a document more precisely than the use of traditional subject headings allows and locating either the document, or its further description. The second is that of naming specific topics within a document, or a number of documents, and indicating their location.

THE QUEST FOR INFORMATION

During the war of 1939-1945 the need for speedier access to detailed information and subsequently the development of computers to store and retrieve identified items of information led to a worldwide interest in the study of "information" as such and in its identification and presentation, particularly in the form of a precise statement of subject and location–that is, of indexing. Textbooks such as Brian Vickery's described for a wider audience the various methods of identifying, coding, and retrieving information in use,[1,2] or, like Robert Collison's, gave detailed instruction for compiling indexes.[3] The comparative efficiency of four indexing systems was evaluated for recall and relevance, specificity and exhaustivity, in an experiment set up in 1957 at the College of Aeronautics at Cranfield by C. W. Cleverdon.[4] The experiment and its methodology gave rise to considerable discussion.[5,6] A series of conferences arranged by Aslib (The Association for Information Management) has brought specialists in language, psychology, and computer science together with practicing librarians, abstracters, and other information providers to discuss the nature of information, the requirements and search behavior of users, and the technology of advanced information retrieval. Begun in 1973, the series had reached its eleventh conference by 1991.[7] Similar topics were discussed in the *Journal of Informatics.*[8]

LOGICAL ANALYSIS

In Great Britain, especially, while the rough and ready usefulness of verbal manipulation provided by such systems as KWIC indexing was appreciated, logical classification was seen as the essential basis for subject indexing. The Classification Research Group (CRG), founded in 1952, having worked for some time on the problems of a general classification scheme, turned its attention to ways of formulating a precise statement of the content of a document.[9] (The group continues to meet and from time to time publishes a bulletin recording its activities.)[10] One member of the group, J. E. L. Farradane, divided items of knowledge into *isolates,* individual entities expressed in uniquely definable terms, and *operators,* the relations between the isolates. His operators were *appurtenance, equivalence, reaction, dimensional (time and space), comparison, association,* and *concurrence.* All subjects, he said, could be analyzed by assigning them to those categories of isolates and operators. By using symbols for the operators, such an analysis could be expressed in linear form producing what he termed an *analet.*[11]

The *British National Bibliography (BNB),* whose classifiers had been founder-members of the CRG, played its part in systematizing indexing. From its inception in 1951 until 1971 the classified bibliography used chain indexing as the means of locating entries dealing with particular topics. Exemplified by Dewey and elaborated by Ranganathan, chain indexing was not systematized for general use until the monthly examples in the *BNB* found their way into library catalogs and its methodology became the subject of books and articles and a part of library school curricula. The chief arbiter of chain procedure was E. J. Coates, who was then responsible for subject cataloging in the BNB.[12]

Briefly, chain procedure provides a term to name the specific subject of a class mark that has been assigned to a document, and qualifies that term by a series of terms naming successive broader classes in the same hierarchy until the subject and its context are unequivocally stated, thus creating a horizontal chain. To satisfy alternative approaches that look for a more comprehensive term, each successive broader class is named and appears as the lead word in its own horizontal chain (pointing to a location in the classified sequence from where the searcher can follow the subdivisions until the required subject is found), and thus, by discarding a link (representing a class) at each entry, a vertical chain is formed. Thus a book on parasites infesting cattle appears in the index under its specific designation, and is also findable through more comprehensive terms, via the following chain-link entries, dispersed, of course, alphabetically among the other index entries:

Parasites	:	Diseases	: Cattle	636.2089696
Diseases	:	Cattle		636.20896
Veterinary medicine				636.2089

Cattle	:	Livestock	636.2
Livestock	:	Agriculture	636

At the top of the entry in the classified sequence, the specific subject appears in the form:

636.2089	Veterinary medicine
636.20896	Diseases
636.2089696	Parasites

Obviously, editorial rules were required to compensate for the irregularities of the classification scheme and also to present the terms consistently and acceptably.

When plans were being made for fully automated production of the *BNB,* a system of indexing was devised that should take full advantage of the computer's capacity to manipulate input data and produce a succinct statement of the content of a document under a number of lead terms, or entry words.[13] Whereas successive chain index entries had allowed for only a single entry that expressed the specific subject of a document, PRECIS, the new system devised by Derek Austin, allowed a summary statement of the subject to appear in the index under a variety of lead terms, elaborated as required–hence the name, derived from its description: PREserved Context Index System.

The system depends upon the analysis of a subject into a number of abstract categories and their interrelationships–the first division being into entity and activity, and then, as required, into object, agent, part, attribute, geographical location, viewpoint, etc. A "string" of terms names the entities and activities, and their relationships are indicated by a code of symbols, "role operators." Terms required by the indexer to be printed as lead terms are indicated as such, and the computer interprets the codified symbols to ensure that no matter what the lead term is, elements from the original string shall appear, either as qualifiers of the term or as a second-line "display." Prepositions are changed where necessary to keep a grammatical structure. The following example is taken from Austin's manual .[14]

Rivers

Pollution by industrial chemicals

Pollution. Rivers

By industrial chemicals

Chemicals

Industrial chemicals. Pollution of rivers

Industrial chemicals

Pollution of rivers

What was virtually a brief indicative abstract provided by the PRECIS string–and so much valued by users of the printed *BNB*– has been replaced since January 1991 by a simplified version designed both to speed up cataloging in the British Library and to recognize that increasingly access to bibliographic information will be through online catalogs rather than through printed media. The new system, COMPASS (COMPuter Aided Subject System), while keeping certain features of PRECIS, such as context dependency and role operators, relies on elements of the complete record displayed on the screen to fill out the subject information.[15,16]

THESAURI

With the use of rigid classification came the need for consistently defined terms. An early model of a controlled vocabulary that combined a faceted classification with prescribed terminology was Jean Aitchison's *Thesaurofacet* for engineering and related subjects.[17] Jean Aitchison also assisted in the compilation of other specialist classifications-cum-thesauri, including a *Thesaurus on Youth* and schemes for UNESCO and for the Department of Health and Social Security.[18-20] In collaboration with Alan Gilchrist she also produced a manual of thesaurus construction.[21] More generalized guides to thesaurus construction have come from the British Standards Institution.[22,23]

The Institution of Electrical Engineers (a pioneer of standardization) has produced exemplary aids for compiling and searching its printed abstracting journals and its computer searchable database for information in Physics, Electronics, and Computers. Cumulative indexes, both author and subject, covering four-year periods dating from 1957, are available for all INSPEC abstracting journals. The *INSPEC Thesaurus,* supplemented by the *INSPEC Classification,* provides an example of the care taken to guide the user by printing an abundance of "lead-ins," or cross-references, and by noting the date on which a term was first used and also any term(s) superseded by the addition of a new term.[24, 25]

A thesaurus in another field has been specially created for the compilation and use of a new printed index to legal journals.[26,27] The index–in fact, separate indexes for subjects, authors, cases, legislation, and book reviews–uses an average of three keywords drawn from the thesaurus per article. The keywords are cited in alphabetical order and rotated so that each term becomes an entry word.[28]

Most thesauri cover restricted areas of knowledge. A wide-ranging thesaurus, though still biased by the nature of the literature it controls, is that prepared within the British Standards Institution (BSI) for international use to give access to the immense range of published standards emanating from standardizing bodies all over the world–the ROOT thesaurus.[29]

Thesauri compiled in Great Britain are held by the Aslib library which aims to collect all thesauri that are published in the United Kingdom. New additions are noted in *Aslib Information,* and a complete list of holdings, including overseas publications held, is in preparation.

Naturally the choice of preferred terms in a thesaurus must depend on a consensus of usage, where that exists, and many glossaries have been compiled by interested bodies, notably by committees convened by the British Standards Institution, on such diverse topics as bibliography, coffee, and quality control. BSI has also published a guide for the selection, formation, and definition of technical terms.[30]

ONLINE INDEXING SERVICES

Thesauri are, of course, only a means to an end, assisting the arrangement of documents and access to them in libraries, or, like the *INSPEC Thesaurus,* serving as guides to compiling and using both printed and online abstracting and indexing services. The latest edition of J. Stephens's inventory of such services in the United Kingdom (1986) listed 430 abstracting and indexing services covering documentary material published as journals, printed lists or cards, in microform, or in machine-readable form.[31] Many more guides, mostly to sources of information on specialist subjects, have since been published, and Aslib's *Directory of Information Sources in the UK* now lists 5,500 organizations, including, of course, those that provide indexing and abstracting services.[32]

Many of the online services now available developed from the initiative of single persons or institutions. *Current Technology Index (CTI),* for example, available since 1981 for online searching through DIALOG, goes back to 1915 when the *Subject Index to Periodicals,* compiled by cooperative efforts was first published by the Library Association to mitigate the loss of *Poole's Index.* In 1962 the *Subject Index* split into *British Humanities Index* and *British Technology Index,* the latter changing to its present title in 1981 to reflect the universal nature of its sources. In 1987 *British Humanities Index* lost some of its social sciences coverage to *Applied Social Sciences Index and Abstracts (ASSIA),* available online through DATA-Star.[33-35]

British Technology Index used a highly sophisticated form of chain indexing developed by E. J. Coates. In this version, Coates used a number of categories for concept analysis, such as thing, kind, part, property, action, instrument, with a fixed citation order and a system of references that allowed alternative access and ensured collocation of related entries.[36] *ASSIA* index entries, designed from the beginning for computer manipulation, are closely akin in their methodology to those used in *CTI.* Publication of the *ASSIA* thesaurus is expected in 1992.

Similarly, *Library and Information Science Abstracts (LISA)* began in 1950 with contributions from a team of enthusiasts coordinated by Muriel and Reginal Lock.[37] H. A. Whatley edited succeeding volumes until 1969 when the word "information" insinuated itself (as it was doing everywhere) into the original title of *Library Science Abstracts,* and professional production, under the editorship of Tom Edwards (now editor of *CTI*), was deemed necessary to ensure adequate coverage, timeliness, and consistent indexing. The abstracts are arranged according to the classification for library science devised by the Classification Research Group, to which a name index and a subject index using chain procedure give access. Reflecting its universal coverage, *LISA* now has an international editorial board. It is available on CD-ROM and via DIALOG.

Around 1970, people who needed up-to-date and collated information about government publications were vigorously expressing dissatisfaction with the need to search several published indexes–somewhat erratic indexes at that–for Her Majesty's Stationery Office (HMSO) publications. They were troubled also by the risk of missing altogether official documents increasingly being published by the issuing departments themselves or even by other bodies.[38] A number of unofficial guides were produced to improve access to certain categories of publication, such as Stephen Richard's index of committee chairmen[39] and Chadwyck-Healey's index to official publications not put out by HMSO,[40] but pressure remained for a centralized database, now clearly warranted by advancements in communications technology. The improved technology led to the conversion of the detailed indexing system that had been developed in the House of Commons library to the computerized database POLIS (Parliamentary Online Information System), available not only at several stations within the Parliament buildings but also to external subscribers.[41,42] POLIS gives access to all papers originating within Parliament together with related documents emanating from outside sources. Thesauri list names of individuals and corporate bodies and titles of publications and also the controlled vocabulary used for assigning subject terms. For searching the database, descriptors may be chosen from the printed thesaurus or from a display on the screen.[43]

BRITISH STANDARDS

At the beginning of the period under review, the British Standards Institution showed little interest in documentation: there were a few published recommendations on making references, on transliteration, and on alphabetical arrangement. By the end of the period, BSI committees were concerned with many of the intellectual aspects of information technology, in addition to specifications for physical media such as legibility of typographical characters and the conservation of documents. Three sets of recommendations highly pertinent to indexing give instructions on: (1) determining which topics presented in a document should be chosen for entry in an index;[44] (2) the choice, form, and setting-out of index terms and their overall arrangement;[45] (3) the detailed arrangement of letters, words, numbers, and symbols.[46] BSI glossaries and recommendations for the construction of thesauri have already been mentioned. They are all shown in a frequently updated list–*Some Documentation Standards*–available from BSI.

Faced with the mammoth task of indexing its own publication BS 1000M *(Universal Decimal Classification International Medium Edition. English text)*, BSI rejected its own recommendations and preferred to derive its alphabetical index by computer-manipulation of the machine-readable file of the schedules, generating a vast number of entries which make few concessions to the user (who must know his classification scheme) but which will be hospitable to emendations in updated editions.[47]

AUTOMATIC INDEXING

Meanwhile the search continues for the techniques of automatic indexing and intelligent retrieval that will minimize human intervention in computerized indexing and so speed up the creation of indexes to books and within databases and finally eliminate the need for human intermediaries between the machine and the enquirer. The experiments in parsing methods and semantic analysis are particularly interesting.[48-50] The Informatics conferences have made important contributions in this area.[51]

Karen Sparck Jones, of the Cambridge Language Unit, who has done a considerable amount of work on automatic indexing, wrote in 1983, "It is evident that the uncertainty characteristic of search systems, deriving from the fact that they are language-dependent access systems to complex information sources, makes for real challenges in any attempt to apply expert systems (or indeed other state-of-the-art artificial intelligence) technology to search interface building."[52] Seven years later, while noting the upgrading of information retrieval techniques to provide more direct access to the information itself rather than to a bibliographic reference, Kevin Jones comments, "It would seem that much of what has been attempted so far in computational linguistics is either too complex or too restricted. A much more pragmatic approach is probably needed."[53]

At present it appears that the most satisfying indexes are still made by human indexers. They may be considerably helped by software such as the MACREX Indexing Program. This program, invented by Hilary and Drusilla Calvert, allows automatic sorting and merging of entries, the checking of references, layout for the printer, and the display of collected entries containing common elements and also of the whole index in its progressive stages of growth.[54,55] Indexers who use microcomputers can keep in touch with each other and learn of recent developments through the Society of Indexers' occasional newsletter *Microindexer.*

THE SOCIETY OF INDEXERS

How different, indeed, is the current situation from the situation 30-odd years ago, when a book indexer of longstanding declared that he was not acquainted with a single other person who worked in the field of indexing! That lonely indexer, G. Norman Knight, convened a meeting in 1957 at which 60 other lonely indexers formed themselves into a society with the objects of improving the standard of indexing, supplying publishers with competent indexers, and improving the standing of indexers themselves. The Society of Indexers lost no time in issuing its own journal, *The Indexer,*[56] arranging training courses and conferences, and offering publishers the names of experienced indexers. Subsequently the Society welcomed as affiliated members the American and Australian Societies of Indexers (founded respectively in 1968 and 1976) and the Indexing and Abstracting Society of Canada (founded in 1977), and continues to welcome members of the affiliated societies in person at conferences and also as contributors to *The Indexer.*

In addition to articles in the journal, members of the society have published textbooks, notably those of Collison[57] and Norman Knight,[58,59] and have also prepared a series of training manuals for individual study, leading, after a demonstration of the student's competence, to the qualifications of Accreditation and Registration.[60] Those qualifications are indicated in the list *Indexers available* circulated annually to publishers and editors. Some members of the Society have also compiled prestigious indexes, but to name examples would be invidious, as has been, perforce, through lack of space, the selection of named individuals and publications earlier in this article.

The Wheatley Medal

The responsibility of publishers to publish good indexes as well as of indexers to compile them is recognized in the annual award of the Library Association Wheatley Medal for an outstanding index first published in the United Kingdom during the preceding three years. Selection of the winner is made by a joint panel consisting of members of the Library Association and The Society of Indexers, with the first medal awarded in 1962.

Full Circle?

The medal commemorates Henry B. Wheatley, himself a great indexer and founder, in 1878, of the Index Society–unfortunately short-lived, "having failed," said Wheatley, "from want of popular support. This want of permanent success was probably owing to its aim being too general."[61] In fact, the aim was quite different from that of the present Society of Indexers, stemming from proposals for a society to work together toward the creation of vast general indexes–a vision perhaps taking shape again as databases grow and efforts are made to facilitate interaction between them.

REFERENCE NOTES

1. B. C. Vickery, *Classification and Indexing in Science,* 2nd ed. (London: Butterworths, 1959).

2. B. C. Vickery, *Techniques of Information Retrieval* (London: Butterworths, 1970).

3. Robert L. Collison, *Indexes and Indexing,* 4th rev. ed. (London: Benn, 1972).

4. Aslib/Cranfield Research Project, *Report on the Testing and Analysis of an Investigation into the Comparative Efficiency of Indexing Systems,* by Cyril W. Cleverdon (Cranfield: [College of Aeronautics], 1962).

5. C. W. Cleverdon, "The Cranfield Tests on Index Language Devices," *Aslib Proceedings* 19 (1967): 173-194.

6. C. W. Cleverdon, "Evaluation Tests of Information Retrieval Systems," *Journal of Documentation* 26 (1970): 55-67.

7. *INFORMATICS (Conferences. Proceedings)* 1, 1973- (London: Aslib, 1974-) (*Informatics 4,* 1976, is available only in *Journal of Informatics* 1, no. 1 & 2 (1977).

8. *Journal of Informatics* 1-3, 1977-1979. (London: University College London, 1977-79).

9. D. J. Foskett, "The Classification Research Group, 1952-1962," *Libri* 12 (1962): 127-138.

10. Classification Research Group, "Bulletin No. 12," *Journal of Documentation* 41 (1985): 75-99.

11. J. E. L. Farradane, "A Scientific Theory of Classification and Indexing," *Journal of Documentation* 6 (1950): 83-99 and 8 (June 1952): 73-92.

12. E. J. Coates, *Subject Catalogues: Headings and Structure* (London: Library Association, 1960; Reissued 1988), 99-148.

13. Derek Austin, "Progress in Documentation: The Development of PRECIS: A Theoretical and Technical History," *Journal of Documentation* 30 (1974): 47-102.

14. Derek Austin, *PRECIS: A Manual of Concept Analysis and Subject Indexing,* 2d ed. (London: British Library, 1984; first pub. 1974), 135.

15. "The New British Library Subject System" *Select: National Bibliographic Service Newsletter* 1 (June/July 1990): 3-4.

16. Neil Wilson, "COMPASS: News from the Front," *Select: National Bibliographic Service Newsletter* 4 (Summer 1991).

17. *Thesaurofacet, a Thesaurus and Faceted Classification for Engineering and Related Subjects,* comp. Jean Aitchison (and others) (Whetstone, Leics: English Electric Co., 1969).

18. Jean Aitchison (and others), *Thesaurus on Youth: An Integrated Classification and Thesaurus on Youth Affairs and Related Topics* (Leicester: National Youth Bureau, 1981).

19. Jean Aitchison, *UNESCO Thesaurus: A Structured List of Descriptors for Indexing and Retrieving Literature in the Fields of Education, Science, and Social Sciences, Culture and Communication* (Paris: UNESCO, 1977), 2v.

20. Jean Aitchison, Paul Brewin, and Joanna Cotten, *DHSS/DATA Thesaurus* (London: Department of Health and Social Security, 1985).

21. Jean Aitchison and Alan Gilchrist, *Thesaurus Construction,* 2d ed. (London: Aslib, 1987).

22. British Standards Institution, *Guide to Establishment and Development of Monolingual Thesauri* (London: B. S. I., 1987). BS5723:1987.

23. British Standards Institution, *Guide to the Establishment and Development of Multilingual Thesauri* (London: B.S.I., 1985). BS6723:1985.

24. *INSPEC Thesaurus* (Stevenage, Herts: Institution of Electrical Engineers, 1993). First ed. 1973.

25. *INSPEC Classification* (Stevenage, Herts: Institution of Electrical Engineers, 1991).

26. *Legal Journals Index* (Hebden Bridge: Legal Information Resources, 1986-).

27. Nigel Smith and Christine Miskin, *A Legal Thesaurus* (Hebden Bridge: Legal Information Resources, 1987).

28. Nigel Smith, "Indexing Legal Journals," *Law Librarian* 20 (1989): 1-6.

29. *ROOT Thesaurus* (Prepared in the British Standards Institution) 3d ed. (Milton Keynes: B.S.I., 1988), 2v. (Vol. 1 classified display, vol. 2 alphabetical list.)

30. British Standards Institution, *Recommendations for the Selection, Formation and Definition of Technical Terms* (London: B.S.I., 1982). BS 3669: 1963 (1982).

31. J. Stephens, *Inventory of Abstracting and Indexing Services Produced in the United Kingdom,* 3d ed. (London: British Library, 1986). British Library Information Guide 2. Updates previous editions of 1978 and 1983.

32. *Directory of Information Sources in the UK*, 6th ed. by Ellen Codlin (London: Aslib, 1992), 2v. (Main vol. and Index vol.)

33. *British Humanities Index* (London: Library Association, 1915- . From 1990 pub. by Bowker-Saur).

34. *Current Technology Index* (London: L.A., 1981- . From 1990 pub. by Bowker-Saur).

35. *Applied Social Sciences Index and Abstracts* (London: L.A., 1987- . From 1990 pub. by Bowker-Saur).

36. E. J. Coates, "Aims and Methods of the *British Technology Index*," *The Indexer* 3 (1963): 146-152.

37. *Library (and Information) Science Abstracts* (London: Library Association, 1950- . From 1990 pub. by Bowker-Saur).

38. Mary Piggott, *The Cataloguer's Way Through AACR2: From Document Receipt to Document Retrieval* (London: Library Association, 1990), 264-267.

39. Stephen Richard, *British Government Publications: An Index to Chairmen and Authors* (London: Library Association, 1974-1984), 4v. covering 1800-1982.

40. *Keyword Index to British Official Publications Not Published by HMSO* (Cambridge: Chadwyck-Healey, 1984-).

41. David Menhennet, "The Library of the House of Commons," *Law Librarian* l, no. 3 (1970):31-34.

42. David Menhennet and Jane Wainwright, "POLIS in Parliament: Computer-Based Retrieval in the House of Commons Library," *Journal of Documentation* 38 (1982): 72-93.

43. Ann Siswell, "POLIS": The Parliamentary Online Information System," *Law Librarian* 17 (1982): 23-26.

44. British Standards Institution, *Recommendations for Examining Documents, Determining Their Subjects and Selecting Indexing Terms* (London: B.S.I., 1984). BS6529. Reissued 1991.

45. British Standards Institution, *Recommendations for Preparing Indexes to Books, Periodicals and Other Documents* (London: B.S.I., 1988). BS 3700.

46. British Standards Institution, *Recommendations for Alphabetical Arrangement and the Filing Order of Numbers and Symbols* (London: B.S.I., 1985). BS1749.

47. *Universal Decimal Classification, International Medium Edition. English Text. Part 2. Alphabetical Subject Index* (London: B.S.I., 1988). BS1000M. Pt 2: 1988.

48. P. Harding, *Automatic Indexing and Classification for Mechanized Information Retrieval* (London: INSPEC, 1982). BL R&D Report 5723.

49. *Automatic Natural Language Parsing,* ed. Karen Sparck Jones and Yorick Wilks (Chichester: Horwood, 1983).

50. C. Korycinski and Alan F. Newell, "Natural Language Processing and Automatic Indexing," *The Indexer* 17 (1990): 21-29.

51. *INFORMATICS (Conferences. Proceedings).*

52. Karen Sparck Jones, "Intelligent Retrieval," in *Informatics* 7, 1983 (London: Aslib, 1984), 141.

53. Kevin P. Jones, "Natural Language Processing and Automatic Indexing: A Reply" [to ref. 50] *The Indexer* 17 (1990): 114.

54. MACREX Indexing Program. Available from Macrex Indexing Services, 38 Rochester Road, London NW1 9JJ and also from Bayside Indexing Service, 265 Arlington Avenue, Kensington, CA, 94707 USA.

55. Drusilla Calvert, "Automatic Indexing," *Stag* 8 (Summer 1991): 15.

56. *The Indexer,* Vol. 1, no. 1 - March 1958 - (London: Society of Indexers, 1958-   ).

57. Collison, *Indexes and Indexing.*

58. G. Norman Knight, *Indexing, the Art of* (London: Allen and Unwin, 1979).

59. *Training in Indexing: A Course of the Society of Indexers,* ed. G. Norman Knight (Cambridge, MA, and London: M.I.T. Press, 1969).

60. *Training in Indexing,* Units 1-5 (London: Society of Indexers, 1988-1991).

61. Henry B. Wheatley, *How to Make an Index* (London: Stock, 1902), 210.

PART VII:
PRESERVATION

Chapter 15

Preservation: A Quarter Century of Growth

William T Henderson

BACKGROUND

For more than 25 years, preservation of library materials has been a growing concern in librarianship in many parts of the world. The comprehension of the problems implicit in the deterioration of the books and other materials in their custody together with the definition of ways by which these problems may be controlled or ameliorated, if not solved outright, has come to occupy a host of individuals. These problems also promise to continue to be prominent concerns in the future. The finite nature of paper library materials together with the multiplicity of interactions both within the finished products and between them and those who use and work with them has given and continues to give librarians, binders, physical scientists, conservators, and many others an extended list of problems all of which cry for solution and all of which have come to be gathered under the heading of preservation.

In 1990 George Cunha[1] sketched the history of the changing emphasis in the preservation of library materials from concern with particular books and documents to concern for and emphasis on whole collections. In the United States there was limited recognition of the problems of disintegrating collections before the appearance of Gordon Williams's report in 1964 recommending a centralized national preservation collection of books to be gathered and maintained under federal auspices.[2] Though Williams's recommendations were never carried to fruition, his statement of the basic problem as it related to books has had wide acceptance and his report continues to be recognized as a major document in the literature of preservation.

It is apparent upon reflection that one reason preservation was not recognized earlier as being as serious and as pervasive as is now the case was the generation-long period of rapid growth both in the size of collections and in the numbers of libraries which began with the end of World War II. This growth masked at least somewhat the effect of the aging of older materials. Librarians were preoccupied by the increase in the size of their collections fostered by the need to keep up with growing user populations, burgeoning staffs, emerging disciplines, and space to accommodate it all. In addition the rapidly expanding population and growing economy seemed to promise unending growth and expansion for academic, public, and other libraries of all types. With all these growth factors still fresh in their experience, it seemed to many librarians that preservation with all its attendant implications appeared to rear itself very suddenly just at a time when it was becoming apparent that the growth period was slowing if not ending. The simultaneous shrinking of purchasing power caused by long-term inflation and an economy no longer expanding at its former rate have made mounting new programs difficult for all and impossible for many at the very time the consciousness of the need for preservation was developing to its present unprecedented level. Despite economic hard times, preservation persists and has gained recognition and adherents as the nature and extent of deterioration in collections has become better understood. Describing or terming preservation as a complex of problems (i.e., using the plural) is intentional as there is wider recognition that paper is influenced by a number of factors, each of which is a problem in itself. Then, too, the field of preservation is broader than books and libraries in that it also includes archives, museums, and historical societies along with other types of organizations and institutions and collections of many kinds of materials. There are a number of interrelationships because paper forms the basis of many of the materials held by and utilized in these institutions. There are other common grounds in that leather, cloth, wood, and metal along with paper are historically important components of artifacts of many types. In our own day, the growth of materials developed by human ingenuity, the plastics and other synthetics used in film, sound recordings, magnetic tapes, and other media and materials all are being recognized as having need of preservation. In each instance it is found that each type of material or medium has its own cluster of preservation needs and problems. Many of the overlappings and interrelationships between and among media materials are obvious and easily recognized while others are more subtle and less obvious to the casual observer. That there are numerous forces acting upon and attacking materials which form the physical items in collections is not always easily discerned. It is heartening to observe rising awareness of the problems involved and increasing activity to observe, describe, and deal with these destructive forces. Research and development continue to result in new techniques, new understandings, and new and differing approaches to the problems. The proliferation of activities within library preservation programs alone illustrates the process. The formulation of disaster prevention and control plans, of staff and user awareness activities, of the monitoring and control of environmental conditions, of reducing ultraviolet radiation, of introducing phased preservation activities, and of other similar program components together with the recognition that preservation is the business of everyone connected with a library (both staff and users) all illustrate the growth of the field, its increasing complexity, and the interrelatedness of its many parts.

There are indications from at least a few quarters that efforts to deal with the problems of books and paper are somewhat more developed than for other materials, such as natural history and biological materials and many kinds of realia.[3] Within archives, libraries, and the fine arts areas in which preservation seems most developed, there remain institutions and collections still relatively untouched by preservation and many areas in which research and development remain to be done to provide basic understanding of particular destructive factors and to solve problems still untouched. However, developments over the last decade are significant. The first of these developments is a general agreement on the nature and extent of both the predominant problems and ways of dealing with them. Second is the advent of programs involving regional, state, and national cooperation in the United States and other parts of the world which are fostering cooperative efforts to find solutions and funding for preservation activities of a variety of kinds at several levels.

FACTORS LEADING TO MATURITY

With a growing recognition of the nature of the problems and with an emerging consensus on ways of dealing with at least some of the major problem areas, preservation has taken on a degree of maturity and achieved a level of recognition among librarians and archivists, and even the general public, which was lacking prior to the 1980s. During that decade three factors which show promise of forming the basis for solutions of several of the more pressing problems began to emerge. These are: (1) the change in manufacturing methods to produce alkaline paper for printing and writing; (2) the introduction of widespread microfilming of brittle and threatened materials; and (3) the development of mass deacidification technology to the point of commercial usefulness.

No one of these developments in itself provides a complete solution to the deterioration of research library collections. Of the three, the now widespread availability and increasing use of alkaline paper is perhaps the most basic. It may eventually mean that those parts of collections originating in the closing years of the twentieth century will have a life expectancy of three to five centuries much as did the products of printing presses in the early days of printing. This promises to be a vast improvement over the much shorter life expectancy of most of the volumes published from the middle of the nineteenth century to the present.

Preservation microfilming, if the present programs are successful, will assure in the U.S. and possibly in other parts of the world as well, a core collection of master film negatives to back up brittle collections on the shelves of research libraries. Microfilming will not replace these volumes, but it will assure the continued availability of their intellectual content. Furthermore, the film has the potential for comparatively easy conversion to digital formats if and when such storage becomes generally accepted, and if the advantages of machine-based use (particularly its concurrent ability to manipulate data) are needed.

The third element, mass deacidification, after more than two decades of development, appears to be on the threshold of becoming a reality. The prospect of a several fold increase in the useful life of still usable, but acidic, books, archives, and other documents is most significant. Along with the use of alkaline paper, mass deacidification gives a new perspective on the future of the book, of repair and conservation work, and of library binding as ways of assuring truly long-term usefulness to books and documents which in the past would have joined the ranks of the embrittled candidates for the microfilm camera. If efforts to strengthen paper as a part of or as an adjunct to deacidification become reality, the way may well be open to preserving massive collections of deteriorated materials in their original formats without recourse to microfilm or other types of reformatting. This also could mean renewed usefulness to materials which are not good candidates for reformatting. Such materials include those things in color or with important halftone illustrations which will not reproduce well on film along with those items in which the paper itself, or the structure of the book or document, are of equal or greater value than the text. Included also in this category are association copies, or materials with intrinsic value or of value deriving from other bases which give the original volume or document importance as an artifact. Items of this sort are already adding to the anxieties of those selecting brittle materials for filming. There is some evidence, at present, of a growing reluctance in the United States to accept the wholesale withdrawal and destruction of volumes even though quite brittle, after they are filmed. This is a major change in attitude from that which prevailed only a short time ago when microfilming was almost wholly thought of as a means of saving the content of newspapers. The rationale for this change in attitude is summed up in Barclay Ogden's *On the Preservation of Books and Documents in Original Form.*[4] It is perhaps premature to contemplate as yet in very great detail the kind of working situation that may prevail when the mass deacidification chambers and the microfilm cameras may be shut down because the great mass of their work is accomplished. Such a condition is not likely for some two to four decades in any but some small and specialized collections; but it will be a time quite different from that which the present generation of the preservation-minded has experienced and will experience for many years yet to come.

Even so, some conjecture on such a future can be informative and perhaps interesting and even exhilarating.

The reformatting of large collections of brittle materials may free space on library shelves for continued growth of the paper collections on long lasting alkaline paper. Also such free space may in some instances permit the remodeling or recycling of buildings to provide really good quarters for the storage and use of microfilm and the new formats which will be coming into ever greater use as the old brittle paper collections are reformatted. Such microform and media centers, with sophisticated environmental controls, lighting designed to aid the user of film reader or monitor, furniture designed for the users of the new media, and staff to service users, media, and equipment could help make the use of microfilm and other alternative formats and media more acceptable and more pleasant than has been the case with the less than ideal work space and unfriendly reading equipment of the past. There is little evidence yet of the development of a perfect microfilm reader but there is evidence that spending one's entire working life with computer keyboard and monitor is not utopia. Eyestrain and physical problems such as carpal tunnel syndrome are all too prevalent indications of some of the results of the changes to the new technologies. In fact the pen-driven computer may prove to be but the latest technological development of what possibly began with a stick in the dust of the earth or a soft rock rubbed on a more solid surface.[5] This may be seen as the rapid completion of a technological cycle when one remembers that in the 1930s those of the generation of the writer were often introduced to pen and ink by way of a steel nib and inkwell! The now ubiquitous ballpoint had a shaky start in the 1940s but by the 1960s had largely replaced both the steel nib and the fountain pen. After the touch screen and mouse, the electronic pen may be something of a surprise.

But this digression has carried us far away from the conclusion of the consideration of permanent alkaline paper, preservation microfilming, and mass deacidification. These three, by first providing long life for new books, by preserving the content of those volumes of the past which are too brittle to survive, and by inducing a measure of chemical stability within older volumes which are still usable before they become embrittled seem to promise a future with a useful if not fully complete written record of the past experience of humanity. With this memory of the common human experience at hand, perhaps the human future can become increasingly humane.

FUTURE NEEDS AND POSSIBILITIES

These developments, however, will not mean the end of the need for preservation of library materials, archives, and other similar collections. In the twenty-first century as in the past, once new books and documents, even those on alkaline paper, will continue to be subjected to wear and tear, accidents, malicious damage and destruction, and the ravages of aging, though this latter factor will be somewhat less catastrophic than in the last 150 years. Repair and rebinding, disaster prevention and control, environmental stability, user awareness campaigns, good shelf maintenance, and many of the other presently accepted preservation activities will continue to be appropriate.

These preservation activities will continue to be needed, but the need for them will at least shift in its emphasis as the nature of the materials changes. Somewhat different kinds and levels of need will come into being because the physical nature of materials will be different as more and more are on stable, long-lasting paper. Repairing, rebinding, and otherwise treating such an item will, of necessity, have to become consistent with the nature of the paper in the document or book. Using conservation materials of similar long-lasting qualities will become mandatory where in the past, with less long-lasting books, it has been advisable or desirable. The new generation of long-lasting books will require repair and treatment with the knowledge and forethought that the repair or rebinding may last as long as the volume and that the longevity of the volume must not be compromised by the repair. High standards and expert work will continue to be in demand in book repair facilities. The ethics and the practical considerations behind this kind of treatment have been worked out already in the application of conservation theory to the formulation of repair and rebinding methods and standards. Their extension to the coming generations of materials on permanent paper will require a degree of refocusing and perhaps some adaptation of practice.

At the same time alkaline books begin to make their presence felt, libraries and other collecting agencies will continue both to receive some materials on unstable acidic paper and be faced with dealing with the unstable portions of their older collections. From both of these groups some materials will be selected for deacidification and some, becoming too brittle for deacidification to be helpful, will continue to go under the microfilm camera. Older collections may undergo repeated screenings for one kind of treatment or another as program emphases change and develop. Procedures for dealing with these groups of materials will be increasingly refined and made routine. In addition, some items from the prealkaline era, both deacidified and not so treated, along with some materials from the alkaline age will gradually find their way into special collections and rare book repositories as their age, scarcity, importance to scholarship, association value, typographic features, and other factors give them value as artifacts. Generally, this complex of collections of core and special materials will continue to gain value and to present their caregivers with increasingly complex problems to solve as the materials exhibit the marks of aging and as their value increases. Rather than reducing, the need for collection maintenance and conservation will grow.

Ancillary to special collections will be collections of copies of the rare and special materials purposely prepared on film, or on paper by photocopy or in modern print editions to serve as surrogates for the originals for the use of lower-level students and scholars and even for the routine use by the specialist in order to protect the originals from as much use as possible. There are intimations of this today in the preparation of use copies of threatened items.

It is possible that as the usefulness of cold storage for stabilizing photographic materials gains recognition, its use in providing an enhanced storage environment for books also may be recognized. Cryogenic storage for especially threatened valuable books appears to be logical and, indeed, it is in use to a limited degree in special refrigerated display and storage cases found in some special collections facilities. Lowering the storage temperature to a subzero level will reduce the innate aging reactions in the components of books to virtually nothing and a cold vault will simultaneously provide ideal security for valuable books and documents. At such time as cold storage gains recognition and comes into use, there will be certain accompanying costs and requirements. Cold storage will be expensive to build and operate, and will require a constant and dependable power supply in a time in which some see the public power supply becoming less dependable than has been the experience in many developed regions during the past half century or more. Because of its expense, such space will be available only for the most valuable and most threatened materials. To achieve the tight pack of materials necessary for efficient use of space, compact shelving will be used and may well have automated mechanical storage equipment to achieve the requisite tight and efficient arrangement of stored items.

Cold storage areas will also require adjacent work areas in which books and documents may be prepared for frozen storage by being sealed in vaporproof pouches in which they may be thawed and acclimatized for use when needed. Because use of items so stored requires special arrangement, the use of surrogates will be recognized increasingly as necessary for many purposes. Quite likely initial reader contact, whether the specialized scholar, the student or casual reader, will be with the surrogate. The original will be kept frozen only to be brought out for the scholar who must examine the paper, details of the printing (or writing, in the case of manuscripts), the niceties of the structure of the volume, and other such recondite matters.

Given the acquisition by a library or archive of freezer space for artifactual storage, it is possible that the presence of such space will bring other artifacts into the freezer. Museums and other units in research-oriented institutions will have a similar need to preserve items of many kinds all of which are at greater risk of degradation and loss at room temperature than if kept cold. Thus the library's frozen book storage may give rise to a center for artifactual storage and use which is multidisciplinary and multimedia; for it may be both more economical and easier to consolidate cold storage in one place in an institution than to build several such units at scattered sites. Be it in the library, alongside the campus frozen food storage plant, in the medical/biological complex or elsewhere, such a center will place library materials and their users in close proximity to other scholars and researchers in such a way that a new kind of multidisciplinary research facility may evolve, one in which those working in apparently widely separated disciplines and with seemingly disparate purposes may discover that they have common interests as well as common needs. From this may come new patterns of interdisciplinary cooperation and sharing, and new and unanticipated patterns of research and study may lead to new knowledge.

CONSIDERATION OF NEW MEDIA

In addition to the continued attention to the preservation of books and other paper documents, libraries and archives will become increasingly involved with preservation of materials in other media. Already apparent is that each medium which humans use for information storage and dissemination has its own cluster of preservation needs. So far many of these needs have been found to be sufficiently similar to those of paper that it has been possible, with a few adjustments, to use and house media materials alongside books and paper documents without too much difficulty. This, however, may not always be the case as is evident in the recommendation that nitrate films not be stored with any other types of material and in the requirement that magnetic tapes and other computer materials be stored and used in their own environmentally controlled and especially clean quarters.

A growing problem of unprecedented nature and great potential importance is becoming apparent. This is the preservation of computer-based materials, particularly those materials which remain in machine-readable form. The development of the computer has been so rapid and the emphasis of development has centered to such a degree on ever more powerful, more efficient, and more user-friendly hardware and software that preservation concerns have been largely ignored. The problem is being recognized among some archivists and librarians and among at least some in the computer industry, and the perception one may readily gain is that here again there is actually a complex of problems which comprise the greater problem.[6] Because the use of computers to store and disseminate information differs fundamentally from such use of paper and print, the problems are quite different; so different, in fact, that the computer is being recognized as being as revolutionary in its own way as was printing in the fifteenth century as a means of disseminating knowledge.[7]

An overriding aspect of the situation is that of system obsolescence. With the rapid development and deployment of succeeding generations of both hardware and software, systems quickly become outmoded and obsolete, requiring periodic conversion of data to new formats in order that they may be accessed by the current generation of equipment and software. Second, the physical media used for storing machine-readable information are all more or less fragile and subject to degradation. Magnetic tape is presently the storage medium of choice both because it is relatively easily copied and handled in computer facilities and because it is more permanent than disks and drums. Even so, tapes must be monitored periodically for deterioration, rewound to assure proper tensioning, and recopied for backup. The dependable storage life of magnetic tape is at present considered to be little more than 20 years. This seems to satisfy computer administrators because within the 20-year period tapes will require reformatting and simultaneous copying in order to assure access to data by the next generation of hardware and software; but 20 years is a far more rapid turnaround time for reformatting than that familiar to librarians and archivists for paper, even paper subject to acid hydrolysis. The implications of this need for continuous monitoring and relatively frequent reformatting have not yet been fully recognized by most librarians and archivists. It will be expensive in that it will be time consuming and will require specialized staff, appropriate equipment for each change in format, and space with appropriate environmental and security controls to house the tape archive. This means a new and different preservation facility in each tape archive. Specific recommendations for the conversion of machine-readable media to tape and for the archival care of magnetic tape are found in the literature. An excellent summary of the history and needs of machine-readable media and microforms is William Saffady's "Stability, Care and Handling of Microforms, Magnetic Media and Optical Disks"[8] in which may be found at the close of each section an enumeration of the archival storage needs of each medium.

Optical discs appear to be more stable than magnetic media both because of their obviously greater physical durability and because the reading mechanism does not actually touch the disc as data are read. However, they are not indestructible and they are subject to "CD rot" or hydrolysis of the reflective layer caused either by impurities in the metallic layer or by the introduction of moisture through a scratch or failure in the plastic coating of the disc.[9] Here, also, as with machine-dependent media of all types, system obsolescence is likely. As disc technology evolves, individuals and institutions may be left with older discs which are not compatible with succeeding generations of equipment.

Questions of what to save in machine-readable form are more complex and involve all the factors already familiar in building collections in the more traditional media in libraries and archives. In addition, questions of copyright, cost, availability, appropriateness to a particular collection, possibilities of sharing collections of digitized data among institutions, the needs of particular researchers and scholars, and the ability and willingness of institutions to take on the responsibility for the long-term storage of this kind of material all will come to bear. Neavill indicates that the selection of electronic materials for preservation will be much more difficult than similar selection of print-based materials primarily because electronic materials must be acquired for preservation while current. Selection for preservation cannot be delayed as may such selection for print because the information will quite likely cease to exist once the current or initial need is satisfied.[10] An example of some of the problems in selecting and making machine-based publications available can be seen in experiences surrounding a single subscription to an online journal. A particular issue of such a journal may be available online only until the succeeding issue replaces it in the publisher's commercial or publicly accessible database. A subscriber, personal or institutional, in order to have back issues at hand must download and store each issue as it is available and perhaps, in addition, print it out, accumulate printouts, and bind and shelve them as traditional paper-based periodicals. Where is the convenience or economy to the subscriber in this? Such a subscription brings only limited access to each issue unless one is willing to assume responsibility for indefinite storage of the downloaded file or the printout.

Large databases such as machine-readable reference sources, which may be updated continuously, present problems both of size and loss of currency if downloaded. There are also questions, as yet unresolved, as to permanent retention of data made available initially on subscription by commercial vendors. If an issuing firm or agency changes its character, or ceases to exist, what will happen to the database which may be of continued value to research and scholarship? Still further are questions of how libraries and archives may share in the retention of machine-based information and make it available to their clients and users. These and similar questions are unanswered as yet and there is little experience on which to depend in shaping policies and programs to provide answers.[11] Neavill, in the two articles previously cited, provides an introduction and initial exploration of these concerns.

There is evidence of recognition of these and related problems of control of machine-based data files in government. *Recordfacts Update,*[12] a newsletter issued by the Office of Records Administration of the National Archives and Records Administration (NARA) contains articles and notices written for the neophyte in this area describing the management of machine-readable records within the government and the National Archives. Of interest in connection with questions of long-term storage of machine-readable records is an indication in a description of Archives II, the new facility in College Park, Maryland, for the National Archives, of space dedicated to the special needs of "nontextual records."[13] Also of interest to those contemplating the establishment of a machine-readable archive is the NARA publication *Managing Electronic Records*[14] which describes initial steps being taken in the National Archives to deal with archival machine-readable information and which also introduces many of the problem areas here under discussion to those managing files and records.

Ethics and operations are closely intertwined in preservation as in other fields, and this close association is evident in this paper. To most librarians and archivists a basic ethical stance is to furnish the patron with the document or publication in its entirety and in its original form if at all possible. The user is then free to utilize the item as the need dictates so long as it is not unduly damaged or destroyed and so long as appropriate credit is given to the document as a source of information. When materials are reformatted for any purpose, when they may be repaired, deacidified, rebound, etc., the conservator or other preservation specialist is under ethical constraints to change the item as little as possible, to remove nothing without documenting it, and to add nothing which will confuse future users. Similar ethical standards and constraints will evolve for electronically stored and disseminated information. Librarians, scholars, archivists, and computer specialists all will have a share in the formulation of these standards. Each medium, whatever its makeup, presents its own problems in this regard and a part of preservation will be to continue to help assure the integrity of the information being copied, reformatted, stored, and disseminated. Just as this requires careful collation and inspection of books and papers along with careful consideration of the needs of each sheet or page, so too in the preservation of electronic media the preservationist will be concerned for the completeness and integrity of the data or information even though it may not be possible to retain the original form or format as the preservation processes proceed.

CONCLUSION

From these considerations it is apparent that the future of preservation of library materials will continue to grow and to change. Traditional paper materials will survive, will be used, and will need continued care. The now traditional media materials of many kinds–microfilm, motion pictures, sound recordings, photographs, art on paper, archives, and others will be joined by increasing numbers of machine-readable materials; and, quite likely other media still unknown will join the list each in its turn. All will proliferate and require care if they are to be of use. The promise is of a future in which preservation will be of increasing importance. The older materials and media may require a degree of rethinking or refocusing particularly of the ethical considerations surrounding their treatment. The new media, particularly those related to the computer, will require both the formulation of an ethical and theoretical base and of operational methods and technologies. The opportunities appear to be unending. The field continues to evolve.

REFERENCE NOTES

1. George Martin Cunha, "Current Trends in Preservation Research and Development," *American Archivist* 53 (Spring 1990): 192-202.

2. Gordon R. Williams, *The Preservation of Deteriorating Books: An Examination of the Problem with Recommendations for a Solution* (Washington, DC: Association of Research Libraries, 1964). Reprinted in revised form in *Library Journal* 91 (January 1-15, 1966): 51-56, 189-194.

3. Lambertus Van Zelst, "Needs and Potential Solutions in Conservation," in *Conserving and Preserving Materials in Nonbook Formats,* ed. Kathryn Luther Henderson and William T Henderson (Urbana-Champaign, IL: University of Illinois Graduate School of Library and Information Science, 1991), 7-22 (Allerton Park Institute no. 30).

4. Barclay Ogden, *On the Preservation of Books and Documents in Original Form* (Washington, DC: Commission on Preservation and Access, 1989).

5. Bart Ziegler, "Computers That Use Pens May Soon Make Their Mark," *The News Gazette,* Champaign-Urbana, IL: 139th Year, no. 330 (June 23, 1991): C-4.

6. See writings by Gordon B. Neavill, "Electronic Publishing, Libraries, and the Survival of Information," *Library Resources & Technical Services* 28 (January/March 1984): 76-89; and "Preservation of Computer-Based and Computer-Generated Records," in *Conserving and Preserving Materials in Nonbook Formats,* ed. Kathryn Luther Henderson and William T Henderson (Urbana-Champaign, IL.: University of Illinois Graduate School of Library and Information Science, 1991), 45-60. (Allerton Park Institute no. 30). Also see articles by Mallinson, Cuddihy, Calmes, and Vogelgesang in *Proceedings of Conservation in Archives International Symposium. Ottawa, Canada. May 9-12, 1988.* Together these materials form an introduction to both the overall preservation problem of computer-based materials and explore a number of the component problem areas as well.

7. Neavill, "Preservation of Computer-Based and Computer Generated Records," 45.

8. William Saffady, "Stability, Care and Handling of Microforms, Magnetic Media and Optical Disks," *Library Technology Reports* 27 (January-February, 1991): 5-116.

9. Mary E. Marshall and Ginni Voedisch, "Compact Discs: Permanence and Irretrievability May Be Synonymous in Libraries as Well as in Roget's," in *National Online Meeting Proceedings–1990,* New York, May 1-3, 1990 (Medford, NJ: Learned Information, 1990), 249-254.

10. Neavill, "Preservation of Computer-Based and Computer-Generated Records," 58.

11. Ibid., p. 57-59.

12. *Recordfacts Update.* 4, no. 1-2 (Spring-Summer 1990)

13. *Recordfacts Update* 4, no. 1 (Spring 1990): 6.

14. *Managing Electronic Records* (Washington, DC: National Archives and Records Administration, Office of Records Administration, 1990).

Chapter 16

Combining Old World Craftsmanship with New World Technology: A Quarter Century of Library Binding in Review, 1965-1990

James Orr

Library binding, with its handcrafted operations and skilled detailed procedures, has made some notable advancements these past 25 years. Automation and mechanization have slowly made inroads, enabling the industry to become more modernized.

Diversity is still a strong factor to overcome in achieving real mechanization in library binding. Binding orders have not changed much over the years. They may consist of one, 100, 500, or 1,000 volumes, but seldom are two volumes alike, except with sets or textbooks. They are not only different in size, format, construction, and paper, but all are received in different stages of disrepair. All have different binding instructions, and not all customers want their books bound the same way. That is to say, some may prefer adhesive binding to oversewing, others may want the old sewing preserved, while still others may want all books oversewed if at all possible. For this reason, library binding still requires a good deal of special handling and skill that can only be done by hand or with semi-automated techniques. In this respect binding is still a craft relying on the binder's skill, knowledge, and experience.

BINDING MATERIALS

Possibly one of the biggest new developments introduced over these past 25 years has been adhesive binding. This is not to be confused with the hot melt adhesives, used by some publishers, that do not have an enviable record for strength, durability, or longevity.

Library binders use an adhesive known as polyvinyl acetate (PVA). This is a clear white vinyl resin that is internally plasticized. This adhesive is applied in a double fanning operation to the spine. It is a slow-drying adhesive but provides a good deal of strength and durability. It has also been found that good bonding can result on coated or slick paper stock if the fibers are properly exposed. There are now special milling machines that can do this.

Polyvinyl adhesive allows a good binding to result, even in cases where the narrow margins that are all too common among many publications today exist. Adhesive bound volumes have proven themselves with exposures to adverse heat and cold and extensive hard usage. In addition, PVA adhesives are neutral with no acidic content. They allow the book to open very freely, eliminating strain and pressure which is especially beneficial for photocopying. For this reason, many semi-brittle books are treated this way.

Promising new adhesive developments include the use of PUR or polyurethane. This adhesive does not have to be fanned on, and when it is cured or dry, it has a remarkable strength. The problem has been the application of the adhesive which, while in its liquid state, is toxic and cannot be handled indiscriminately. Machines for its application have been developed and are presently undergoing some rigorous testing. The trend continues to favor more and more adhesive binding.

IMPACT OF AUTOMATION

New developments in automated binding preparation have been introduced within the last ten to 12 years. Binders are providing computer-automated binding preparation systems. This entails the bindery furnishing the library with the software, usually consisting of the library's binding title base, outlining how the title is bound as to color, lettering, sequence, trim size, and any other information that may be pertinent to the binding process. The library, in preparing a binding shipment, calls up the title by name, call number, or other code arrangements and inputs all variable information. The data are then transmitted by wire to the binder who makes up the binding tickets which will be waiting when the shipment arrives. In our own case, we furnish our customers with the computer and software, the modem, and a printer as well as maintenance for both the program and the hardware. A variation on this procedure would be to have the library put these data on a floppy disk that accompanies the binding shipment, as a number of binders currently do. Some binders now extend these processes even further by tying in scheduling, processing, and billing to their own in-house production.

The ubiquitous rub-off or sample patterns formerly used to match binding lettering alignment, styles, and patterns has all but disappeared in favor of numbers corresponding to scale assigned lettering slots. The once popular lettering pallets tied in with lead slugs cast from the interior linotype machines are all but extinct now, except possibly in some very small shops. Sophisticated new stamping machines with rotary stamping wheels, operated by formatters tied in with computers, and in some cases automatically fed, do all the cover stamping. Demands for decorative bands and head-and-tail lines are few in number, and for legibility, the majority of all lettering is in white.

Group F buckram is still the accepted standard for covering material, and whenever possible, illustrated covers are procured for children's books. Years ago binders may have stocked as many as 30 different buckram colors for binding books and magazines. Today, binders try to limit their inventory to about 20 basic colors. In our own case, we have a "graphic klear" cover for books, which consists of laminating the dust jacket to the hard cover case, thus providing a very strong cover with attractive color graphics.

CONSERVATION AND PRESERVATION ISSUES

The job of the library binder has always been to preserve and conserve the printed word, and in fact, that is the premise the industry was founded on. In 1978, a renewed emphasis on preservation occurred in libraries the world over due to the mass breakdown in their collections resulting from the acid sizing and ground wood that was introduced to papermaking between 1810-1880. These conditions were further complicated by poor environment and handling, which caused millions of books to literally self destruct. Universities and institutions established conservation and preservation courses, graduating professional conservators who took up positions in most of the major libraries. As a result, binders saw different binding requests being made from many of their university and public library accounts. Many were now requesting that volumes have the old sewing retained, no trimming, adhesive binding, hand sewing to tape, binding flush to bottom, or recasing–not that these were new requests to binders, but they were more in demand than ever before.

Some conservation techniques were more helpful than others. Binding flush to bottom could be counterproductive inasmuch as the leaves now are coming in full, direct contact with the dirt or dust particles on the shelf. Heavy use of such a volume, on and off the shelf, could be very damaging. Adhesive binding proved it could minimize the stress on semi-brittle volumes, prolonging their utility, and for this reason has been extensively used on this category of work. Requests for acid free materials prompted binders to issue strong demands to their suppliers for quick compliance in meeting these standards–and today the use of acid-free or neutral material is common. Binders were also called upon to laminate, encapsulate, and make slipcases or phase boxes in order to house the books that were very brittle and not capable of being bound.

Deacidification processes were introduced by independent companies and the Library of Congress in the last 25 years. Binders looked at these in conjunction with the binding process to see which could be used as an adjunct. Limited processing, such as Wei T'o, were introduced but not on a large scale, except a few who attempted to act in a dealer-jobber capacity. The whole problem of deacidification is quite involved, to say nothing of the added logistics and handling. For now, most binders are leaving this to the individual companies.

Today binders afford their customers a number of options in handling their binding requirements: oversewing for heavy-duty wear, adhesive binding for stress-free openability, through-the-fold sewing to tape for material in signature form, singer sewing for flats (3/8″ or under), hand oversewing for narrow margins, overcasting and retention of old sewing on rare or special volumes. Lamination and encapsulation of old, brittle, or special pages, hinging, stubbing, and mending with precision, skill, and dexterity are still the trademark of a professional library binder. The customer still makes the final decision on how the work is processed, but because of the diversity of materials, it is impossible for the customer to see and evaluate the many intricacies that occur. For this reason, reliance on the binder for proper handling should also prevail. Good communication between library and binder must exist. Periodic visits to the bindery by the library staff provide good insight as to advancements and opportunities to reevaluate current methods for updating, change, or minor alterations in binding specifications. Most binders, in addition to good customer service, provide an additional liaison through their sales force by making periodic visits throughout the year, checking on performance and customer satisfaction. The majority of all orders are picked up and delivered by the binder, with binding schedules running about 28 days, or as special incentives two weeks. Rush orders average about two weeks.

LIBRARY BINDING INDUSTRY

The library binding industry is a small industry, with total sales somewhere between $90 and $125 million, which also encompasses some prebinding. The largest binding expenditures are made by university, college, institutional, and large public libraries. The potential market consists of approximately 115,000 libraries of all types. This market, while large, is always confronted with tight and stringent budgets, and some libraries have little or no existing allocations at all for binding. While books and publications have proliferated in the last 25 years, binding budgets have not necessarily increased accordingly. Library binding, like most businesses, is very competitive and is not one that produces large profits. For library binding to continue as a viable enterprise, ways must be found to minimize more of the manual operations, which commonly occurs with more accepted uniformity and standardization. Certain titles could all be bound in one color, one style, and one lettering pattern. If libraries are willing to do their own preliminary collation for magazines and books, limit colors, and accept uniform sizes, this would enable binders to find those essential ways of keeping costs from making dramatic increases. This is not to advocate shortcut methods which reduce quality but rather to maintain sound methods of binding, through simplified procedures that reduce handling.

Today there are about 40 to 50 library binders nationally (this also incorporates in-house binderies operated by some universities and public libraries). The many small binderies operating years ago are diminishing. Bigger firms are buying them up, or they are leaving the business altogether. In today's market a certain volume is required to stay profitable. Large capital expenditures must be made to procure the available automated machines and methods that enable binders to be competitive. Many of the small firms do not have the required capital resources.

The medium-sized bindery has about 40 to 50 employees, and most of these firms belong to the trade association known as LBI or the Library Binding Institute. The main function of the association has been to establish high quality binding standards,[1] promote the many benefits binders offer, and act as general liaison with library organizations. In order to be a member of LBI, a binder must submit samples to ensure that the binding is in conformance with the established binding standards. If the work does not measure up, the binder cannot become certified.

A number of binders today perform other services in addition to library binding, such as edition binding, prebinding, microfilming, special conservation work, and job binding. The future for library binding holds a great deal of promise in adhesives, improved automated handling in both processing and preparation, and greater benefits from automated systems due to interfacing with the libraries' own hardware and software programs. Binding budgets are subject to many restraints. Unless adequate funding is available to correspond with the ever-increasing proliferation of books, journals, and all printed material, binding growth will be limited and binders will be forced to diversify. If, however, libraries are able to promote their cause so that their binding budget requirements are met, library binding will expand along with new equipment and materials to meet the challenge.

REFERENCE NOTE

1. *Library Binding Institute Standard for Library Binding,* 8th ed. (Rochester, NY: Library Binding Institute, 1986).

PART VIII:

EDUCATION AND PROFESSIONAL DEVELOPMENT

Chapter 17

A Quarter Century of Cataloging Education

Arlene G. Taylor

INTRODUCTION

What was it like to study cataloging over 25 years ago? Realizing that I was a library school student then, I pulled out the notes and assignments from the three cataloging courses I took in 1964, 1965, and 1966. There they were–about 200 3 × 5 inch "p-slips," neatly typed or handwritten in ink in correct card catalog format: call number in the upper left corner; main entry, body of the entry, physical description paragraph, and notes, all exactly paragraphed (with hanging indention when title was the main entry); tracings at the bottom. I had forgotten that we spent so much time meticulously writing or typing so many of these on nonerasable paper before the invention of "white out." Some had been made into complete card sets–the unit card was typed or photocopied again and again with a different entry from the tracing typed at the top each time. There were handmade check-in cards for the serials, and finally, there were authority record cards and many references. Errors and alternative approaches were marked with red ink or pencil.

Recovering from the shock of all those "p-slips," I turned next to the class notes. My first course was taught by Allie Beth Martin in an extension course from the University of Oklahoma. I was introduced to the 1949 ALA and LC rules for choice and form of entry and description, the eighth edition of Sears subject headings, the eighth abridged edition of the Dewey Decimal Classification (DDC), and the 1942 ALA filing rules. I was required to memorize the 100 divisions of DDC (an exercise that has stood me in good stead to this day)! This was a very practical how-to-do-it course.

My second course, taught by Kathryn Luther Henderson at the University of Illinois, was a much greater mix of theory with practice. Here was the basis not only for applying the 1949 ALA and LC rules to individual items but also for understanding underlying principles and for comprehending entry as essential for collocation. Professor Henderson gave us a thorough background in the history of cataloging. We learned about card, book, and microform catalogs in classified or alphabetical arrangements. Following a substantial grounding in the sixth edition of the Library of Congress Subject Headings (LCSH), we studied Library of Congress Classification and the seventeenth edition of DDC. Although original cataloging was emphasized, we also learned how to find cataloging in the *National Union Catalog* and to adapt it to fit the item in hand, conforming to specified "local policies." There was considerable concentration on the aspect of cataloging that we now call authority work, although it was not called that, and the process did not seem to have a name then.

My third course, taught by Oliver T. Field at the University of Illinois, covered the administration of catalog departments and the cataloging of the following special materials: archives (including manuscripts), maps, music, "phonodiscs," serials, pictorial materials, motion pictures, and rare books. Finally, there was a unit on catalog maintenance.

From my reading of the literature, my experience seems to have been fairly typical of the mid-1960s. A required introduction to cataloging and classification was followed by one or two advanced elective courses. When there were two advanced courses they were usually divided into cataloging of monographs and cataloging of "nonbook" materials.

COURSE CONTENT

What has changed in the last quarter century? Obivously, there have been major technological changes: "white out" has come and gone and catalog records are now in the form of computer print-outs. And the years have added editions: we are now using the *Anglo-American Cataloguing Rules,* second edition, 1988 revision (AACR2R); Sears, 14th ed.; Abridged DDC, 12th ed.; full DDC,

20th ed.; printed LCSH, 16th ed.; and the 1980 ALA or LC filing rules. But these are substitutions, not major additions. While AACR2R *does* represent a major shift in philosophical understanding, it is actually easier to teach than the ALA and LC rules because of its greater logic.

There have, however, been major additions to the material to be covered and virtually no subtractions. Since 1966 we have had the development of LC's Cataloging-in-Publication (CIP) program, the International Standard Bibliographic Descriptions (ISBD), and the Machine Readable Cataloging (MARC) formats. Bibliographic networks have developed and have drastically changed the way in which local cataloging is done. Cooperative cataloging has taken on greatly increased importance. The online catalog has become the format of choice. Computer files, audiocassettes, videocassettes, compact discs, and three-dimensional materials have been added to the list of nonbook materials that students should learn to catalog. Many more subject approaches are available, such as specialized subject thesauri and PRECIS. Much of the theory of subject analysis has developed in the area of our field known as information science, and this must be integrated into the traditional curriculum. The concept of authority control has become a widely-accepted approach to catalog creation. Finally, the amount and quality of research in the area of bibliographic control has increased dramatically, giving a great deal more theoretical framework to be introduced.

NUMBER OF COURSES

At the same time that the material to be covered has increased, the amount of time allowed for cataloging education in library schools has decreased. In her 1988 article on cataloging education, Roxanne Sellberg stated: "The 1960s was a decade when traditional structures were challenged and the criticisms leveled then produced some significant changes during the 1970s.... A number of schools reduced their cataloging requirements, and 11.7 percent dropped cataloging altogether from their required core curricula."[1] This change came about partly because of the development of computers and bibliographic networks. There was a widespread belief that the Library of Congress would be able to catalog everything and that it would be available via computer to everyone. There was experimentation in some library schools with dropping cataloging from the required "core" courses and with combining various cataloging concepts into other courses (e.g., incorporating discussion of use of catalogs into reference courses).

In the 1980s the realities of the economic situation made it clear that the Library of Congress could not catalog everything and, in fact, was able to cover a smaller proportion of materials than before. By the end of the 1980s there was a realization that the computer was not going to solve libraries' cataloging needs without trained humans to input the data correctly, and some cataloging courses were reinstated. Most library schools now offer two or three courses, one of which is required.

A few library schools have developed extended master's programs for the purpose of allowing students to specialize in one or more areas and to participate in a specialized internship. One such area of specialization is that of "bibliographic control," which incorporates cataloging and classification and also includes broader aspects of the process of creating, arranging, and maintaining systems for bibliographic information retrieval. One extended program has developed the following courses: Introduction to Bibliographic Control; Descriptive Cataloging; Subject Analysis; Technical Services; Indexing and Abstracting; Serials Librarianship; Music Cataloging; and Seminar in Bibliographic Control. Whether such specializations will become a trend remains a question.

PROFESSORS

One aspect of cataloging education in the last quarter century that has not changed is the effect of the professor on the learning process. In a recent article announcing that Professor Henderson has been awarded the Campus Award for Excellence in Graduate and Professional Teaching at the University of Illinois at Urbana-Champaign, it was stated that a 1970 graduate had written, "Beyond doubt, Professor Henderson has been the major influence in my professional career. . . . She provided detailed feedback to each student and at the same time she conveyed her love of her profession and the endless excitement she found in it."[2] A 1990 graduate wrote, "Combined with her obvious skills in teaching, Professor Henderson's personal relationship with her students puts her into the small class of teachers who can claim lasting impact on their students' professional and personal lives."[3] Those statements could also have been written by me, a 1966 graduate. These personal attributes did not change in a quarter century. But some of my colleagues who also went to library school over a quarter century ago did not fare so well. They came away with the idea that cataloging had to be endured and that it had no future application for them. Librarians who had this experience, unfortunately, sometimes tell the clerks and students who work for them that if they go to library school they will hate cataloging, but the rest will be fine.

I strongly believe that, while many students arrive at library school already prejudiced against cataloging, their attitudes can be modified by caring professors who are excited by this area of librarianship. But because we have had a shortage of professors fully prepared in this area, some schools have assigned the cataloging course(s) to be taught by persons whose main interests lie elsewhere. Unfortunately, dislike or disinterest in a subject can influence students as much or more than enthusiasm. It is to be hoped that having returned to a period when it is generally accepted that students need *some* exposure to the concepts of bibliographic control, more people will soon be prepared to teach with enthusiasm in this area.

TEACHING METHODS

Methodology used in teaching is another aspect of education that is greatly dependent upon the personality of the professor. Lecturing works well for some, while dividing classes up for group work works better for others. Some professors can use visual materials effectively. The availability of visual teaching aids has increased in the last quarter century. In the 1960s visual aids had to be created by an individual professor. Now there are commercially prepared transparencies and videos available for use. Videos can be as unsuccessful as films were a quarter century ago, however. Unless they are very professionally done, students who have grown up in an age of music videos will laugh at awkward amateurs trying to be actors. Videos also become outdated quickly and students have a tendency to laugh at out-of-style clothing. Equipment for visual materials has changed considerably in the last 25 years. Audio- and videocassette players have been developed, as has equipment to project computer screens for viewing by an entire class. Slide and overhead transparency projectors are much more sophisticated.

A teaching methodology that came and went for teaching cataloging in the last quarter century was the case study method. It was tried widely in the 1970s and a couple of case study texts were published, but this happened at the same time that courses in cataloging were being cut from curricula, and students did not have enough cataloging knowledge to analyze cases successfully. In extended programs with specializations case studies perhaps can be used more successfully, especially after fulfillment of an internship requirement.

LABORATORY WORK

Virtually all cataloging courses require supplementary laboratory work and have done so for much longer than the last quarter century. But there have been major changes. In the 1960s cataloging labs consisted of cataloging tools such as copies of LCSH, DDC, LC Classification schedules, and the rules for entry and description. In addition there were copies of books that had been chosen to represent knotty cataloging problems. Some labs had typewriters (occasionally electric!). Lab work resulted in typed catalog cards. Gradually, computers were introduced into cataloging lab work. In the 1970s computer-assisted instruction (CAI) was used successfully. "Programmed instruction" allowed students to move ahead by reading material and answering questions. If the questions were answered incorrectly, the student was required to review the material. Correct answers moved the student to new material. As computerized instruction has gotten more sophisticated, programs have been developed that resemble cataloging workstations.

In the 1980s most library schools acquired the ability to access major databases, such as OCLC and RLIN. Now laboratory work includes learning to search these databases, and instead of typing catalog cards, students enter cataloging records into computers in MARC formats. Some library schools have acquired the software for integrated library systems so that students can work with acquisitions and serials records in addition to learning about online catalog construction. Cataloging tools in book format are still in evidence. However, LCSH and name and title authority records are now also available online. The standard book tools have been joined by MARC manuals, various computer manuals, and interpretive manuals such as the *LC Rule Interpretations* and the LC *Subject Cataloging Manuals.*

THE FUTURE

Cataloging education in the future will continue to change rapidly. We must face the challenge of creating bibliographic control for intellectual entities available online in addition to those in concrete physical formats. Our current system of classifying in order to provide shelf order, for example, is not helpful for providing access to a hundred "books" all stored on the same compact disc. Classification, therefore, must be approached as a means for intellectual access. Future catalogers must deal with whether and how there should be bibliographic records as surrogates for intellectual entities that are accessible online. Will there be, instead, indexes from names, titles, and subjects that point directly to online works? How will online works be related to offline counterparts?

Future catalogers must also improve subject access. There is currently much dissatisfaction with our subject approaches, the basic structures of which were developed a century ago. Whether changes will consist of structural changes to current systems or will be characterized by complete replacement of current systems is still unknown, but cataloging education will be affected either way.

Cataloging education will continue to deal with rapid technological developments. Cataloging workstations eventually will incorporate online access to all cataloging tools, as well as to massive databases of bibliographic records and to the intellectual works themselves. The economic implications of providing access for students to such workstations will have to be faced as well.

International cooperation will gain greater visibility in efforts to obtain universal bibliographic control. As a result cataloging education will require that students be introduced to such concepts as UNIMARC (Universal MARC), the work and publications of the

International Federation of Library Associations and Institutions (IFLA), multilingual online systems, systems for inputting nonroman alphabet languages, and classification as a means for multilingual subject access.

As was mentioned earlier, library schools may have to extend the length of their programs to give time for additional coursework and internships in order for students to be prepared to work in the area of bibliographic control. They will certainly have to face the fact that the amount of material to be covered cannot be given justice in two courses and, if the time is not extended, then librarians must reconcile themselves to the necessity of teaching this material to new librarians themselves.

Although we have made progress in returning the concepts of bibliographic control to the curriculum, more needs to be done to convince all library educators and librarians that a basic understanding of the structure of bibliographic control is absolutely necessary for all librarians. Lois Chan once made the analogy that consulting a reference librarian who does not understand the catalog is like consulting a doctor who does not understand the nature and function of drugs, having never studied pharmacology in medical school.[4] And it is not only understanding catalog structure that is at stake. Administrators cannot make informed decisions about tomorrow's technology without a thorough grounding in bibliographic control. The course in library schools that is required of all students must concentrate on providing that grounding in bibliographic control theory and practice, with later courses providing the details of creation of the catalog structure for those students whose imaginations are fired in that direction.

REFERENCE NOTES

1. Roxanne Sellberg, "The Teaching of Cataloging in U.S. Library Schools," *Library Resources & Technical Services* 32, no. 1 (January 1988): 33.

2. Curt McKay, "Henderson Named Most Outstanding Graduate Teacher," Graduate School of Library & Information Science, Library School Association, *Newsletter* no. 9 (Fall 1991): 1.

3. Ibid.

4. Lois Mai Chan, "[Article in] Catalogs and Catalogers: Evolution through Revolution," edited by Tillie Krieger, *Journal of Academic Librarianship* 2, no. 4 (September 1976): 177.

Chapter 18

Continuing Education and Technical Services Librarians: Learning for 1965-1990 and the Future

Eloise M. Vondruska

For anyone who received a graduate degree in library science beginning in 1965 through about the early 1970s, the subsequent appearance of new technologies, new standards, and new services that have become primary to technical services activities has demanded that technical services librarians participate in continuing education to be knowledgeable and current. The expansion of information and the need to access and control information effectively in all of its myriad new formats are further reasons that require that continuing education be ongoing in the technical services librarian's career. The graduate degree may have once served a lifelong career satisfactorily, but now it is the commencement point for lifelong learning.

However, continuing education is more than new fact-based knowledge being added to the core of facts and theories of graduate studies. An essential component of continuing education is a broader understanding of those core facts and theories, as it comes after experience in the working world. Continuing education completes the cycle of learning based on assimilation of facts and accommodation to the environment. Viewed in this way, education is by definition a continuing process. One does not become educated, but one is always becoming educated. This chapter examines this two-fold approach to continuing education. First, some of the changes in technology and standards in technical services librarianship that have occurred over the last 25 years have made some fact-based continuing education a necessity. Second, regardless of the changes in the knowledge base, continuing education is examined for how it provides a component of the educational process that is initiated in formal graduate coursework.

The extensive literature of continuing education for librarianship often has focused on the relative merits of different forms of continuing education activities: formal vs. informal, courses for credit, professional reading, networking and conferences, and so on. Continuing education has been offered by professional associations, state agencies, graduate library schools, and others. Continuing education provides personal development and morale boosting. Advancement in the profession can result from a broadening of one's knowledge and skills. Some organizations formally reward individuals who have earned advanced education credits through promotions and salary advancements. Of course, these kinds of benefits depend on the individual and the employing organization. Also, continuing education needs depend on the individual's length of service in the profession, and on the state of the profession at any one time. (Remember the rush of AACR2 workshops?)

An extensive history of library continuing education is provided in *Continuing Education for the Library Information Professions.*[1] The efforts in continuing education implementation, standardization, and evaluation discussed in that work generally relate to the profession as a whole, or by type of library. Similarly, continuing education as an aspect of education by type of library is covered in the comprehensive collection edited by Herbert S. White, *Education for Professional Librarians.*[2] Some of the literature of the last 25 years that provided insights into continuing education and technical services librarians, in particular, is discussed in more detail in White's work.

Prior to the late 1960s, there were few studies on continuing education for librarians. In 1969 Elizabeth W. Stone published the results of a major survey of library school graduates of the classes of 1956 and 1961.[3] The study was undertaken to identify some of the factors that motivate or deter librarians from continuing their professional development after receipt of a master's degree in library science. Stone's findings revealed that librarians of that time showed a disparity between what they were doing and what they thought they should be doing for optimal professional development. More librarians were involved in informal activities than formal ones. Based on the study, Stone offered one recommendation that continuing education be the responsibility of a central organization. Her study and its other recommendations emphasized that new knowledge needed to be acquired after library school (especially true during automation's advent in librarianship). She also suggested ways to motivate librarians to participate in formal continuing education activities. Administration and automation were major areas suggested as topics for continuing education needed at that time.

The growing importance of continuing education for librarianship, due in large part to rapid technological changes, was acknowledged throughout the 1970s. The mid-1970s brought the establishment of the nationwide CLENE (Continuing Library Education Network and Exchange), and today's nationwide efforts continue through the American Library Association's CLENERT (Continuing Library Education Network and Exchange Roundtable), as well as through the continuing education activities of other specialized library associations or sections and divisions of professional associations.

Another viewpoint on the nature of continuing education and the professions in general (including librarianship) was written about extensively by adult educator Cyril O. Houle. He suggests the use of the term continuing "learning" rather than continuing "education."[4] This word change places the emphasis on the individual directing the study actions, instead of on the person providing the instruction. In outlining the continuum of professional education, he begins with general education, shows how it moves through specialized education, and concludes in continuing education. He suggests that there are at least four purposes of continuing education: (1) maintenance and modernization; (2) preparation for change; (3) induction into new responsibilities; and (4) refresher training. All four aspects are relevant to technical services librarians' goals for continuing education. Learning an automated process to perform an existing manual procedure is a form of maintenance and modernization. Learning a new set of cataloging rules is preparation for change. Mastering administrative and budgeting concepts before a job promotion to a management position helps the transition to new responsibilities. And attending an annual professional conference could encompass general refresher training.

The dynamic and rapid growth in information and changes in information handling that have occurred in the last 25 years have made continuing education for technical services librarians a basic tenet of career librarianship. While the popular perception of libraries may be that they are static, conservative, and quiet institutions, those who have worked in technical services jobs in libraries since 1965 quickly could dispel that stereotypical perception. Those librarians who have worked since the 1960s have much evidence to support the concept of libraries as dynamic, progressive, and noisy environments. The technical services procedures of 1965 are quite different from those of the 1990s. Just think of a baker's dozen of now tried-and-true acronyms central to technical services activities: AACR2, CD-ROM, CLSI, LUIS, MARC, NOTIS, OCLC, OPAC, PC, RAM, RLIN, and WLN–how many of these terms existed in the library lexicon in 1965? These terms do not appear in the 1965 index to *Library Literature,* and by midpoint of this 25-year odyssey, only a few of these terms appear in the *Library Literature* 1978 index. By 1990, however, some of these terms command pages of entries in the index. These terms are but a small sampling of this acronym-riddled age of librarianship. How could today's librarians communicate without this vocabulary? Technical services librarians would be mute without these terms, and the nature of technical services work would be quite different without the technologies and standards represented by these terms.

But what of the second approach to continuing education, not as it teaches new facts, but rather as it provides new meaning or understanding about what is already known? Continuing education seen in this light is part of a cycle of learning. Graduate library school teaches students a core of theories and facts. Many library school students have little library work experience. But after graduate training and some professional experience, the technical services librarian has an entirely new perspective on the theories and facts of the classroom. Continuing education pursued after on-the-job experience makes the work that follows easier and more meaningful. Much effort has to be applied to the initial stages of learning theories and facts, and then acquiring experience, but continuing education leads to a synthesis of facts and experience that leads, often, to new theories and ways of doing things.

This model of continuing education is not in conflict with the traditional view of the sequential nature of education, what might be called the "snowball" approach, but puts a spin on that snowball. In the snowball approach, the learner starts with general knowledge and specific facts and rolls along to collect experience and then rolls along to acquire more new knowledge and facts. This second perspective of continuing education sees it as a circle that is revolving and evolving. There is a beginning, the attainment of general knowledge and facts, but it curves around to be used in on-the-job experience, and then curves again to acquire new facts through continuing education. But after learning new facts and reflecting on the experiential setting, there is often a period of evaluation and synthesis that leads the curve back to provide a new base for general knowledge and specific facts at the beginning of the circle.

Now as the millennium approaches, what form will continuing education for technical services librarians take in the future? Without a doubt, it is necessary for the library technical services professional to pursue continuing education, be it formal or informal. Technological innovations in information handling continue to spiral and branch out into new forms. The need for continual learning will spiral and branch out similarly. Coupled with the unfortunate trend of the demise of many library schools, it becomes even more probable that as the ranks of library and information science graduates diminish, the practitioners in the field will have an even greater responsibility to be knowledgeable about new and evolving technologies, standards, and information services in order to provide the best service to their constituencies.

Seen in a slightly different light, besides participating in continuing education, the technical services librarian should consider that there are benefits to be gained from being a provider of continuing education. Through association committee work, a technical services librarian can be involved in assessing the continuing education needs of one's colleagues, and can be instrumental in designing programs and services to meet those needs. A secondary benefit derived from continuing education committee work is experience in organizational and communications skill building.

Continuing education lets one step back to examine what else needs to be learned in order to move forward. What kinds of topics will require learning? The theories at the core of the field of librarianship taught in graduate school must be supplemented by continuing education. Consider some areas that undoubtedly will be continuing education topics in the 1990s and beyond.

Technical services librarians will continue to study the use of bibliographic utilities in support of technical services activities, and the services offered by the bibliographic utilities will continue to evolve. It seems incredible to remember that one of the benefits OCLC was heralded for in its early days was to produce catalog cards inexpensively, compared to today's environment where card catalogs are being closed and/or removed in favor of online public access catalogs. And yet, those OCLC custom-produced catalog cards were a great innovation and benefit and are remembered fondly!

The new generation of automation for integrated library systems and the new powers of microcomputers demand that technical services librarians continue to learn. No longer are technical services librarians faced with just adopting an integrated system, but they must consider converting to second- or third-generation integrated systems. Supervising this kind of activity has come to be learned mostly as on-the-job training and through continuing education programs. This is to say nothing of the technical services librarian who changes jobs, and now faces working with a different name brand integrated automated system. Some technical services librarians are building careers moving from system to system. Of course, each system has its own protocols that require continuing learning. And many technical services librarians make the transitions from library work to employment with a vendor and then back to library work. All the while, the interplay of experience in the different environments allows the professional to broaden the range and depth of understanding of librarianship's theories and facts.

In the area of selection and acquisition of materials, the ever increasing use of automation in various phases of acquisitions work will change as the automated systems change. For libraries acquiring international materials, the establishment of the unified European Community in 1992, as well as the changing face of nations throughout the world requires new avenues and needs for acquisitions of materials.

Certainly, the evolution of the use of the *Anglo-American Cataloguing Rules,* 2nd edition, requires ongoing education for catalogers. New MARC formats for holdings information and for classification require new study. And, the discussion of the merits of a subject cataloging code may lead to formalizing standards for subject cataloging that may need to be learned. Even without such a code, the adoption of new terminology in subject headings as reflective of new concepts requires continuing learning. Or, perhaps the future of cataloging may involve a totally new approach. Artificial intelligence and advanced computing power may allow for cataloging source information such as the title page, the title page verso, table of contents, and index to be scanned electronically, without the need for human interpretation of data and application of rules and structure to the information. Or, cataloging-in-publication could continue its evolution to be created by the publishing source and encoded in a barcode so that all the information could be scanned into the local library's automated information system.

Technical services librarians also are aware of the fact that many of the rules and standards that direct our activities were created while a paper environment was still paramount. While the paperless society is not yet here, information storage continues to develop in that direction. Many of the standards and rules created for access and bibliographic control of a paper environment often conflict with, or are of secondary importance to, an environment where access and bibliographic control are computerized. Also, the source information itself may be computerized. Some information no longer appears as printed paper documents, but exists only in computerized or microprint forms. Technical services librarians must know how to acquire, catalog, access, process, and preserve information in all of these new formats. But as the context of the rules and standards that govern technical services activities changes, the rules and standards themselves may need to be changed, and thus relearned. These new formats for publication and dissemination of information require more and more technical services librarians to become multimedia (multi-informational?) experts.

Finally, the vast resources of our nation's libraries that still exist in print, our invaluable brittle and decaying books, demand that today's technical services librarians be knowledgeable in the field of optimal techniques for handling and processing materials (books, audiotapes, laser discs, computer files, etc.) for preservation. These are just some areas of technical services that will require continuing education attention in the future.

How should continuing education for technical services librarians be offered in the future? There will always be a need for seminars and coursework to master new concepts comprehensively. Graduate schools, state agencies, and professional associations will need to continue to sponsor such efforts. Professional reading and networking are other avenues for continuing education that will continue to have merit. A newer form of continuing education is the use of electronic bulletin boards for communication and knowledge-sharing. The day should come when every technical services librarian's desk will include a personal computer, or a terminal that provides a gateway to databases with bulletin board access. What new ways of learning can one imagine? The best thing ever learned in school is how to learn. That is what continuing education is all about. Continuing education and technical services librarianship, like a garden, is a process–always growing and undergoing redesign. Seeds are planted, weeds are pulled, and the long-awaited harvest brings the fruit of our labors. The technical services librarian, like the gardener, has two roles to play, to plant the seed, and to enjoy the harvest, to be the teacher and the student. Direct your own course of study, but realize that it will never end. Like a garden, it passes through seasons, sometimes dormant, other times sprouting lots of new growth.

REFERENCE NOTES

1. William G. Asp, Suzanne H. Mahmoodi, Marilyn L. Miller, Peggy O'Donnell, and Elizabeth W. Stone. *Continuing Education for the Library Information Professions* (Hamden, CT: Library Professional Publications, 1985).

2. Herbert S. White, ed. *Education for Professional Librarians* (White Plains, NY: Knowledge Industry Publications, 1986).

3. Elizabeth W. Stone, *Factors Related to the Professional Development of Librarians* (Metuchen, NJ: Scarecrow Press, 1969).

4. Cyril O. Houle, *Continuing Learning in the Professions* (San Francisco: Jossey-Bass Publishers, 1981).

Chapter 19

Recollections of Two Little-Known Professional Organizations and Their Impact on Technical Services

Lawrence W. S. Auld

INTRODUCTION

The fact that the topic of this chapter was suggested and that the text was written appears to validate the assumption that professional associations have an impact on technical services. The opposite might be argued, that it is the technical services, as represented by certain individuals, that have an impact on the professional associations. This is analogous to the historian's problems of whether strong leaders shape events or great events call forth leaders. Whichever, the leaders and events can be identified. Similarly, both library leaders and professional concerns can be identified but, often, the causal relationships are not clearly defined.

An investigation of the impact of the professional associations on technical services in libraries during the last quarter century can be approached in several ways. One, obvious but impractical in this length chapter, would be to track the activities of the associations, seeking to determine what unique contributions were made by each. Another would be to track each aspect of technical services separately, looking to identify the combined contributions of the various associations. The approach chosen for this chapter is simply to recount the stories of two professional groups. Although neither group was exclusively devoted to technical services, both influenced technical services more than administrative or public services, because most automation projects during that period were based on acquisitions, fund accounting, serials and binding control, cataloging, and circulation. While these ultimately affected the ability of the libraries' clientele to access materials and information, as virtually all library operations do, the immediate target was, for the most part, the improvement of internal library processes.

By looking at only these two organizations, many changes which occurred outside the interface between the professional associations and technical services have been omitted, although they were highly significant in their own right. Also, much of the historical fabric providing the background and context of these two organizations must also be omitted here due to space limitations.[1] In short, this is a highly selective overview based on secondary sources together with personal recollections. In this way, future scholars will have ample opportunity to mine the archival record in order to expand, confirm, and/or refute what follows.

The principal changes that have affected technical services since 1965 can be summarized with such overlapping headings as AACR, ISBD, MARC, catalog formats, shared cataloging, networking, OCLC, collection development, inflation, preservation, and continuing education. With the possible exception of inflation, it is difficult if not impossible to discuss any one of these areas without also discussing one or more of the others, so even these broad headings suggest a taxonomy of considerably greater precision than is warranted by reality.

The two professional groups that have been chosen for examination are COLA (the Committee on Library Automation) and the LARC (Library Automation, Research and Consulting) Association. For each, the initial context is described, the group is followed from its inception to its disappearance as a separate entity, and an attempt is made to assess the impact of the group.

COLA

While Ralph Parker is often credited with developing and also writing about the first instance of library automation in 1936,[2] it was not until the 1960s that the automation of library processes became feasible for more than a very small handful of special, essentially experimental libraries. IBM's 1400 and System 360 series and similar competitors' machines, announced in the late 1950s and early 1960s respectively, were the host computers for the first generation of automated library systems. A few early library automation personnel no doubt formed invisible colleges, but most of those who were just starting in this new line of library work were working alone.

In 1964, Howard Dillon, then automation librarian at the Ohio State University Library, suggested that it would be helpful if there were a regular forum in which persons working with library automation could share their ideas and experiences. The Committee on Library Automation (usually referred to as COLA[3]) was formed with Dillon as the initial leader and *de facto* honorary godfather after he was no longer directly involved in library automation. COLA was unaffiliated with any other organization but, nevertheless, used free meeting rooms at American Library Association (ALA) and American Society for Information Science (ASIS) meetings.

To meet the simple requirements for COLA membershp, one had to be involved "hands on" with library automation, not be a library director, and was required to share ideas and experiences with the membership *in writing* one or more times a year. One library director was heard to observe that one also had to be something of a "wild duck." Among the early members of COLA who come to mind were Richard De Gennaro and Susan Martin (Harvard), Ralph Shoffner (Library Research Institute–Berkeley), Velma Veneziano (Northwestern), Charles Payne (University of Chicago), Don Hammer (Purdue), Don Bosseau (University of California–San Diego), David Wiesbrod (Yale), Allen Veaner (Stanford), Herb Ahn (University of California–Irvine), and Connie Dunlap (Michigan).

At the outset, with attendance under two dozen, sharing was done informally with lots of questions, answers, and discussion. The consistent reappearance of several persons suggests that the exchanges were valuable, at least to those participants. Then, as growing numbers of libraries began to automate and more librarians heard of COLA, the attendance began to increase. By 1970, what had been a small, relatively intimate group had grown to a crowd with more coming in each year, and informal discussion was giving way to planned program sessions.

In the minds of some, COLA was out of control. It needed more formal guidance, and it was large enough that it was attracting the attention of ALA and ASIS, particularly in terms of meeting room needs. The core membership identified four alternatives for the group: become a part of ALA, probably as the COLA Discussion Group of the Information Science and Automation Division (ISAD, now LITA, the Library and Information Technology Association); become a special interest group (SIG) in the American Society for Information Science (ASIS); continue without any change; or simply disband. Only the first two alternatives were given serious consideration and the outcome was never really in doubt, for it was estimated that about three-fourths of the COLA members also belonged to ALA, while only about one-third also belonged to ASIS; a few belonged to both. In terms of numbers, the choice was clear; become a part of ALA. However, non-ALA members said that they would give up attending if COLA joined ALA, just as non-ASIS members said they would not attend if a liaison with ASIS were to be agreed upon. Strong feelings were expressed, and it was clear that some important members would be lost whatever the decision. In the end, a majority voted to join ALA, and, under the chairmanship of Don L. Bosseau, COLA was reconstituted as the COLA Discussion Group of ISAD. Its purpose was to ". . . report research and development experiences in library automation and provide a forum for informal exchange of technical information," while "membership in the group is limited to persons engaged in the design and implementation of automated systems and who are members of ISAD. Normally only one person per institution will have membership."[4]

The first meeting of the newly organized COLA Discussion Group was a three-hour session January 17, 1971, in Los Angeles. The group was described as being "designed to be a forum for open and frank discourse in the area of library systems development. It should prove, as well, to be an excellent arena for newcomers in the field to meet and talk with experienced library systems personnel." In spite of the membership limitations noted above, it was specified that "guests are welcome to participate."[5] Presentations were given by Hugh Atkinson who described LCS, the online circulation control system which began operation at Ohio State University Library in December 1970; Larry Auld who described LOLITA, the online book order and fund accounting system at Oregon State University Library; and Mary Jane Reed who described the serials control system at the New York State Library.[6]

The summer 1971 program in Dallas featured James Aagaard and Velma Veneziano who described Northwestern University's interactive computer-based system for library circulation and technical services;[7] James Sokoloski who reported on the University of Massachusetts online book acquisitions system, computer-based cataloging, and the acquisitions and processing system for 28 college and university libraries in the state of Massachusetts; and Fred Kilgour (Ohio College Library Center) and Fred Bellomy (University of California Library Systems Development Program) who gave progress reports on their "regional development programs."[8] The summer 1972 program featured Charles Payne who described briefly the development of a data management system for the use of the University of Chicago Library; Ronald Miller who outlined the growth of the New England Library Information Network (NELINET) and described the developments of the past year; John Kountz who reported on the results of his work in the Orange County (California) Public Library and expressed an intent of carrying this catalog and circulation control work into the California State University and Colleges as a base for further developments; Kenneth Bierman who discussed the service initiated and being offered by the Oklahoma Department of Libraries; and Maryann Duggan who reported that the Southwestern Library Interstate Cooperative Endeavor (SLICE) originated the services offered in Oklahoma.[9]

Two years later in 1974 Brian Aveney, Chair of the COLA Discussion Group, included in his report to the ISAD Board an informal proposal that the Group be merged with the MARC Users' Discussion Group (MUDG).[10] Another two years later Sue Martin, now Chair of the Library Automation Discussion Group,[11] reported to the Board "that there had been little discussion and no opposition to the proposal to combine the Library Automation Discussion Group and MARC Users' Discussion Group [MUDG]." A decision was postponed in recognition of Henriette Avram's concern that the merger might cause problems of communication between MARBI[12] and the MUDG.[13] At its next meeting, "Ms. Martin reminded the board of the previous discussion of merging COLA and MUDG. She stated that it seemed to be the feeling of those present at the COLA-MUDG meeting that MUDG does have its place." Therefore, she " . . . suggested that the proposal of merging the two groups be withdrawn."[14]

In 1981, when the LITA Board approved a merger of the MARC Users' and Library Automation Dicussion Groups, the latter's origins were recognized in the phrase "formerly COLA."[15] In its present organization, LITA does not have any discussion groups. However, at least three of LITA's committees and nearly all of LITA's 22 interest groups are related to one or another aspect of library automation.

From this brief account, it can be seen that the work of COLA and its members over its 17 years of activity contributed measurably to the evolution of LITA's interest in the various aspects of the use of computers in the technical and public services of libraries. It is interesting to speculate on an alternate ASIS scenario and consider the possible effect of the addition to that association of a COLA SIG. Would a COLA SIG have flourished and attracted significantly greater numbers of librarians to ASIS? Would this have resulted in ASIS developing in a direction closer to the day-to-day interests of librarians? Or would ASIS have adopted its agenda of largely theoretical research apart from librarianship anyway? As one of the COLA members who voted to become a part of ALA, I felt that COLA's interests, which were oriented primarily toward applications rather than theory, were more closely allied to ALA than to ASIS. I do not think COLA would have significantly increased ASIS membership, nor would COLA have had the necessary strength to have steered ASIS in another direction. Further, if COLA had not gone to ALA, then a comparable group would have been formed in ALA, effectively siphoning off any potential COLA membership in ASIS. In retrospect, I think the COLA membership made the best decision.

LARC

This brief account of the LARC Association must begin with an even briefer account of the development of the Los Angeles County Public Library's book catalogs, for experience with one of these catalogs was the principal motivation in the creation of LARC.

In 1952 a majority of the branches of the Los Angeles County Public Library, including some of the larger and newer branches, were without card catalogs. After exploring alternatives, the Library chose to produce printed book catalogs using punched cards and IBM unit record equipment. The bound volumes, divided into author, title, and subject sections, were not pretty, but they did provide much improved access to the library's holdings throughout its branch system. The first edition of the *Children's Catalog* was completed in that same year, while the first edition of the *Adult Catalog* was completed in 1955.[16]

In 1963 the Library contracted with the Econolist Company[17] to produce an improved set of book catalogs which were also expected to be more economical. Econolist used Varityper machines to create one, two, or three lines of proportionally-spaced text on tabulator cards which were then punched with sequence numbers for machine sorting and control. A sequential camera photographed the cards, creating film masters of the page images from which the catalogs were printed.[18] The results were quite handsome. Nevertheless, the project encountered financial problems and the Econolist Company eventually filed for bankruptcy.

In 1967, the library was seeking bid proposals for optical character recognition conversion of its catalogs to machine-readable form.[19] At the same time, the Council on Library Resources gave Los Angeles County Public Library a grant of $38,000 to study computerized library applications with the results of the study to be used in converting the library's book catalogs to a new computerized production method.[20] Finally, ten years later the library announced that it was converting its master catalog to Computer-Output-Microfilm using ROM 3 COM Terminals.[21]

During the period that the Los Angeles County Public Library was working with the Econolist Company (1962-1965), its Vice President and General Manager was Frank S. Patrinostro. Frank

Samuel Patrinostro was born in Florida in 1929, served with the United States Army Air Force from 1946-1949, received an A.B. degree in Journalism from the University of Miami (Florida) in 1954, and did graduate studies at Northwestern University. In the 1960s he was identified as a research specialist in information systems in urban governments. Apart from his work, he was active in People to People of the United States. Following the demise of the Econolist Company, he was the manager of sales for the western region for the Science Press (Ephrata, Pennsylvania).[22]

After their experience working together, the one point on which both the Los Angeles County Public Library and the Econolist Company agreed was that the cost estimates were too low and that the final costs were significantly higher than expected. From the library's point of view, it was described as having "encountered a cost problem resulting from the deficient planning on the part of the production firm estimating the work."[23] The "cost problem" was a project which cost more than double the amount originally budgeted.[24] Patrinostro responded, saying that "virtually every factor given me by the library failed to hold true" and citing examples such as the actual count of subject entries being 300 percent greater than he had been led to believe and the count of author entries being 75 percent greater.[25]

Out of this experience, Patrinostro developed the belief that the full details of library automation projects, especially those with problems, should be made available to the library profession so that others could learn and benefit from these experiences. He was particularly concerned that projects that had developed problems were too often hidden from view and even, in some cases, denied.

To this end Patrinostro founded LARC in 1968 and was actively, some would say aggressively, promoting the organization at the 1969 ALA Annual Conference in Atlantic City. Part of his sales presentation focused on the well-known and tacitly acknowledged false starts by libraries as they attempted to introduce the computer into their operations. It was important, he said, that information about these failures should be shared so other libraries could have the benefit of these experiences and thereby avoid making the same mistakes.

His point was well taken, and LARC recruited several prominent persons into its membership. Reaching a stable organizational structure took about two years. In early 1969 the chairman of the board was Herbert K. Ahn who was assisted by fellow directors Dave G. Everett, Catherine MacQuarrie, Ray Hogaboom, and Frank S. Patrinostro.[26] Later in the year no chairman was cited, and the "interim directors" were Catherine MacQuarrie, Ray Hogaboom, Frank S. Patrinostro, John Blanchard, and Harold Jasper.[27] LARC had its first election of officers in late 1969 or early 1970, and the association's first president was Barbara Markuson during 1970. She was followed by H. William Axford (1971), C. Edward Carroll (1972), H. Joanne Harrar (1973), W. Carl Jackson (1974), and Don L. Bosseau (1975). Patrinostro served as Interim Executive Secretary until 1970 when he became Executive Secretary.

LARC described itself as "a non-profit professional association dedicated to defining the use of automation and research in library technology." The specific objectives were "to provide colloquiums designed to acquaint library school students with the techniques of practitioners in the library automation field; training classes designed to acquaint working librarians with systems planning, analysis, and design; continued publication of *The LARC Reports* as a primary source of documentation for planned or implemented library automation projects; assistance to libraries planning library automation projects; instructional materials for the use of advanced projects in the field of library automation; [and] establishment of an exchange for materials on library automation."[28] Beginning in 1973, the Association's statement became, "The LARC Association is an international non-profit organization incorporated to promote continuing education and training in library automation through research, workshops, meetings, and publications and to provide a forum for the worldwide exchange of information about library automation and related developments."[29]

The LARC Reports began in 1968 as a plain quarterly publication without a cover or advertising. The first report was by Patrinostro and dealt with "Why Research and Study Teams Frequently Fail to Meet Objectives."[30] The second report, titled "The Third Conversion of Book Catalogs for the Los Angeles County Library," was a reprint of the library's request for proposals together with two unsigned commentaries by Patrinostro.[31]

Volume 2 of *The LARC Reports* began with an unsigned editorial which severely criticized the library automation efforts up to that point and laid out the LARC agenda.

> During the past decade many of us have hurried full of illusion, all the sails of hope spread wide, to meetings, seminars, books, articles, virtually everything we thought might help us correct and refine our concepts of library automation. All too frequent, we found something incredible–namely, that most of these things had nothing clear to say about how automated techniques can be applied to library operations. . . .
>
> The LARC ASSOCIATION is committed to the difficult task of discovering with unimpeachable clarity, that is, with veritable evidence, what things, facts, experiences, phenomena among all those that exist can help librarians in planning or implementing automated projects. . . .
>
> We take up this task not out of mere curiosity . . . [n] or as a scholar . . . No: In this task of discovering what automation is and how it can serve libraries THE LARC ASSOCIATION is dedicated to the quest of finding new and better ways of keeping librarians abreast of new knowledge and new techniques so that what we learn in school does not become incurably obsolete.[32]

Beginning in 1970 it was planned that each issue would ". . . have an issue editor and each issue will, in general, be devoted to papers relating to a single automation topic, thus providing for a fuller treatment of important areas."[33] They would be "A practical and timely source of documentation on planned or implemented automated library projects."[34] More than 30 accounts of library automation had appeared in *The LARC Reports* when they ceased publication in 1975.

The Association also began publishing *The LARC Newsletter* for its members in January, 1974. The *Newsletter* was one of at least 11 journals with which ERIC/CLIS established abstracts agreements about 1973. These journals were to announce the availability of ERIC material to their approximately 100,000 readers. "ERIC/CLIS monthly input to *Research in Education* was sent to the editor of these journals who selected items and printed a list of ERIC/ CLIS accessions of top priority and interest to their readership."[35]

And this was just the beginning of an ambitious publication program. *Network: International Communications in Library Automation* appeared briefly. Then, no less than six series were initiated with the number of volumes in each varying from 1 to 12: *A Survey of Automated Activities in the Libraries of the World, Computerized Serials System Series, Computerized Acquisitions Systems Series, Computerized Circulation System Series, Computerized Cataloging Systems Series,* and *Series on Automated Activities in Health Sciences Libraries.* Finally, at least 11 monographs were issued independently of any series. The LARC Association also sponsored and cosponsored a number of institutes with the proceedings appearing in one or another of the above.

On October 1, 1975, Patrinostro announced that the LARC membership had voted, by a 3-1 margin, to merge the organization with The World Information Systems Exchange (WISE), a new organization of which Patrinostro was the founder and director-general. The overall aims of WISE included "[t]he collection and dissemination of information on the application of new technologies to professional practice and procedures" in such fields as agriculture, chemistry, government operations, and population management. The plan was for LARC to become the Library and Information Science Division, one of the 14 operating divisions of WISE.[36] No further mention of either LARC or WISE was found in the literature.

Following his work with LARC, Patrinostro became manager of the western region for Control Data Technotec from 1976-1980. He then became a communications company executive and consultant, serving as the president of Technical Communications Associates in Sunnyvale, California.[37]

At the very least, LARC successfully accomplished two things, one at a personal level, the other at a professional level. First, it provided the platform which allowed Patrinostro to vindicate himself as the former manager of the failed Econolist Company. Second, LARC attempted to identify the world's library automation projects and to publish detailed descriptions of many of them. While the first is essential to understanding the LARC Association, the second would not have happened without Patrinostro's providing the necessary focus and drive. LARC's continuing education efforts, important to the participants at the time, are now largely subsumed in the association's publications.

CONCLUSION

In addition to the American Library Association and the Special Libraries Association, librarians participate in a multitude of other professional organizations, mostly thematic (e.g., the Medical Library Association and the Catholic Library Association) and local (i.e., the state and regional associations). Over the years, a variety of attempts to form new associations to meet particular needs have been mounted. Some have managed to survive, if only marginally, while others have disappeared. Two of those that disappeared have been described briefly in this chapter.

REFERENCE NOTES

The following are the secondary (i.e., published) sources used in this chapter. As a member of COLA and an observer of the LARC Association, I have also relied somewhat on my recollections of the events described.

1. For a general overview of the work of the associations, see their published proceedings and other accounts. Particularly useful are the annual summaries of the year's work in several areas of technical services published in *Library Resources & Technical Services*.

2. Ralph Halstead Parker, "Punched Card Method in Circulation Work," *Library Journal* 61 (December 1, 1936): 903-905. Although Parker's circulation system was based on punched cards processed with unit record equipment, its influence can be traced directly to today's sophisticated integrated library systems.

3. A file of COLA materials, spanning the period from 1965 to about 1970, is available among papers deposited by the author in the Archives of the University of Illinois at Urbana-Champaign Library.

4. "COLA Discussion Group," *JOLA Technical Communications* 1 (August 1970): 6.

5. "ISAD COLA Discussion Group," *JOLA Technical Communications* 2 (January 1971): 5.

6. "ISAD COLA Discussion Group," *JOLA Technical Communications* 2 (April 1971): 2-3.

7. Today we now know this system as NOTIS.

8. "COLA Discussion-Dallas," *JOLA Technical Communications* 2 (September 1971): 1-4.

9. "COLA Discussion Group Meeting Summary–June 25, 1972," *JOLA Technical Communications* 3 (March-April 1972): 3-4.

10. "COLA Discussion Group Report," *Journal of Library Automation* 7 (September 1974): 222.

11. Sometime between 1974 and 1976 the COLA Discussion Group was renamed the Library Automation Discussion Group. Whether this change was official or unofficial is not clear from the published record.

12. Machine-Readable Bibliographic Information Committee, an interdivisional creation in 1974 of the then Resources and Technical Services Division (now Association for Library Collections and Technical Services), the Information Science and Automation Division (now the Library and Information Technology Association), and the Reference and Adult Services Division.

13. "Highlights of ISAD Board Meetings," *Journal of Library Automation* 9 (June 1976): 164.

14. "Highlights of the ISAD Board Meeting," *Journal of Library Automation* 9 (September 1976): 245-246.

15. "Highlights of LITA Board Meetings," *Journal of Library Automation* 14 (June 1981): 133.

16. Catherine MacQuarrie, "IBM Book Catalog," *Library Journal* 82 (March 1, 1957): 630-634; Catherine MacQuarrie and Beryl L. Martin, "The Book Catalog of the Los Angeles County Public Library: How It Is Being Made," *Library Resources & Technical Services* 4 (Summer 1960): 208-227; John D. Henderson, "The Book Catalogs of the Los Angeles County Public Library," in *Proceedings of the 1963 Clinic on Library Applications of Data Processing* (Champaign: University of Illinois Graduate School of Library Science, 1964), 18-33; William Spence Geller, "Duplicate Catalogs in Regional and Public Library Systems," in *Library Catalogs: Changing Directions* (Chicago: University of Chicago Press, 1964), 57-67; Joseph Becker, "Automatic Preparation of Book Catalogs," *ALA Bulletin* 58 (September 1964): 714-718.

17. The Econolist Company specialized in printing checks and other materials.

18. Catherine MacQuarrie, "The Metamorphosis of the Book Catalogs," *Library Resources & Technical Services* 8 (Fall 1964): 370-378; Joseph Becker, "Automatic Preparation of Book Catalogs," *ALA Bulletin* 58 (September 1964): 714-718.

19. "The Third Conversion of Book Catalogs for the Los Angeles County Library," *The LARC Reports* 1, no. 2 (1968): 1-19.

20. "Computerized Techniques," *Library Resources & Technical Services* 11 (Summer 1967): 382; "Los Angeles County Public Library to Study Computerized Techniques," *Library Journal* 91 (August 1966): 3673.

21. "LA Public Library Moves to COM," *Journal of Library Automation* 10 (December 1977): 377.

22. *Who's Who in the West,* 15th ed., 1976-1977 (Chicago: Marquis Who's Who, 1976): 564.

23. Quoted by Patrinostro who described it as having appeared "last year" in *Library Resources & Technical Services.* See his "Why Research and Study Teams Frequently Fail to Meet Objectives," *The LARC Reports* 1, no. 1 (1968): 2.

24. Frank S. Patrinostro, "Why Research and Study Teams Frequently Fail to Meet Objectives," *The LARC Reports* 1, no. 1 (1968): 2.

25. Frank S. Patrinostro, "Commentary-1," *The LARC Reports* 1, no. 2 (1968): 20-21.

26. [masthead], *The LARC Reports* 2 (March 1969): [3].

27. [masthead], *The LARC Reports* 2 (September 1969): [3].

28. [advertisement], *The LARC Reports* 3 (April 1970): [ii].

29. [masthead], *The LARC Reports* 6 (1973): [1]; "The Library Automation Research and Consulting (LARC) Association," *The Indexer* 8 (October 1973): 205.

30. Frank S. Patrinostro, "Why Research and Study Teams Frequently Fail to Meet Objectives," *The LARC Reports* 1, no. 1 (1968): 1-4.

31. Frank S. Patrinostro, "The Third Conversion of Book Catalogs for the Los Angeles County Library," *The LARC Reports* 1, no. 2 (1968): 1-23.

32. "Editorial," *The LARC Reports* 2 (March 1969): [4].

33. "A Notice to Readers," *The LARC Reports* 3 (April 1970): [iv].

34. "Larc," *International Library Review* 3 (October 1971): 454.

35. Joshua I. Smith, "ERIC Clearinghouse on Library and Information Sciences," *The Bowker Annual of Library & Book Trade Information.* 19th ed., 1974 (New York: R. R. Bowker Company, 1974), 29.

36. "LARC to Merge with World Information Systems Exchange (WISE)," *Program* 10 (January 1976): 30-31.

37. *Who's Who in the West,* 22d ed., 1989-90 (Wilmette, IL: Marquis Who's Who, 1989), 524.

PART IX:
FUTURE

Chapter 20

The Effect of a Transition in Intellectual Property Rights Caused by Electronic Media on the Human Capital of Librarians

Richard W. Meyer

The impact on intellectual property rights brought on by the emergence of electronic publications, exemplified by online journals, portends some significant need for human capital (skills) appreciated by technical services librarians. This may be revealed by conjecture on the future based on experience with printed journals and by examination of recent activities in the online, electronic environment. This chapter proceeds as follows. First, the nature of the journal is described in order to form the basis for affirming the needs of the scholarly community. Second, a brief examination of property rights institutions, with particular regard for intellectual property, is compared with the current state of the electronic environment to illuminate the nature of the transition which is under way in sharing of scholarly information. Third, suggestions are made on the implications these issues impose on the working technical services librarian's base of skills. Fourth, the chapter concludes with a summary.

THE ROLE OF JOURNALS

Although a variety of models have been employed to describe the role of journals in scholarship, a simple taxonomy readily emerges from a moderately thoughtful examination of the shelves in any academic library. In the academic environment, where much of the development of new knowledge originates, four elements of the role of journals present themselves. Although there may be other roles, those that are essential to scholars can be labeled: communication, archiving, gatekeeping, and human capital appreciation.

The results of scientific research, new knowledge and advances in technology, are communicated among interested parties as a way to keep each other up to date on progress. For this purpose, *Physical Review Letters* intends to convey information on who is doing what and where in physics research. However, casual observation indicates that more efficient alternatives exist for the purpose of communicating current activity in scholarly pursuits. In addition to traditional conventions or meetings, letters, and mailing manuscripts to each other, the electronic forum has also emerged as a convenient medium for informal communication. In fact, as with many of its counterparts, *Physical Review Letters* has evolved from communication of work in progress to communicating the completed results of research.

The cumulative collection of journal issues over time provides an historical record of knowledge. While this function satisfies the demand of historical research, it may be of little continual concern to the ongoing process of research. The value of journal issues to scholars declines with age. As a result, the initial stages of new research projects often pay little attention to older volumes. However, the archival role of journals is important enough that some thought must be applied to how that role will be fulfilled in an electronic milieu.

Scholarly journals play an important role as gatekeepers, which lower the costs of information searching for scholars actively pursuing a line of research. The results of work in specific disciplines are concentrated in narrow areas by individual journal titles. The segmentation of and collection of knowledge into discrete titles reduces search costs to individuals seeking to keep up with work in distinct areas. Scholars can do a major portion of their literature searching (either on-going or ex-post) by reviewing a few basic journals in their discipline. It is important to keep in mind that scholarly publishing is segmented into discretely titled journals focused on a narrowly defined discipline, largely for the economy this provides both the author and reader.

The last, and perhaps most telling, role of scholarly journals has to do with human capital appreciation by those who publish in them. Human capital is defined as knowledge, expertise, or skills that may elevate the value of the possessor to a potential employer. Employers pay higher salaries to those with higher levels of expertise. The status of a journal–its recognition among peers, which is often a reflection of the reputation of the referees–may accrue capital to the individuals who publish in the journal. This human capital can be turned into wealth accrual captured in tenure and promotions by faculty.[1] To achieve tenure or a promotion depends largely on a quantifiable record or reputable research. That is, scholars must supply evidence of items published in refereed journals.

With the possible exception of the archival role, scholars depend upon the journal literature in several important ways. Traditionally, they have communicated with each other through publication of research results. They have reduced the effort in finding information relevant to their research with discipline-specific journals. They have accrued expertise, and consequently created a low cost measure for evaluating the quality of each others' work, through publication in refereed journals. In order to fulfill these roles, the property rights institution referred to as copyright emerged as a means of providing an incentive for creativity. However, scholars typically assigned copyright to the publisher of the journal to which they have submitted the report of their research. In an environment where electronic publication may emerge as a more efficient means to fulfill the roles described here, copyright may need to be replaced with a new property rights institution.[2] The potential for this new institution to emerge is suggested by an examination of the basic nature of property rights in regard to electronic information. In turn, that revelation may suggest the need for acquisition of new skills by technical services librarians.

PROPERTY RIGHTS AND INTELLECTUAL PROPERTY

Copyright is a property rights institution which was established for the benefit of society as a whole. In order to stimulate creativity, governments have endowed monopoly ownership on the expression of ideas to the originators of those expressions. Thus when an author produces a work, once copyrighted, he or she is afforded protection under law from piracy of his or her expression by others who might profit from his or her labor. Curiously, however, in the scholarly community it is common practice for authors to freely assign copyright to the publisher of the journal in which his or her article appears.

The author of a work of fiction will retain (or at most share with the publisher) copyright, because his or her earnings as a writer are determined directly by the sales of the publication. In the scholarly community, different incentive and reward structures confront the author. The academic scholar receives rewards for his or her creation indirectly through tenure and promotion review. The higher the quality of his or her work, the more likely tenure, or promotion to a higher level position with greater reward, or relocation to a better paying position at another academy. The scholar has an incentive to trade his or her property right to a publisher in return for at least two valuable services that the publisher provides to the author.

First, the reputation of the journal endows a level of prestige on the author whose paper is accepted. This prestige derives in part from the reputation of the editors and reviewers and in part from the extent of the audience reading the journal. To a certain extent, it is this prestige that the scholar acquires, which is responsible for achievement of tenure or promotion. Second, the publisher provides the means whereby the author's expression of an idea may be distributed into the marketplace of ideas; in effect, dispersing his or her expression as widely as possible to the community of scholars who have an interest in the particular product of the individual. The publisher bears the costs of consolidating similar material together, printing it, and delivering the printed information.

It is an essential mission of the scholarly community to create and disseminate ideas.[3] While the individual expressions of ideas may be stimulated by the protection of copyright, the ideas themselves belong to the intellectual commons available to every member of society.[4] Recognition of the effort of a scholar's work by as many users of the commons as possible fulfills an essential desire of the scholarly author. The scholar's incentive is to have his or her expression be as widely known as possible. Wide recognition elevates promotion opportunity. Therefore, whenever an easily entered forum is available, which will achieve this scholarly end, widespread acceptance by the scholarly community is inevitable. Use of the electronic network provides an easily used means for scholars to widely distribute research. Within this electronic commons there may be no need for copyright assignment to publishers. Copyright actually protects the interests of commercial publishers (including scholarly societies) who have borne the costs of printing and providing gatekeeper service. In the electronic forum, these costs may be borne by the author or his associated institution. Currently, institutions are assuming these costs without any promise of financial return, or with only the promise of peer regard endowed on its members. In this environment, copyright may need to be replaced with another property rights institution.

Voluntarily contributed listservers on the electronic network, which are provided by academic institutions, are emerging at a rapid pace. Listservers are essentially points of consolidation of E-mail messages on a given topic. Any message contributed to the listserver is quickly distributed to all the subscribers. In addition, by 1991 over 25 journals and nearly 100 newsletters were available to researchers using BITNET.[5] A thorough explanation of how these journals work has been provided on the basis of experience with the *Public-Access Computer Systems (PACS) Review* elsewhere.[6] It is easy to see that these listservers provide a new means to scholars for dispersion of expressions. The network of volunteered listservers provides a marketplace of ideas that operates like a common property institution. Comment on the basic nature of common property institutions may support the assertion that copyright may give way to another form of property rights institution in the electronic environment that can better support the goals of scholars.

In older societies, common property often provided an efficient means of organizing pasture land or fishing grounds. The shift away from common property to individual holdings in modern society can be shown to be the result of a change in the equilibrium balance between transactions costs between common property users and costs of excluding other people.[7] For example, in the case of the early American colonies, where building a fence was expensive (an exclusion cost), and communicating herding arrangements or stock identification between numbers of a small user population was easy (low transactions cost), the common pasture was efficient. In the Western United States of the late 1800s, where large pastures were required because of low grass density (high transactions cost), and when barbed wire became available cheaply (low exclusion cost), common pastures gave way to individual holdings. Although this is an oversimplification of the issue, the choice between individual holdings and common property appears to be driven by the equilibrium between transactions costs and exclusion costs. As exclusion costs rise or transactions costs decrease, this equilibrium shifts away from individual ownership toward common property ownership. This principle applies to the academic milieu of sharing scholarly information.

Publication in print media to which copyright is assigned represents an equilibrium balance where individual ownership predominates. In the print environment, exclusion costs are low and readily monitored by means of the copyright convention. Journal referees and editors form a convenient locus for each journal to monitor selection of items for publication. On the other hand, transaction costs in the form of communicating with each other among a large pool of scholars are high. In the electronic environment, the reverse tends to be true. Exclusion costs are higher because electronic systems make piracy of ideas easy.[8] The ease of downloading huge blocks of text into one's own word processor may facilitate plagiarism. Transaction costs are lower in the electronic environment. Print media are cumbersome to distribute and provide slow means of communicating. Elimination of printing and distribution effort in the electronic media represents a lowering of transaction costs. The electronic forum transfers the costs of printing to the readers, thus eliminating the need for one of the services provided by publishers. Should a controlled vocabulary be applied to articles before they are published, another key service, that of gatekeeper, is assumed by the providers of the electronic network. Furthermore, once familiar with using an electronic mail system, scholars may maintain virtually day-to-day contact. It is not uncommon to hear others speak of receiving dozens or even hundreds of electronic messages daily, particularly from list servers dedicated to subjects of particular concern to the receiver.

Communication among scholars has grown substantially with the advent of BITNET and the Internet. Scholarly papers that may have been shared in their prepublication form through the mail, are now shared in draft form through electronic networks. This allows rapid revision of individual points of view, means for more frequent revision of drafts, and closer joint research. Associated with this, there is a higher level of risk that expressions of ideas may be fixed in time. A point of view once shared may be so completely transformed by iteration, that a given author may be able to completely reverse the reported results of his or her research, with no record retained in the electronic system to record this transformation historically.

The effort to exclude others from pirating an idea also is substantial. So many individuals have access to the worldwide network of computers, that users of BITNET and Internet are frequently surprised by inquiries and comment from readers of their work from all over the world. This increase in exclusion costs along with the closely associated decrease in communications effort (transaction cost) have been accompanied by an associated movement of the equilibrium to a smaller number of commons. Instead of needing several periodicals in the print realm to share ideas, scholars may find it readily possible to accomplish the same amount of work with only one forum in the electronic environment.[9] Thoughts of librarians on the issue of online public catalog interfaces may be discussed in the printed literature within several publications. On BITNET, the same issue may easily fit within one listserver.

In the electronic environment, the need is diminished for some agent to handle the gatekeeping function previously handled by publishers. The power of electronic search engines to sort through massive amounts of information makes it possible to afford lumping all the articles on one broad subject area into one major file. This would function much the same as indexes now available online that group access to all the work in the discipline. As a result, the electronic networks' information base may be dominated by a few commercial firms with large databases. For example, Chemical Abstracts Service could group all the articles in chemistry into one file available on the network from their computers. However, this potential may depend upon a political decision of colleges and universities or government. Should universities, or government agencies, decide to retain ownership of the intellectual property produced by their faculties, the future of commercial publication enterprises could be limited to the print realm. Instead, the forum for sharing scholarly work may result in individual listservers established on each campus or agency into which all the scholarly output of the campus or agency is commonly placed. Peer review and refereeing functions, which establish the level of prestige associated with a work, may be measured by the attached commentary rather than the brand name of the printed journal counterpart. In fact, at this point in time, new electronic journals appear to be the work exclusively of academic institutions, while several government agencies are making individual documents available online.

Subject-oriented listserver journals are emerging at a great rate. These are contributed by academic institutions. Even if the federal government does not restrict commercial firms from offering electronic journals on the public computer network, this milieu may be dominated by noncommercial publishers. What may be most significantly distinct about journals in the electronic forum is that institutions bear the cost of providing them. Subscriptions to all the listservers to date on BITNET are free. The incentive structure here makes it likely that electronic journals will be broad based, nonduplicative in nature across offerers, and voluntarily contributed by academic centers. Indeed this appears to be happening as is witnessed by the University of Houston's *Public-Access Computer Systems Review,* the University of North Carolina's *Newsletter on Serials Pricing,* and so forth. There is little incentive for academic institutions to pay publishers (in the form of yielded copyright) to provide services, when there is no need to overcome the costs of printing and distribution.

Evidence drawn from a look at the federal government sector enforces the contention that the emerging model will change the property rights institution in the direction described above. For example, two significant government agencies, the National Aeronautics and Space Administration (NASA) and the National Science Foundation (NSF), offer a large number of text files via the Internet from their computers. NSF offers the *Science and Technology Information System* (STIS) and NASA has hundreds of descriptions of shuttle and satellite components, systems, and procedures on one of its computers. In both cases the documents are available free of charge to anyone through the Internet or dial access via anonymous file transfer protocol (ftp). Considering the mandate with which government agencies are faced for disseminating information, this is a logical approach. All government agencies are required to distribute copies of their publications to depository libraries so that the public has free and ready access to this information. Recently, cost saving measures have been introduced by some of these agencies. Rather than distribute printed copies, some are now distributing CD-ROM versions of their documents. Earlier cost saving efforts exist in the form of microfilm distribution. The most effective cost saving measure available may be to offer the documents to the public as machine-readable files through the Internet. This eliminates all the costs associated with printing and mailing. A user interested in a NASA publication may download the index from the NASA computer, read it on his or her microcomputer or terminal, then download only those documents of interest.

This scenario implies a significant change in property rights control. Keeping track of who downloads a document is easy with a computer and offers two benefits. First, this information yields a potential measure of value in the form of how many copies are downloaded. This measure is, of course, relevant to the tenure and promotion review process. Second, this information provides means for cost tracking and payment. Whoever downloads, pays. Whether the computer in question belongs to a government agency or publisher or academic institution is irrelevant. Regardless of whether the publishing agency is a single academic institution or major governmental agency, there are cost incentives that vector in the direction of an on-demand publication scenario. Evolution to this sort of environment implies some substantial modification of the current mechanisms used by technical services librarians to provide control of the literature.

ELECTRONIC INFORMATION FORUM
AND LIBRARIAN SKILLS

Experiments with numerous alternatives to the scholarly journal do not appear to be very successful.[10] However, for the rest of this chapter, it will be assumed that the current forum of new networks provides an environment in which success of many electronic journals is imminent.[11] (The issue of graphics is ignored on the assumption that it is a technical problem likely to be resolved and has no significant impact on the model considered here.) It may not be explicitly necessary to retain the pure analog in the form of discretely titled electronic journals. An individual research paper stored on the NASA computer should be just as easy to cite or retrieve as one contained in an electronic journal analog on an academic computer. In order to fulfill the fourfold role ascribed above to printed journals, their electronic counterparts must communicate, organize, disseminate, and archive. An electronic journal which does these functions is not hard to imagine. Thorough description of how electronic journals function have been provided by others.[11] In the electronic environment, there will need to be segmentation of the scholarly literature into subject, probably implicitly by broad subject descriptor. This could easily be as broad based a subject as all space-related documents of NASA or all the publications of a land grant college. For these journals it will be necessary for the readers to be able to subscribe so that articles are automatically delivered to individual E-mail addresses. Scholars will require a simple method of submitting articles through an online electronic system. Some means need to be available to determine the existence of other journals to which the potential reader holds no subscription. In a similar fashion, readers will require the ability to easily find articles when only a citation is in hand. Obviously, a capability to print issues or articles is required. Additionally, it would facilitate the peer review process if articles were selected for inclusion in electronic journals by editors assisted by referees and could be appended with the comments of readers.

It is interesting to note in the light of the property rights issue assessed above, that among the first network-available electronic journals there are several on bibliographic and related topics. Those with the skills to develop a viable electronic journal are adept with bibliographic subtleties as well as computer utilization. Librarians have the bibliographic expertise, and they appear to be equally adept with computer skills. This is important, since each of the distinct roles played by scholarly journals has its counterpart in new skills that must be developed by librarians.

Communication Role. The effectiveness of the electronic environment as a means for distribution of scholarly information has been demonstrated to every user of BITNET or the Internet who has sent and received electronic mail. Skills developed by librarians using utilities like OCLC have some relevance to learning the basics of electronic communication. Although commands vary, common elements emerge. Users of NOTIS, for instance, have found it valuable to share information via a listserver available over BITNET, which is set up for messages dealing exclusively with NOTIS. This server is actively used by librarians throughout the U.S. Once a librarian learns how to use one listserver, any number of others can be addressed with equal facility. This expertise is likely to be drawn on by other librarians as well as faculty.

Gatekeeper Role. The distinguishing characteristic needed to effect a search (gatekeeper) mechanism on a network full of listservers containing articles on a multitude of subjects is a controlled vocabulary. Defined terms such as author's name, place of origin of the publication, subject, and so forth may need to be attached at the time the creator submits a work for publication. The much-vaunted concept of hypertext depends upon built-in links between text in one passage and text in another passage or even article. Even with sophisticated intelligence, computers will need some similarity in terminology to make these links. This suggests that choices of terms which would be used to link one item to another would best be made before an article is published, rather than after. If the property rights argument that journals will be offered and published by academic institutions is correct, this suggests a new relationship for librarians with the rest of the faculty. It may be necessary for scholars to submit their work to the library for librarians to standardize terminology at the time an article is ready for publication. In other words, librarians may do their work when an article is written, not when a journal is received.

Archival Role. Several concerns emerge with regard to the archival role of scholarly journals in an environment conducive to change. Electronic publication offers the opportunity for continued revision of an individual article in response to changing information or whim of the author. Should a scholar discover an error in the text of an article, or revise a procedure such that research results are different, or simply decide to rescind an article for personal reasons, modification of the medium is inevitable. Librarians will be faced with an environment that may or may not have integrity. To handle this contingency, it will be necessary to invent a citation form that is capable of tracking a dynamic entity. For example, a change in name (for example, due to a change in marital status) easily could be attached to the existing electronic article. Librarians will need to be able to associate this change with a change in their citation. Similarly, appended statements by readers will need some notation in the citation. It is very likely that comments could be added by a reader who is more distinguished than the original author. As a result, some articles may be retrieved, not for the author's contribution, but for the commentator's. A citation form to collocate commentary on the work of others would have some practical use in this environment.

Furthermore, the journal not downloaded requires the surrogate identifying it to the user to carry full information on how to access the content. This portends some additional skills by librarians that will need to be translated into some explicit information on the locally loaded index. Once again, this information could easily need to track a dynamic entity. Once a call number is applied to a printed journal, the user can usually track it down in the stacks even if it is shifted at some time. In contrast, what prevents an agency holding a particular group of documents online from transferring them to another or deleting them altogether? The implication is that indexes will need to be continually monitored for replacement.

Alternatively, it seems possible that scholars may share ideas through E-mail and revise them up to the point where these expressions are submitted to a formal electronic journal. Should that be the case, the burden on librarians may be lightened, but this is not likely. At a given point in time, an article may appear to be thoroughly accurate even to scrutiny by a panel of peers. However, theory usually gives way to new theory over time, as new sources of evidence are revealed, or better thinking is applied. As a result, what once appeared accurate may be revised. Therefore, the citation capable of tracking a dynamic entity will still be needed.

Furthermore, consideration needs to be given to who carries the archival responsibility. In contrast to the printed realm, it seems likely that economical efficiency points to the originator. Economies here suggest that librarians must maintain backfiles of electronic journals for their own originating institutions. In the case of printed journals, vendors seldom maintain an inventory of backfiles for long. Typically, they remainder their stock to specialists. Therefore libraries acquiring backruns find it seldom possible to acquire them from the original publisher. Publishers only save backruns of journals for as long as it is profitable. As soon as the marginal cost of retaining an article exceeds the marginal profit from it, they will purge it from their files. This implies that the archival function will remain with libraries for electronic journals, but that the mechanism may be different. That is, the publishing agency will retain the function of archivist. Due to their existing expertise, it appears likely that they will assign that role to librarians within their organization. This role clearly complements the gatekeeper role in which the cataloger applies subject descriptors before a document is made available, rather than after the journal is received.

Human Capital Role. If the property rights equilibrium establishes journals volunteered by academic institutions as the norm, it will be necessary for some unit of each campus to establish the institutions that will facilitate accrual of capital by researchers. In the print realm, scholars contribute their work to the journals which will associate the highest degree of esteem to their efforts as possible. Catalogers, or whoever is involved in managing these journals, will have to acquire skills appropriate to producing high quality. In part, this can be contributed by soliciting editorial overview by reputable scholars in the various fields. Additional quality may be contributed by the degree of efficiency employed by the journal managers. Efficiency will be affected by the source of material contributed.

Staff with the University of Southern California indicate that it takes about 45 minutes per issue to load the *Chronicle of Higher Education* to their online system.[12] Much of the time involved relates to editing the digitized text received from the publisher into the correct record structure needed for the text retrieval software used at USC. This suggests that there might be awesome amounts of time associated with subscribing to just a few online journals if full text is routinely loaded locally. In effect, it appears that downloading and local storing of full text may not be a viable approach. Instead, librarians will better serve their patrons by developing in-house expertise with searching out articles maintained on the network in other locations. The implications of this approach are twofold. Librarians will have to develop effective routines for coding standard handles and uploading articles. They will also need to push for standards among the units responsible for providing institutional databases of articles. Fortunately, librarians have made substantial progress through agents such as the MARC record for standardizing their work. This standardization will need to apply to the user interface as well.

The scenario portrayed to this point indicates that the norm will be for institutions to retain copyright and to load their scholarly contributions to systems (listservers) locally maintained. Scholars at other institutions would subscribe on a subject basis to those journals of interest. This implies that an individual scholar would have to invoke subscriptions to as many as 3,000 listservers maintained at other institutions. The likelihood of this happening would be increased greatly either by efficient mechanisms in place to invoke the subscriptions and screen the articles or by subject specialization at the individual institutions. Rather than offering smorgasbord collections of all campus output, individual universities and colleges may choose to solicit and load only those articles on general topics for which they already have a high level of expertise. The latter appears to be the case to date. Most of the journal titles made available over BITNET have a decided subject focus.

Currently, librarians are discovering and exploring a wealth of information available through the Internet. Some of these publications are individual documents (such as Supreme Court decisions or NSF research program announcements) and some are electronic journals which collect several articles together under a common title. A dilemma exists in the form of the question, are these to be selectively downloaded and locally mounted or not? In terms of print media, libraries traditionally acquire a selected segment of the literature. However, in the case of online resources, it may be possible to download indexes to virtually all the resources and then assist users with file transfer of desired items. This then raises additional questions. Who monitors the process at any individual library? Is it a systems analyst or programmer or is it a cataloger or reference librarian?

In addition to the four roles, there are options available to the profession on ways to handle electronic journals. The library will need to play a facilitator role–helping individuals find their way into this form of literature. This implies further acquisition of computer skills by librarians. They will need to become aware of all the journals available online, their addresses, the technical details of their file structure, how to log into them, and so forth. In some cases users will need to be taught to download documents on their own and in some cases librarians will have to download these to local files and provide a system to access them.

Clemson University has mounted several commercially available databases and some locally produced full-text files under the BRS Search^TM software. Most of the commercial files are periodical indexes, but this service includes the *Academic American Encyclopedia*. The campus telephone directory and a list of jobs available are among the full-text files created on campus. It is interesting to compare the growth in number of connects to these different files. Over the period January to June 1991 the number of accesses to the encyclopedia quickly leveled off at 200 per month, compared to 600 per month for the list of jobs available and 1,500 per month for the campus directory. This suggests that online downloading and storage of full-text material produced off campus may not be as valuable to users as intuition predicts.

CONCLUSION

It is probably unsafe to assume that electronic journals will eliminate the continued publication of printed journals. Instead, the electronic versions will simply be another add-on. Traditionally, every new communication technology has expanded the amount and variety of resources. Neither printing nor typing eliminated handwritten manuscripts. Even with a word processor in every office, pencils seem to still have use. This suggests that librarians will not be able to forget what they know about cataloging traditional materials, but will have to acquire additional skills on top of the old ones. Those tasks and skills required to handle printed resources and media will need to be augmented by skills for the special handling of electronic materials.

Predictions on the future of libraries at the starting point often overlook a clear understanding of what a library is. The appropriate base from which to predict what something will be in the future is to know what it truly is now. If we understand that a library is a means of putting a set of boundaries around the knowledge that users lack, we can predict that it will be important for libraries to continue to exist in the future. Somebody will have to put the boundaries on electronic information. These may not be librarians, but given their existing expertise, it seems probable that librarians are in the best position to emerge as the agents of control. Currently, librarians possess the bibliographic skills to control the organization of discrete information elements. When the information elements become dynamic electronic media, librarians will have to be able to provide new types of mechanisms. For that, they will have to be prepared with human capital that includes searching the networks to manipulate, organize, and make electronic information available.

REFERENCE NOTES

1. Arthur M. Diamond, Jr., "What Is a Citation Worth?" *Journal of Human Resources* 21 (Spring 1986): 200-215.

2. Francis Dummer Fisher, "The Electronic Lumberyard and Builder's Rights: Technology, Copyrights, Patents, and Academe," *Change* 21 (May/June 1989): 12-21.

3. Steven W. Gilbert and Peter Lyman, "Intellectual Property in the Information Age," *Change* 21 (May/June 1989): 23-28.

4. Harlan Cleveland, "How Can Intellectual Property Be Protected?" *Change* 21 (May/June 1989): 10-11.

5. Michael Strangelove, "E-journals and Newsletters Directory," BITNET communication, May 5, 1991. Available via BITNET from PACS-L@UHUPVM1.

6. Charles W. Bailey, Jr., "Electronic (Online) Publishing in Action," *Online* 15 (January 1991): 28-35.

7. Barry C. Field, "The Evolution of Property Rights," *Kyklos* 42 (1989): 319-345.

8. Cleveland, "How Can Intellectual Property Be Protected?" 10.

9. Lauren H. Seiler, "The Future of the Scholarly Journal," *Academic Computing* 4 (September 1989): 14-16, 66-69.

10. Anne B. Piternick, "Attempts to Find Alternatives to the Scientific Journal: A Brief Review," *Journal of Academic Librarianship* 15 (November 1989): 260-266.

11. Seiler, "The Future of the Scholarly Journal," 66; and Bailey, "Electronic (Online) Publishing in Action," 31-32.

12. Karl Geiger, personal communication, May 5, 1991.

Index